DOWNLOAD NEIG
to access a special messac
of *Life Remixed*™ Ma

C000235885

How does it work?

1. Install the free **Neighbur Vue** app (orange logo) onto your smartphone, iPad or tablet from the Apple or Google Play stores (take special note of the correct spelling).

2. Open the app and allow **Neighbur Vue** to access photos and media on your device and continue to follow the instructions.

3. Scan/point your camera lens over Mark Wilkinson's face below.

4. Once the video starts, tap the 'unlocked' icon 🔓 to lock the content onto your device.
   UNLOCKED

5. Move your device away from the book, then sit back and listen to Mark's message.

If the link is unavailable view the message at:
www.markwilkinsonofficial.com/life-remixed

'*Life Remixed*™ wouldn't have been possible without Mark Wilkinson making a critical decision at the lowest point of his life. Let's face it, our results are the culmination of the decisions we make or don't make. For anyone looking for hope, this book offers an abundance of it. And, with hope, you have options.'

Bob Proctor
Best-Selling Author of *You Were Born Rich*

'Mark Wilkinson is a great embodiment of the teachings in *The Secret*. In *Life Remixed*™, he shares his inspiring journey of overcoming life challenges through consciously shifting his thoughts, feelings, and actions to achieve miraculous results.'

Marci Shimoff
#1 *New York Times* Best-Selling Author
Happy for No Reason and *Chicken Soup for the Woman's Soul*

'*Life Remixed*™ offers a subtle, fresh, and straight-talking approach to self-development intermixed with funny and honest tales from Mark's life and music career. The fact that you can meet Mark through augmented reality at the start of the book really connects you to truly visualise everything he's gone through and achieved.'

Peggy McColl
New York Times Best-Selling Author

'*Life Remixed*™ has the power to change your life. The mind impacts the body, and the evidence is here within the pages of Mark Wilkinson's book. No matter what aspect of life you're in, this book can help, and trust me, you don't need to be a fan of house music, DJing, or even self-development to appreciate it. It's time to remix your life!'

Judy O'Beirn
CEO & Founder, Hasmark Publishing International

'Mark has taken the highs and lows that life has thrown at him and managed to remix them to not only survive but thrive! This book is a testament to his gift of "remixing" and a guide for anyone who has experienced adversity and is looking to remix their own life.'

Harry Singha
Speaker, Mentor, Philanthropist

'Mark's passion in *Life Remixed*™ shows that nothing can stand in your way. When you're determined enough to recover from pain and financial issues, you can achieve it. Mark will show you how to rethink your life, move outside of your comfort zone, have faith, and go for it.'

Lorraine Hahn
Former CNN International TalkAsia & BizAsia Host,
CNBC Anchor

'I was there for lots of the highs, but not so many of the lows. To be honest, I didn't realise how low it went for Mark. Whenever we saw each other, it was always just jokes and laughter. Reading the book made me realise just how bad things had gotten, and I have nothing but admiration for the way that Mark has turned it all around. Up, down, and back up again, with all the twists and turns along the way. An inspirational read.'

Darren Rock (Rocky)
DJ/Producer/Remixer, X-Press 2

'Having shared many great moments with Wilkie over the years, and some darker moments too, and now being on the same journey of discovery with new experiences and even greater moments is fantastic to see. We've remained great friends throughout. I always admire people who are able to make huge changes in their lives. Wilkie has passion and motivation, and has completely changed everything. Wow!!!'

Brandon Block
DJ, Producer, Author, Goal Mapping Coach,
Smart Recovery Trainer

'Mark's story is so inspiring that, together with his teachings, this book will change your life. The comeback tale Mark reveals highlights a powerful truth: no matter how difficult life gets, there's always a way back. And not only a way back to surviving, but also thriving too! Let Mark take you on a hilarious, mind blowing ride into creating your happiest and most abundant life imaginable'

Will Foster
Author of *The Happiness Gap* – Hay House

'As someone who has had to change direction in life (there aren't too many old cricketers around), I can fully relate to *Life Remixed*™ and see how it applies in my own life.'

Tony Murphy
Managing Director at Hamilton Deed & Ex-Surrey Cricketer

'*Life Remixed*™ rocks, sometimes hilarious, sometimes tragic, and always, always real. Ask yourself, would now be a good time to start your own life remix?'

Jason Cundy
Talk Sport Radio Host
Former UK Premier League Professional Footballer

'Mark's is a story that I am so grateful has been told. It is a raw, honest, and inspiring account of finding purpose when all seemed lost and one that I think we can all relate to. Life can knock us down sometimes, and Mark's journey of getting back up from the canvas has been nothing short of remarkable. His lust for life is infectious, and he truly embodies everything he talks about in this book. As is not always the case with music tracks, Mark's remixed life is even better than the original. Highly recommended reading.'

Ian Collins
Managing Director at Safety Coach International Ltd

'*Life Remixed*™ is an honest account of a journey and a powerful illustration of the connections between body and mind. Mark's commitment to face the consequences of his behaviour and the determination with which he embraced the difficult changes are inspiring. As someone who specialises in cleansing and detoxification, I know the extent to which we somatise our traumas and why healing and recovery must start with the willingness to let go of our addictions. However, what strikes me the most about Mark's journey is that he had the courage to ask for help and the humility to accept the help that was given with gratitude! I recommend *Life Remixed*™ to all those looking for evidence that healing and recovery are not just possible but within reach.'

Anne-Lise Miller
Cleansing & Detoxification Specialist
Health-Style for Life, Author of *Too Young To Grow Old*

'It is one thing for someone to show their vulnerabilities. It is quite another thing to help understand how they can turn their challenges "into successes by following in the footsteps and lessons learned of someone like Mark. Putting it all together in a way that entertains, engages, and provides both thought and action, Mark has really nailed it. This is a must-read for anyone sincerely wanting to improve their personal and professional life. It is also a must-share to others that you know want to do the same. Believe me – they will thank you!'

Rob Fisher
President and Director of Operations, Fisher Improvement Technologies

'I want to congratulate Mark on writing *Life Remixed*™. One of my personal mantras is there are no can nots, only will nots, and Mark has proved it to be true many times over in such a human and honest way. I'm glad we met and are still connected to this day.'

Brian Miller
Kinesiology Coach, Better Body Management

'A real-life story of triumph that shows you how to understand, embrace, and overcome challenges through a positive mindset and action – and it's a really great read as well.'

Davin and Atuksha Poonwassie
Founders, Simple Crowdfunding

'I have known Mark since the hedonistic days of London clubland. We worked together at Flying Records shop in Kensington Market, where our friendship grew, and our love of football, music, ponytails, and naughty pairs of glasses bonded us! We were grafters going on to become successful DJs playing music all around the world as well as producing records, promoting clubs, and pushing our boundaries to the limit – and having the time of our lives. Our paths went off in different directions for a while until 2005, when I was shocked to see the usual bubbly, energetic and lively Mark in a terrible physical state at a friend's wedding. When he says he was ill, I, for one, can vouch that this is no exaggeration. He could barely walk. To see him recover and rebuild with his passion for life and to become what he is today is truly amazing, and I'm so proud of him. Never give up. Mark didn't, and the support he has given to me in recent times has been amazing. *Life Remixed*™ is a must-read.

Steven Harper AKA Lofty
DJ/ Producer / Coach, Chilli-Funk

'*Life Remixed*™ is alluring, captivating, and compelling. It's an astounding story of overcoming debilitating physical and emotional pain.'

Angelica Lopez
CEO Adevar Investigative Group

'This book reads like my very own personal journey in life (without the DJ parts). It's honest and real. I can vouch for the life-affirming changes that daily practices provide. The power of self is the greatest power we need to harness in life, and *Life Remixed*™ is a genuine example of how you can make a difference in your own life. Be careful what you wish for.'

Paul Bryenton
Company Director, Human Power Consultancy Ltd

'As a true believer in the power of gratitude and manifesting your goals, I believe this book gives you clear and practical steps for starting your journey towards creating the life of your dreams.'

Olivia Corrie
Company Director, Frontline Communication Training Ltd

'A cross between an episode of *The Inbetweeners* and a Tony Robbins seminar.'

Daniel Wilkinson
Mark's Brother

'Mark offers a seamless remix of joyful hedonism and spiritual guidance. No matter your past, no matter your present, *Life Remixed*™ will enable you to design the life you want, right now. You'll laugh, gasp, and reach for your journal all in one page.'

Charlotte Cramer
Author of The Purpose Myth

'*Life Remixed*™ has all the nuances of redemption and resurrection. Mark skilfully weaves in poignant anecdotes while transporting you into his former world as a leading international DJ. Mark shows us that traveling down a dark road can eventually lead you into the light. Utilizing the metaphor of music for life, you will begin to create the melody of your own as you learn to keep your subconscious soundtrack in check. Get prepared to remix your life!'

Pashmina P., M.Ed,
International Bestselling Author
Founder, the Online Author's Office

'I first met Mark DJing on the London club scene. I was new to London, having arrived from Sydney due to the allure of the music and lifestyle in the '90s. As Ministry resident DJ, he was never far from the action and always had a smile and some inspiring words to share. We always got on great. I've seen him rock dance floors. One night at the legendary Turnmills nightclub, he was a god behind those decks – and then on the other side of success, I've seen him broken and struggling to walk.

I'm so impressed by his comeback in *Life Remixed*.™. Mark's positivity is relentless. Keep reading as this book could change your life.'

Damian Gelle
Founder SW4 Festival Clapham Common, London, UK, and the Electric Gardens Festival, Australia

'I met Mark back in early 2012 when we were both working at the London Olympics. This interaction was in Mark's role as a Health & Safety Manager for the Olympic Stadium. Life Remixed™ shows his instant likeability factor and communication manner that makes him the kind of man you want to work with. He very clearly sets out his standards and desires on any task, and he rightly expects results. He is always available and willing to support and assist you at any time to ensure these targets are met. This, I believe, is why post-London 2012, we have been naturally drawn together as our personalities just click on any project we turn to. I thoroughly enjoy Mark's zest for life and infectious desire to grow and be so positive every day. You will be pushed to find a more proactive, positive person who can interact on any level delivering with both personality and professionalism. I wish Mark ultimate success with *Life Remixed*™, and I look forward to watching him grow even further. Keep reading!

Paul Whiting
Head of Fire Response, London Olympic Stadium Test events 2012
Director, EMFS Group Ltd

'Unlike other rags-to-redemption stories, Mark doesn't just give you the sunshine at the end. He takes you through every gut clenchingly won lesson that he's learned along the way.'

Kieron Bain
jacKofKats from Don'tstayin.com, Creative Director,
Direct Sales Copywriting

'He always went where angels feared to tread, always headstrong, never listened, but he's still my boy.'

Gill Wilkinson
Mark's Mother

LOOKING BEYOND THE DANCE
TO FACE THE MUSIC

LIFE
REMIXED™

MARK WILKINSON

Editor: Kathryn Young
kathryn@hasmarkpublishing.com

Cover Artist & Layout Design: Anne Karklins
anne@hasmarkpublishing.com

DEDICATION

MY HEARTFELT THANKS go out to the following people who are the closest to me and have been there through all of the challenges.

My wife Emma, who is my biggest supporter and in recent years has been the driving force behind getting this whole idea of *Life Remixed*™ out into the physical and online world. Without her, my story may not have been published and would surely not have helped as many people as it already has.

My loving Mum (Gill) and Dad (Charles RIP).

Dan, my wonderful brother.

Mabel, my wonderful Gran.

All my family: Barry, Chris, Peter, Sarah, Geoff, Matt, Lisa, and their partners and families – I love you all.

Those very close friends who have always been there, never judging me as I stumbled through my early years making so many mistakes – from messing around in parks, dancing around in fields, and partying on the sand – I love you all too.

Special mention to those closest to me at each time of my growth: Guy, Rocky, Dave, and Paul.

TABLE OF CONTENTS

ACKNOWLEDGEMENTS

MY HEARTFELT GRATITUDE and thanks to all the people who have believed in me, especially those who believed in me even when I didn't believe in myself!

Kevin Green, Danny Rampling, and Lewis Senior for the three-part foreword. Each has known me at different times throughout my *Life Remixed* journey, and their input has been invaluable. Thank you, gentlemen.

Brian, Anne-Lise, Dave W, Rocky, Diesel, Ashley, Lofty, Blake, Peri & Debbie, Ian & Renie, Jeffrey, Dawn, Matt, Ian and Bernadette, Regan, Norman, Norman Fatboy, Norman Jay MBE, Brandon, Mat & Seb ModDev, Roy & Julie, Lynsey, Flying Records London (Charlie, Jo, Max & Ali, Dean, Scott, Clive, Keith, Mick), Boys Own London (Terry, Pete, Andrew (RIP), Steve & Cymon), Ministry of Sound London (Justin, Hector, CJ, Paul, Jeremy, Avi, Adam, Simon, Gareth), Paper Recordings Manchester (Ben, Pete, Miles & Elliott), Sign of the Times London (Fiona, Paolo), Kinky Disco London (Roscoe, Derek Dehlarge), Full Circle Colnbrook (Phil, Fi, Martyn), Shave Yer Tongue Bracknell (Moira, Scott), Back 2 Basics Leeds (Dave, Mickey, Huggy, Ralph), Milky Lunch Norwich (Jay, George, Ben) Wobble Birmingham (Phil), Faith (Dave & Stu), Shine & Thompsons in Belfast (Alan, Stevie, Batesy), L'America Cardiff (Craig & Dave) Bed (Simon) & Niche (Dazz) in Sheffield, El Divino & Villa Eddie Ibiza, CJ, Ricky, Andy W, Jamie T, Mi-Soul & Mi-House radio, and all the clubs in SW England who booked me back in the day (Ben, Mike, Kev, Jim, Dave). The singers, Steve, Tara, Errol, Denise (RIP) & Rose. Everyone in the Balearic network. All in Phuket Thailand (Mark, Lisa, Massimo, RDG, Russell & Poom, RDR & Emily, Dan, Steve (RIP), Byron, Rung & Doris (RIP).

Paul, Bowling Searley, Kev, Leo, Paul B, Olivia, Guy, Rachel, Mae & Tom, MK & Dani, Jase, Deano, Laura & David, Steve & Louise, Peteski, Ian R, Kieran, Alex, Tony, Damian G, Boney, Woody, Kirsty, Tim & Fleur, Keith, Andrew, Mo, Caroline, Rachel, Lee B, Lee H, Lee S, Dion,

Rob & Ray, Brian & Ainsley, Morgs & Trudi, Brian & Claire, Darren, Lee, Craig, Rual & Pearl, Kathryn, Rick & Lorna, Fi, Tyler, Izabelle, Gemma, Michael, Madison, Gary & Maria, Darren & Helen, Tony & all @ Hamilton Deed, Chris, Noel, Andy, Jon, Dave J, Mick H, Dave V, Paul, Nico, Mark & Trusha, Will & Connor, Parish & Estelle, Mark & Minori, Chris PGA, Charley, Reza, Dan O2, Hilary, Phil West, Graeme, Torq, Graham, Robby, Jonny, Simon, Stoods, Heather, Sean, Jim, Mac, Paul, Richard, Alex, Bryan, Kevin and Michael, Gilly, Jamie, Tom, Nick, Sunil, Lucy, Charlotte, Giovani, Dean, Heather, Sarah, Barry MACS, Lesley, Dave, Dave H, Joe, Dimple, Harry, Paul D, Louise, Tony Robbins, Bob Proctor, Rhonda Byrne, Will, Sophie, Rose, Fred, Mikalis, Mike B, Pashmina, Davin & Atuksha, Des & Lisa, Pam, Dovile, Ariane, Eliza, Denise, Dr Jones & Mr Hampton, Judy, Dave, Jenna & all @ Hasmark Publishing International.

And every other DJ and club promoter in the UK and worldwide who took the time to book me to play in their wonderful nightclubs and, just as importantly, buy and play my records on their dancefloors – big love to you all.

Plus, all my worldwide clients and all the amazing authors in the recommended reading section for sharing their gifts!

Apologies if I forgot anyone! I'll make it up to you in the next book, promise.

FOREWORD PART 1

BY DANNY RAMPLING

I first met Mark in 1996 through the London house music scene, and we've gradually become friends ever since. When we met, Mark was already a leading London DJ, record producer, and resident DJ at the Ministry of Sound nightclub. Consequently, we played at many events together, including Ministry of Sound, Turnmills, Bagleys, The Cross, and Pacha in Ibiza, as well as many other great nightclubs across the world.

My own journey into DJing started when I first discovered the Balearic sound of Alfredo playing at Amnesia in Ibiza in 1987. Three friends and I brought the music back to London in 1988 in what has been described by many as the UK's first Summer of Love. It was an incredible time, with the energy of the people, the crowds, the passion, the excitement, the love, the smiley faces. What a time it was to be alive! Clubs were packed every night of the week across the city. I started the now legendary night 'Shoom' at the Fitness Centre near London Bridge to packed crowds week in and week out. Similar to Mark, I've been fortunate enough to make a career in music while travelling the world playing music to packed, happy, smiling crowds.

During 2005, I decided it was time to take a break from music and played a final set in London at Turnmills with Frankie Knuckles playing before me (RIP Frankie – FK Always). What I hadn't realised was that 18 months before this, Mark had developed an undiagnosed disease and was in chronic pain and barely able to function physically.

After the Turnmills party, Mark wrote a thank you letter to me, via *DJ Magazine*, for my DJ career up to that point, informing me that the uplifting music that I played that night had reawakened his love for music and life itself. I felt humbled and proud that the music had helped a friend recover his mindset after a serious disease, and therefore, profoundly transform the course of his life. We kept in touch throughout the next few years as there was much synergy developing between us.

By 2010 I had returned to being a DJ, and we both co-produced a record titled Night and Day that still receives plays by a broad range of DJs, in clubs, and on radio. The track was released on Kidology London, the label founded and owned by Mark. I have produced many tracks in my career, and working on this track with Mark is one that really stands out. The close quarters of the recording studio are where I became aware of his organisational skills, his methodical work ethic, his ambition, passion, focus, and attention to detail. During our discussions, Mark's quest for self-development following the incurable disease diagnosis became more apparent. We shared a great rapport with both music and self-development, which we have both invested time into studying.

I hold the utmost admiration and respect for Mark for overcoming these challenges and completely changing the course of his life. He has become a successful business operator with multiple profitable businesses and financial stability. Mark is now a dynamic business, wealth, and life coach, which resulted from his commitment to working smart and recreating himself with multiple streams of income. I'm sure a solid marriage with his wife and business partner Emma also helps to keep Mark grounded.

Investing years in therapy and self-development while studying with the world's finest coaches has clearly worked for Mark. Life is full of twists and turns and is very much about passing the knowledge of one's life experience and skills on to others. Helping others to achieve greatness through life mastery skills is a blessing. Passing on education and candidly sharing experiences with others is the essence of life and shows true leadership skills.

Life Remixed™ is the inspirational story of a life transition. Mark chronicles the roller-coaster ups and downs of being in the London limelight, of having the DJ lifestyle of fame, money, hedonism, and all the fun of the 1990s party decade. He describes the nights of being adored by fans and having the time of his life, and then being catapulted into the new millennium away from the enviable and desirable DJ lifestyle to the absolute lows of disease and financial insolvency.

I cannot imagine the mental and physical challenges of being contained at home in chronic pain with an undiagnosed disease; however, I saw Mark turn the corner into the road to recovery, becoming self-integrated and inspiring others. He's a shining example of how we can all make changes and recover from any setbacks that life may present.

Life Remixed™ is an outstanding story that follows Mark from DJ hero all the way down to health and financial zero and then follows him back up to success again. Mark has turned a negative period of challenges into a stable, positive life path. He has achieved this through his mindset and self-belief while taking massive daily action. This book is a candid and empowering story that shows we all can achieve our true greatness by thinking, feeling, and manifesting the life we deserve. We can be, do, and have whatever we think about.

It's time we all followed Mark's example and designed the life of our dreams!

Well done for writing this book, Mark.

Danny Rampling, 2020
DJ, Music Producer, Film Consultant, Radio 1 Presenter
Published Author of *Everything You Need to Know About DJing and Success* (Aurum Publishing)
www.mixcloud.com/dannyrampling

FOREWORD PART 2

BY LEWIS SENIOR

When Mark asked me if I would write one of the forewords for *Life Remixed*™, I immediately said yes but first wanted to read the book. Having been through it from cover to cover, I now have a further appreciation of just what an interesting and challenging life he has lived, and at the time of writing, he's still young, just turned 50!

As you read *Life Remixed*™, depending on when you came into this world, you will be able to relate to various aspects of his experiences, because in reality, we are all born 'imperfect'. There's always work to be done, regardless of gender, race, age, creed, religion, heritage, or skin colour, and thanks to such a diverse lifestyle described in the book, you will find many answers to your unanswered questions.

The beauty of Mark's story is that not only is he blessed with a level of vulnerability he is prepared to share with the world, but also through an incredible amount of self-awareness, personal development, and determination, Mark has taken some intentional actions and made a great life for himself, his lovely wife Emma, his family members, business partners, and colleagues.

It is great to see that he hasn't stopped there, as he works at expanding his network daily. Consequently, more and more people are being impacted by his positivity and dedication to helping others learn from his own trials, tribulations, learnings, and strategies for success.

For context, allow me to share that having worked in the oil and gas industry for over 30 years, in 2004, three partners and I founded a coaching organisation based on personality diversity technology called Equilibria. Primarily, our organization focuses on safety and productivity in high-risk industries by raising levels of understanding that the personality of each individual can significantly impact how they react or respond in any given moment. Our foundational self/team/others awareness tool is called E-Colors. It's because of our work that Mark connected with me nearly ten years ago.

Mark had already started his self-development continuum by the time we met. I flew into London Heathrow from the US (where we have several clients) and met him for our first face-to-face meeting. He was already working at the airport, so it was interesting to hear some of his story to date, which you will get to read in the ensuing chapters.

It became apparent to me very quickly that Mark was someone who was determined to make some significant strides in his life, and with the type of personality he had, it wouldn't be a stretch for him to become an Equilibria team member. Unfortunately, at the time, there was a dip in oil prices which impacted our activity, and we didn't want to have him join us without having guaranteed work opportunities. However, the connection was made, and as Mark will describe in one of the chapters, he began to understand that a lot of his choices actually were completely in line with what we describe as a personality style with Yellow/Blue tendencies.

People with these propensities are best described as *Relating Socialisers*, typically focused on people rather than tasks, have a strong desire to help others, like to be liked (even better, loved), are emotionally driven, don't like confrontation, and struggle to say 'no' for fear of upsetting someone. Actually, several people whose E-Colors are Yellow/Blue describe themselves as 'party animals'. If you knew Mark back in the day, do any of the behaviours described here sound like him?

Fortunately, we kept in touch, with Mark attempting to leverage his newfound knowledge within a company he was working for, which is when both Laura and David Senior (also with Equilibria) got to know Mark. From then on, he built his knowledge and mental muscles utilizing our online learning system, not only from a safety perspective but also applications for leadership, teamwork, effective communication, and self-management.

Over the years, we continued to keep in touch, particularly as we saw on social media his frequent visits to the hospital for knee operations. Then, this year, we reached out to Mark as we had further developed our actionable intelligence with a much more robust personality diversity report and follow-up program, which we thought he would find interesting both for him and his business.

I have nothing but admiration and appreciation for Mark and believe that his first book, *Life Remixed*™, will be yet another significant milestone in a journey of resilience and determination to better himself and those around him. He brings joy and happiness to virtually everyone who comes into his sphere of influence.

In my mind, I have dubbed him the 'London Lighthouse', keeping us all off the rocks while providing a clear vision for a bright future. Read on, and I am sure you will agree.

Lewis Senior (Yellow/Red), 2020
CEO and Co-founder Equilibria, Executive Senior Coach
Published Author of *At the End of the Day*
readourbooktoday.com

FOREWORD PART 3

BY KEVIN GREEN

I first knew of Mark in 2017 when he came into our Kevin Green Wealth (KGW) world via a three-day training event at a Heathrow hotel. He's told me since that he heard me present before this event when I shared the stage with Tony Robbins in London at Excel. I'm very happy he was there!

At six feet four inches, Mark is instantly recognisable, and I saw that he came to every KGW three-day training event after that. He was committed to learning and growing and understanding all the opportunities available to him within the KGW network. One of the first times I remember seeing him, though, his knees were so bad with arthritis that he was having trouble walking. However, I could see that he was determined. It was almost as if he knew that by following my strategies, he could recover his health. He also played the long game with us, as he mentioned very early on to one of my team that he'd like to become a KGW coach. Over the last three years, Mark has been such a committed learner he's become someone who I know I can rely on and someone whose company I enjoy.

Mark grasped the messages given to him from the KGW stage quicker than just about anyone. He is obviously blessed with a good level of intelligence, and he has the work ethic to go along with it. Mark and his wife, Emma, have now started their own UK property portfolio, and I know Mark fully understands the Rich Rules to success. He is deeply inspired to keep growing and giving service to as many people as possible. Between them, Mark and Emma now have multiple businesses and continue to learn and grow within the KGW team. In 2019 we shook hands on Mark becoming a KGW coach, and he's now guiding new clients through the program to learn my strategies so they can live the life of their dreams.

Mark and Emma continue to go from strength to strength themselves with further plans to expand their current companies.

Mark is up for everything and fun to be around. *Life Remixed*™ is his story of being a young, headstrong, worldwide DJ and music producer, and then sinking and going through some hellish health and financial challenges to become the successful man he is today. I know his desire to do something important in the world is strong. His passion is to do as much as he can to help others avoid or recover from a crisis, and he's already well on his way.

Congratulations on completing this *Life Remixed*™ book, Mark. Well done. Keep going and keep growing.

Kevin Green, 2020
Multi-Millionaire, Entrepreneur, and Business Coach
www.kevingreen.co.uk

INTRODUCTION

IN EVERY CRISIS, THERE IS AN OPPORTUNITY

HAVE YOU EVER SUFFERED from poor health, lack of wealth, unhappiness, anxiety, or even sunk into a depression? Are you currently stuck or feel like you're not reaching your full potential in life? If any of that is true for you, you're in the right place, as I've lived through all of that.

In these pages, you will find proven solutions that will make your life better, even when situations or circumstances seem to be the worst they can be.

This book is the record of the journey that I took to realise my full potential, rising above the mediocre person I used to be to become the person I am happy and grateful to be today.

In this book, you'll find life remix strategies that will help change your life for the better. Some of it may make you feel uncomfortable, but please know that it's OK. Nothing of note was ever achieved inside a comfort zone. So please don't immediately accept or reject anything I write. My personal request is that you read through it all with an open mind and then try the success strategies out for yourself. Once they work and you see things changing for the better, it will become much easier for you to make life's bigger decisions and stick to them.

For my part, I am looking forward to the day we meet, and I get the chance to work with you towards your ultimate health and happiness. I'll always be interested to hear more about what you're looking to achieve.

These days I own multiple businesses, and I'm a self-development, leadership, wealth, business, and life coach. However, trust me, it wasn't always this way!

When I was younger, I lived another dream life as an international DJ, record producer, remixer, and record label owner until one day in my mid-thirties, out of nowhere, my life sunk into an absolute disaster. I physically collapsed, was then diagnosed with an incurable 'dis-ease', and later suffered a bankruptcy.

At fifty years of age now, thankfully, I've been extremely successful at remixing my own life (multiple businesses, wealth, marriage, harmony, success, and focus), and my aim is to help others improve their lives too. I offer straight-talking, simple strategies, and positive support to help people who are experiencing many types of issues, including addictions, health, relationship, and financial challenges.

I'm so grateful now that I am happy, healthy, wealthy, and in a great marriage. I know I can help you move towards your goals.

It's time to remix your life. Keep an open mind, and let's go!

Big love, Mark x

www.markwilkinsonofficial.com
www.liferemixed.co.uk

THE MISSION

MY MISSION for writing this book is simple. I would like to inspire others to improve their lives. My goal is for everyone to live a really great life, to truly love, and to learn to live and enjoy the present moment. Once learned, this is the way to enjoy every moment of your life (not just struggle through as I did for many years). I would love for you to be able to feel true joy and happiness and to earn your own fortune along the way. I enjoy being able to share this joy and knowledge and inspiring and creating amazing experiences for everyone that I meet. As you'll come to see, my mission not only helps other people achieve great lives, but it also allows me to live to my life's purpose. And for that, I am extremely grateful to you for buying this book and coming to say 'Hello' when we can meet in person.

THE DESCRIPTION

SINCE I'VE STARTED THIS PROJECT, I've been asked many times, 'What exactly is a remix?' So let me explain. A remix is when I take the vocals and musical parts of a pre-existing track and rearrange them into something new. I add to the parts I like, remove or change the parts I don't, and something new is created. This then becomes the 'Mark Wilkinson Remix'. Your life remix is exactly the same. You keep the parts you like about you and your life, you remove the ones you don't, and you create new things that you truly love. Committing to this process means that you feel great about your life in all areas: happiness, health, wealth, and relationships.

I've also had several people ask me to define 'house music'. House music is a genre of electronic dance music characterised by a repetitive four-on-the-floor beat and a tempo of 120 to 130 beats per minute. Head to my Mixcloud page to find my DJ mixes and great examples.

www.mixcloud.com/markwilkinsonofficial
To those that already know, have a smiley face.

THE REMIX OPPORTUNITIES

AT THE END OF EACH CHAPTER, you'll find bullet points that list *Life Remixed*™ opportunities for you to think about and put into action. You'll need to commit to your own life remix to be able to answer some of the questions and get yourself moving towards your new ways of thinking, feeling, and acting that will lead to your new and improved life. I can testify here and now that the results are well worth the effort.

CHAPTER 1

ANOTHER ONE BITES THE DUST

History has demonstrated that the most notable winners usually en-
countered heart-breaking obstacles before they triumphed.
They won because they refused to become discouraged
by their defeats.

– B.C. Forbes, Founder of Forbes Magazine

Have you ever woken up after a broken and extremely painful night's
sleep, sat on the side of your bed, and known that whichever way you
move your body, any attempt is going to be so excruciatingly painful
that it would just be easier to give up? If you can answer yes, then you
understand my journey; if not, then welcome to Life Remixed™.

– Mark Wilkinson

A Little Party Never Killed Nobody.

– The Great Gatsby

ONE LATE SATURDAY AFTERNOON IN 2003, I was thirty-three years old, and it was yet another recovery day after a big, loud, and very intoxicated late night out in one of London's top nightclubs. I was making some food in the kitchen of my basement flat in Marylebone in Central London. I'd recently sold my house in the suburbs and moved five minutes' walk from Oxford Circus to live the DJ dream, to be closer to all the nightclubs where I was playing my favourite house music most nights of the week. It meant I could enjoy (even more than I had already up to that point) the full-on party lifestyle that I was committed to living. I was at the height of my DJ and production career and also in my physical prime, or so I thought.

As I made my way back from the kitchen to the sofa, my right leg gave way beneath me. With an almighty crash, I fell against the wall in the front room and landed in a heap on the floor. Now, I've always been a tall lad. When I was young, my mum used to tell all the people we met that I wasn't allowed to stop growing until I was six feet four inches, and guess what happened: exactly that! That's the equivalent of 193 cm, and I'm not a skinny bloke either, usually weighing in over 100 kg (15.5 stone or 217 pounds), so my fall was a long way down with some serious weight behind it! By the time I hit the floor, I hit it hard. I lay there in agony, really not understanding what just happened. I was shocked and covered in the contents of the tray of food I'd been holding. As I lay there, I couldn't help but think to myself, *Really? REALLY? What the … is going on?*

This was not a normal occurrence, not at all. It had never happened before, at least not while I was sober, and being honest, rarely when I was drunk or out of it either! It certainly hadn't happened whilst at home or at work. Up to that point, I'd had a 16-year professional career as a London DJ. I was lucky enough to be based in the epicentre of London at exactly the right time and at exactly the right age! I loved the journey of playing house music all over the world. And no matter what time zone I was in or how out of it I got, I was always in control of myself and always, always steady on my feet.

Good balance had been a blessing. One of my earliest memories was when I was four years old and came out of playschool and asked my mum if she'd buy me a bike. I remember she said to me, 'You can't even ride a bike! Can you?' So I said to my friend, 'Lend me your bike, please.' And I shot off up the road into the distance. Mum stood there opened mouthed as I disappeared around the corner and completely out of sight. You'll get to see that I've always been the headstrong type. The bike meant freedom, and this was my first experience of it.

Back to the life-changing day of my collapse. As I fell against the wall and onto the floor, all I could feel was this searing pain up the back of my right leg. It felt like fire, like a hot poker had been rammed inside my leg. I shouted as I fell, and the tray of food I was carrying went flying. I immediately knew it was bad. It felt bad, and as I lay there, I could feel the pain pulsating and getting stronger. The back of my right leg was throbbing. It felt like it was burning up and from the inside out. As I tried to get up, I realised there was no strength in my leg at all, like it had stopped working, and it was obvious I needed some help.

Thankfully, my brother Daniel was there. He's four years younger than me and has always been the more sensible one. My friend Dave had lived in the flat before us. It was on Weymouth Street, just off Harley Street, and near Oxford Circus. When I needed a place to crash in a hurry, I'd often stay there. When Dave decided to move into a new place, the Weymouth Street flat became available. Of course, I jumped at the chance to rent it. It's right in the centre of London, close to all the clubs that I worked in when I worked in the city. It was too good to pass up. It was a two-bed basement flat, so I asked my brother if he fancied some Central London living for a while. He was working up near London Bridge so he could walk to work every morning, which made it a no brainer for him too. The buzz of living a five-minute walk from Oxford Circus was too much for me to resist. I was getting over a recent heartbreak, so I needed something new to happen. I still remember the excitement I felt moving in. For me, it was just so I could go out to DJ at 11pm and get home quickly, usually a little bit worse for wear with the company of an attractive woman. I'd be getting home a lot cheaper than a £40–£50 cab ride back to the suburbs, too, and it suited Dan, so a win-win.

Anyway, as I hit the floor, I think he thought I was messing about. He said, 'Are you alright?' half laughing. 'Come on, get up.' When he stood up and looked over the top of the sofa at my pained face, food everywhere and all up the walls, alongside my pathetic and unsuccessful attempts to try to stand up again, it was then he realised that I was in real trouble. He rushed over and kept saying, 'Are you OK? Are you OK?' I was in shock so I don't remember answering him. He helped me back to my feet and slowly over to the sofa to help me lay down. 'What happened?' he said. I just looked at him blankly and said, 'I have no idea, bro.'

I didn't know it then, but this was the first day of an 18-month physical decline into a full-on health crisis. The next year and a half saw me spiral down into a pit of agony, both physically and mentally.

All my joints developed severe pain and began to freeze up, meaning I was unable to stand, walk, or move around as any normal healthy guy in his early thirties should be able to do. Across my whole body, not just my leg where it started, but everywhere, every joint was stiff and painful. I had to start living off painkillers every three hours at first and then more and more of them as the pain worsened. I could hardly sleep without shouting out in pain when the Ibuprofen wore off during the night. Everyday life became more and more difficult until eventually, life just became a struggle for survival, especially for a lifelong self-employed DJ and record producer. I was used to partying hard without having to think too much, but I soon realised there's no sick pay from nightclubs either.

Our basement flat was 40 steps from Harley Street in London (I counted them), which is the London base for some of the best (and most expensive) doctors in the world. As I'd only recently moved up there, I didn't have access to a National Health Service (NHS) physician right at the time when I needed one most!

Being the independent type, I'd never really asked anyone for much help previously in my life, so I tried to soldier on through the pain and kept self-medicating with the painkillers and thinking perhaps it'll wear off. But soon, the Ibuprofen stopped working, and after a while, I ended up having to take them every hour to lessen the pain. My stomach started having terrible cramps because of the painkillers, and I knew I was taking way too many, but the pain all over was so excruciatingly bad, it felt like I just had to do something. I had to take something to try and survive this agony.

I've been asked why didn't I go to an accident and emergency (A&E) department. To be honest, after the initial collapse, it was such a slow burn, a day-by-day deterioration over weeks and into months, it just didn't occur to me. I just kept on 'trying to be normal'. Maybe I didn't want to trouble anyone. Maybe it didn't feel like an emergency. Whatever the reason, I wasn't asking for help from anyone, let alone from the right people, and in hindsight, I made a huge mistake there.

As it was a short walk away, I did start to pay to see some private doctors in and around Harley Street. The problem was they took my money, but none of them ever came close to diagnosing me correctly. I saw numerous doctors and had lots of expensive tests, but all to no avail. None of them prescribed me anything that worked, so my abuse of the painkillers went on and on and on.

Along with the pain, other strange things started to happen. I suffered a savage and unhealthy weight loss, losing four stone (56 pounds or 25 kg) in two weeks! I was skin and bone and looked very unhealthy. I went from my usual slightly overweight party self to skinny-as-a-rake 'sick boy' in almost the blink of an eye.

With the physical decline in full flow, I continued to spiral downwards mentally too. The worst times were when the suicidal thoughts came into my mind. Too many times, I thought to myself that this pain just isn't worth it, that a life like this isn't worth living. From being such a happy young DJ now brought down to being a man who could barely shuffle around in his own home, I asked myself over and over, 'Is this it? Is this the pain I'll be suffering for the rest of my life? From age thirty-three to whenever I die, am I going to be in this much pain?' If that was true, then I'd gone from *living the DJ dream* to *this isn't worth living anymore* in one foul hit. In eighteen months, I'd gone from loving life to wanting to finish it. Mental.

I don't think I would have ever actually gone through with suicide. As a kid, my mum told me that it would be a selfish thing to do. Someone else would have to find me and then deal with the aftermath. Besides that, I don't think I'd actually have been brave enough to go through with it. I did think about a few different ways: taking pills, crashing my car on a motorway, jumping off a bridge or a tall building. Luckily though, I've always had a problem with heights, so I wouldn't have liked it up there at all! The thoughts were very real, though; I have to admit that, and they were really awful.

Up to this point, I thought I'd been a decent enough guy, an OK friend, but maybe not always the best son or brother, not the best boyfriend either. But also, as a DJ, I was the man at the front, the leader of the night, getting everyone involved, keeping the energy up, keeping up to date with the music, making the party happen, making sure every weekend people had a great time and also having a lot of fun myself in the process. I'd managed to build a decent income for myself, too, and up to that point, I'd navigated 16 years of working in the music business. I'd made money as a DJ, promoter, record producer, remixer, and record label owner. Trust me when I say it wasn't the easiest or most balanced existence, but I'd been successful, the bills were always paid, and I'd enjoyed a lot of it.

Deep down, I always knew I was masking something, though, a definite lack of confidence, a lack of belief in myself and also in my music, both DJing and production, that we'll discuss later in this book. On the outside, I didn't take life too seriously. I laughed off my insecurities as much as possible or used alcohol or drugs to get out of my head and forget everything. Looking back now, I just didn't want to acknowledge the negative emotions within me that lead to my addictive and bad behaviour and all the stupid mistakes and the self-destructive actions that I ended up suffering from because of my lack of confidence.

On the face of it, I was too busy enjoying myself and loving the fun parts of my life: travelling the world playing music for club goers to dance the night away, getting the VIP treatment wherever I went, getting given whatever was going, having loads of female attention, and getting well paid for all this!

So, this moment of physical collapse was a huge shock to me, and the ensuing 18 months of undiagnosed pain was savage, awful. At the height of the pain, it's easiest to describe my day like this:

10pm before leaving the house – Take painkillers and, assuming I could face it, go and play a gig to earn some money. My regular gigs got me a stool to sit on so I could still play and at least still survive! I'd continue to take painkillers every hour or two to get me through the club night.

Anytime up until 6am or until after the gig – Take more painkillers, go to bed, wake up every one to two hours in agony. My ribs were particularly painful in my sleep. It felt like someone was stabbing me. I'd often wake up with a scream of pain throughout my broken sleep.

12 noon, wake up, still exhausted – Take more painkillers, sit up, try very slowly to stand up, feel the agony in every joint right through my body. You name it, there was searing pain, and in some areas, lots of swelling. I couldn't touch or be touched, and even trying to shake hands with anyone was agony. It felt like my hand was on fire.

Whilst awake and throughout the rest of the day – Keep taking painkillers every one to two hours, shuffle to the sofa, watch TV, play PlayStation, nap, make food, or better still hope someone would bring me some food, until 10pm, and then start all over again.

With all the painkillers I was taking, it wasn't long before I was getting savage Irritable Bowel Syndrome (IBS) pain in my stomach. (More on that later as my problems had started there when I was 26; but I didn't listen to my body at all back then.) Every day everything just got more and more difficult to do, and as it did, my fear kept growing that I'd never be 'normal' again, never be the life and soul of the party again, never be happy again. I'd been in the thick of it since I was handed my first sip of alcohol by an adult when I was 14. Now, at 33, I was sinking fast, quickly becoming a sickly recluse. I was stuck to the sofa or in my bed. The necessity of pain management was stronger than any conscious choices I could make. It was so challenging for a man like me because it wasn't the me that I'd known all my life up until that point.

In fact, as I began to grow through this health challenge and a few other life challenges that I'll share with you as we go through our life remix, I began to realise that all my greatest doubts, fears, and worries had come to pass. Everything that I had worried about my whole life was now a reality. My physical health had completely gone, and I'd always worried about my DJ bookings drying up as I got older. What if my career wouldn't last into my later years? I'd worry about not having any trade or assets behind me, no other income. What would happen when my music wasn't cool anymore, and the bookings and money ran out? Well, here it was, showing up in my life, right on time. I was so ill I wasn't able to earn anything like the money I needed, and any small amount of cash that I had behind me was quickly diminishing. The mask of happiness that I showed to the world most of my younger years had disappeared.

How had this happened? What had happened? How was I ever going to recover from this? And why me? Why did it happen to me?

These are questions that I had to find the answers to if I wanted to survive this. The alternative was just to give up. I was basically forced to look at my own life and ask myself some deep and altogether better questions. I now know that this happened exactly as it was meant to in order to move me towards a better life. However, there was still a lot to learn!

So, here we go then – *Life Remixed*™. In the following chapters, I'll share with you: this is how much fun we had, this is how bad it got, and this is how I fixed it. I'm going to share the highs and lows of an incredible DJ and music career, all the way from the beginning right through to learning how to remix and make changes in my own life for the better. Every strategy in this book is something you can use for yourself. For me, all of this was essential in order to recover from a painful nightmare.

· · · · · ·

CHAPTER 1 – REMIX OPPORTUNITIES

- When you understand the power of negative thoughts, you'll never allow another one to stay in your mind for long.
- You create exactly what you're thinking (and feeling).
- Always look after your body, because you only get the one.
- If I could create all this crap with an overwhelming amount of fear, doubt, worry, and negative thinking, what could I create if I changed myself to think only positive thoughts?

My first official photoshoot at age 2.

For more photos from Chapter 1, go to www.markwilkinsonofficial.com/life-remixed.

CHAPTER 2

GOOD TIMES

Strange, how the best moments of our lives we scarcely notice except in looking back.

– Joe Abercrombie

Don't cry because it's over, smile because it happened.

– Doctor Seuss

IT WAS 1990, I WAS 20 YEARS OLD, and I got a phone call.

'Hi, who's this? Oh, OK, Hi.

You want me to DJ? Where? In Paris?

When? Next weekend? For £1,000?

(Let me have a think about that). Yeah, OK!!'

I was still living at the family home with my mum, her partner, and my brother in the leafy suburbs of South West London. I'm sure it'd be cooler to say I was brought up in a much rougher and tougher part of the world. But being honest, Hampton Hill was a lovely part of the London Borough of Richmond upon Thames bordering onto Bushy Park.

I had answered the phone, having set up a separate landline telephone number in my bedroom so that I could talk privately to my mates (and girls) whenever I wanted without the unwanted attention of the rest of the house. The hideous brick-sized mobile phones were still a year or two away, so the separate line in my room would have to suffice for the time being.

At first, I thought this must be one of my mates on a windup, playing a joke. The voice on the other end of the phone said, 'Hi, I'm a club promoter from Paris, and I've heard great things about you.'

I tried to hide my excitement about a weekend return flight to 'Gay Paree' with a £1,000 fee! But who cares? This was big time! What a result! My first love was sitting next to me on the bed when I took the call, and she was very impressed. This was all great for my young and as yet uncontrolled ego!

My dad, who was 50 when I was born in 1970, sadly had died the year before in 1989 and left me some money. It wasn't hundreds of thousands, but it was enough for a 19-year-old to have some fun and freedom in London at that time for sure.

Living a Young Man's Dream

The summer before in 1988, acid house, a subgenre of house music, had hit the London clubs. Four London DJs (Paul Oakenfold, Danny Rampling, Nicky Holloway, and Johnny Walker), in a now well-documented story, had come back from Ibiza the year before and started playing the music they'd heard on the White Isle all over London clubland.

This was perfect timing age-wise for me as I had turned 18. Clubland was vibrant and buzzing every night of the week. The combination of the energy of house music, with its four-to-the-floor drum beat, coupled with the drugs LSD (acid) and MDMA (ecstasy), had people dancing all night, every night. Sometimes even when the music stopped, they were still going! I'm sure I saw a bloke dancing to a car alarm in the street once.

So I did what it felt like every 18-year-old was doing at that time (well, some of us anyway!). I gave up the day job at the Bank in Twickenham, and I went out to every single club I could possibly find that was playing the music I loved. I royally partied my arse off and danced the night away with thousands of others. We were young and free, partying night after night and generally right through into the next day, the day after that, and sometimes the day after that. (Thankfully, there weren't any mobile phones with cameras around back then!)

I also made sure to buy everything else a young man needed for his newfound passions: cars – an Orange Ford Cortina Mk5 followed by a blue Ford Escort to get us to every party we could find – and, of course, some DJ equipment for my bedroom. At the time, it was two Citronic belt-driven (basically crap!) record decks and an old 2 track mixer so I could learn to blend the music together. I was happy. I also set about buying more and more music on vinyl and getting out and about in clubland as much as possible. I was in every club and record shop that was open!

From the beginning, I honestly didn't think about or expect to make a career from clubbing or music. I was just enjoying myself. However, I've always been the sociable type, so I got to know a lot of people quickly and easily. I fast became known in London clubland. I suppose being six feet four inches meant I was pretty noticeable in a crowd. You only had to say, 'Wilkie, the tall lad with the glasses', and they all knew who you meant.

It was a time of pure hedonism. In case you don't know what hedonism means, according to the Oxford dictionary, it's *the theory that pleasure (in the sense of the satisfaction of desires) is the highest good and proper aim of human life* – and I felt it. We were actually living it and loving it, pure joy and pleasure. Music was my true joy, and in my young life, earning money through music was almost effort-less. Apart from the odd dodgy promoter who I'd have to chase around the club or try to get him to come round from his self-inflicted haze to pay me so I could go home, it was all pretty easy living the young man's dream.

As I didn't have to work for a while, I now had the majority of my days free. I hung out in record shops buying all the tunes on vinyl I'd heard the night before. This suited my sociable side as I got to know all the staff, and they started to save me the vinyl exclusives. As soon as I got home, I recorded DJ mixes onto cassette tapes. With record producers now using computer programmed drums on records, it became much easier to keep the beats mixed in time, much easier than the disco music of the 1970s with its live drums played by actual human beings!

With my home setup in place, it was possible to have continuous music mixed and recorded onto cassette tapes, which I'd then mass-produce for all my mates. I made regular Mark Wilkinson DJ mixes that I gave out in bars and nightclubs for people to listen to in their cars or at after-parties. When I got savvier, I'd target club promoter friends who could listen to my tapes and maybe even give me a booking. Had to be worth a try.

As part of my love for music, people, and nightclubs, I made sure I went out and listened to as many DJs as possible. I heard more and more of them with their musical choices, and there were a few who really inspired me when they played. My first inspiration was Andrew Weatherall. Back in the late 1980s, he was playing a lot of US and Italian house music. He had tracks that other DJs just didn't have or couldn't get hold of. I remember he used to cover up some of the centre labels of his records so other DJs couldn't see the artists' names and titles when peering over the DJ booth for a sneaky look. Hey, it's a jungle out there and a competitive business, even back then! However, Andrew always managed to have the most upfront tunes and was very much in demand to DJ because of that and his excellent beat matching and mixing. He was an inspirational guy who has recently passed away and left a musical legacy that I and many others could only dream of having. RIP Andy.

Here are some other inspiring DJs that I remember:

- Danny Rampling – Danny is the founder of Shoom and largely responsible for introducing house and Balearic music sounds to London. Thank you for the foreword, Danny.
- Terry Farley – Terry had a great choice of tunes.
- X-Press 2 (Rocky, Diesel, and Ashley) used to play on six decks and three mixers to expand their sound and produced a few club classic tracks along the way.
- Frankie Knuckles – Frankie was the founder of house music from his days at The Warehouse in Chicago. Frankie played wonderful

uplifting American soulful house sounds that mixed together seamlessly for hours. I miss Frankie to this day (RIP).

- Tony Humphries – Tony could mix tracks together in key for longer than any other DJ we knew, and he used his New York City (NYC) radio show to reach deep into London's club scene. We got those tapes of the Humphries mix show from a place in Kensington Market.

- CJ Mackintosh – CJ is a DMC World DJ Mixing Champion and by far the best (in my opinion) British Ministry of Sound resident. CJ mixed wonderfully and chose top vocal tunes week in, week out. You always knew when CJ took over the main room sound system. We called him 'The Guvnor'.

- Norman Jay MBE – Norman is best known for his sweet soulful sounds and for the legendary 'Good Times' at Notting Hill Carnival. He was awarded Member of the British Empire (MBE) in 2002 and has recently written *Mr Good Times*, well worth a read.

- Roger Sanchez – Roger plays uplifting US music from NYC. He's a four-time DJ Awards winner and Grammy award winner.

- Sasha – I was really impressed the first time I heard Sasha. He was incredible at the Sunday night club Shave Yer Tongue in Bracknell, where I played regularly. The first time we heard Sasha in the South was when he came down from his residency in Stoke on a Sunday night after being featured on the front cover of *Mixmag* with a halo around his head! They called him the first superstar DJ. Memorable.

These great DJs had their own styles of music and mixing, and they consistently rocked the floor week in, week out wherever and whenever we heard them. Like thousands of others, I travelled all over London and the South East of England during this iconic time to hear my favourite DJs and their music. What memories. Incredible and happy times.

I wasn't always impressed with every DJ I heard, though. I used to stand to the side of the dance floor and listened intently to what they were doing, their musical choices, their mixing, and whether they were engaged with the dance floor. In all honesty, I quickly realised that I could be as good if not better than some of them on the circuit (obviously in my own opinion here!). As a clubber, a bad dancer, and a musical appreciator, I always wanted to have the energy kept high. I believed that when I got my turn and played my tunes, the crowd would come with me on the uplifting journey. Most of the time, they did, which is one of the reasons I got booked so much right from when I started out.

I would watch and listen to the other DJs carefully. Sometimes they'd deliberately play some deeper, more downbeat records to give the crowd a rest and then be able to lift them back up with a big tune a few minutes later. Although that was OK, that wasn't my style. I was fairly confident from listening to all my favourite DJs and speaking to friends in clubs that a lot of others felt the same. They wanted to be uplifted by the music and not educated by a DJ playing records that they didn't know or even like. It seemed that certain DJs on occasion would play purely for themselves and not the crowd.

I knew the uplifting Italian piano anthems of the time ('piano scream ups' as they were known) were massive with the crowds, and they were also my favourite tunes, so I made sure I played plenty of them. The reactions of the crowds were amazing as it was such happy and joyful and uplifting music. I loved the pianos and the vocals. I got off even more on the crowd going wild to the music I chose. The tracks made people cheer and dance on tables or on the bar. It was such a buzz for me looking around the club seeing every person moving to the beat. Simply put, I would play all the tunes that I would want to hear myself on a night out, and pretty soon, I started to get a name for myself.

I kept on practicing at home and giving those DJ mix tapes away. I just wanted to share my musical choices and my mixing skills and for people to be as happy and buzzing as I was with the amazing music that I was buying and listening to. It didn't take long before I had learned to beat-match vinyl really well (a bit of a skill in those days before digital and sync buttons), blending tracks into each other seamlessly. Putting sound effects and vocal acapellas over tracks to make my own recognisable DJ sound was a real bonus. (A unique selling point, a marketing team would call it today!) So, I had my own sound of DJing, and the feedback I got from people who'd heard my tapes was great. This was well before social media, so it was cool that the verbal feedback came from far and wide, and my name was getting around. People were talking to each other, saying, 'Have you heard that new Mark Wilkinson mix tape?' It wasn't long before the phone was ringing, and my first paid DJ gigs came through.

I got into DJing through an absolute love and passion for music. As a clubber, I saw the joy in people's faces when they were dancing and cheering. I would also watch the DJs when they were rocking a dance floor, and as I became friends with more of them when they got booked for a huge gig and saw their joy, excitement, and enthusiasm, I thought to myself, '*I want some of that*' and knew I could do a great job.

Without losing my own style, I started modelling myself on some of the big-name DJs that I've already mentioned. Musically and stylistically, I took the best from each of them and added my own brand of uplifting energy. I was loving it and growing into a confident DJ who could rock a crowd and enjoy himself immensely along the way. This was shaping up to be some kind of ride! I was in London, the epicentre of the house music explosion, at exactly the right time and at exactly the right age, with all the tools and skills necessary to bring joy to dance floors.

Back to the Beginning

I was born on 3 September 1970. As I was growing up, Mum often shared with me that it was the same day that World War II broke out back in 1939. Actually, to be pedantic, I've discovered since that it was the same day that Britain declared war on Germany. I didn't know it at the time, but the aftermath of WWII was going to affect my family deeply.

Some of my earliest memories are still things that are important to me now. I remember my mum's shock with me disappearing up the road on my best friend's bike that day. (She hadn't seen me learning to ride in nursery school earlier that morning!) In 1975, when it was discovered that I couldn't see the words written on the board properly at school, the local optician couldn't diagnose me properly, so I got sent to the Eye Hospital in Elephant and Castle for my first glasses prescription. Ironically, the world-famous Ministry of Sound club is situated right around the corner from the Eye Hospital, and I would have my own turn as a resident DJ there some 20 years later.

1976 and I remember first hearing music on Mum's record player in the downstairs living room. She was mostly listening to Elvis and The Beatles at the time, and I found the melodic songs wonderful. I remember the feelings of joy and elation just listening over and over to my favourite songs. I didn't love the ballads. I wanted to hear the faster and more uplifting songs every time. It was always about the energy, the buzz, the feeling for me! Around the same time, I was taken to my first Chelsea match by a family friend, and Mum and Dad bought me my first record player for my room.

The impact of these early formative years on all of us is clear to me. To this day, I still wear glasses. I still love music, travelling, riding my bikes and motorbikes, and of course, my love for Chelsea Football Club remains.

As much as they loved me, and I loved them, my early memories of Mum and Dad were a challenge for me. I didn't understand why at the time, but I remember being told that life was difficult, that we had to be fearful, that the world was a scary place, that we didn't have enough. Usually, these worries were around money.

My mum lived 100% for her boys. She worked so hard for Dan and me. My dad didn't earn enough money to keep us all, so sometimes she'd work two or three jobs at a time just to make ends meet. She even did a cleaning job for a while, which I know she disliked immensely. And bless him, my dad was highly intelligent but didn't have enough confidence in himself to earn enough money, which meant my mum worked her butt off to look after us.

However, despite their very best efforts, I was being raised in a 'lack mentality' environment. As far as my parents could see, we never had enough of anything, money was always tight, and I always remember the fear of *someone might break in* or *we might lose the house*. It was a lot of fear and lack for a young lad to deal with.

It obviously didn't always help that from an early age I was demanding and headstrong. One day, it even cost my mum her wedding ring finger! If you're squeamish, please jump these two paragraphs, and also, I'm really very, very sorry, Mum! The story goes, I was around two years old when we were at the park, and I got overly confident and ran up the steps of a really tall slide. The problem came when I got to the top and completely bottled it and lost my nerve. So there I was, stuck at the top of the slide, shaking like a leaf.

My mum had to leave the pram at the bottom of the slide and come up after me. She got up to me and sat us both down so that we'd slide down together. She pushed us off from the top, and as we came down, she caught her wedding ring finger in a metal washer on the side of the slide and horribly ripped off the top of her finger. Disaster! She must've been in so much pain! I can't even imagine it. She had to wrap it in a tissue and, as this was 1975, walk back to the house to get to a phone to get some help. Again, I'm SO sorry, Mum!

When I knew him, my dad struggled a lot with life. He was 50 when I was born and didn't have good physical or mental health. He died at 69 when I was just 19 years old. He had his first major heart attack in 1979 when I was nine years old. I was so young I really didn't know what was happening. I just remember my brother and I got sent to a friend's house while our dad was taken to the hospital. Then we all went up to the hospital most days to sit around for hours to see how he was doing. To be honest, I didn't want to be there. I'd rather be out on my bike, listening to music, or playing football in the park with my mates whose dads weren't in hospital and suffering these major life traumas.

As I grew into a teenager, I found it all more and more difficult to deal with. You've heard of fight or flight, right? Well, with the benefit of hindsight, a lot of what happens over the next 25 years is my flight mechanism kicking in, escapism of the highest order.

With all the health issues my dad was having, I'm surprised my parents even considered it, but they did discuss trying to get both my brother and me into the private school Hampton Grammar (as it was called then) on Hanworth Road. It's a very well-known posh boys' school, and perhaps my life would have been very different had I gone there. My dad even wanted to get me in on an army scholarship and to send me straight off to the army after the 6th form. Mum wasn't having any of that, though, and she won. I do know that they did their level best to get us the best education, but they couldn't scrape the money together for both my brother and me to go to the posh school, so we both ended up in the comprehensive school, Rectory, next door.

Have you ever seen The Inbetweeners television show? If you know what teenage boys are like and you're not easily offended, then give it a go. It's a hilarious comedy about the adventures of a group of lads in the suburbs, and in all honesty, it absolutely could have been written about me and my mates. The character Will seems to be loosely based on me (except the bit when he shits himself in the exam room, of course!). 'Briefcase wanker' was a real thing for me. My mum's father had been an accountant, so she did what she knew best and sent me to a rough-and-ready comprehensive school on my first day, aged 11, looking like a mini-accountant, complete with flares and a briefcase in tow. Needless to say, the other kids hammered me from day one!

It only took three months of me being there amongst all the other cool kids to start to blend in a bit better. To stop me from getting verbally battered daily, I started wearing sta-pressed, Farah, or waffle trousers. Throw in a diamond-cut Pringle jumper or a Lyle & Scott with a loosely done up tie with a tie-pin through the collar of my shirt, and I was doing OK. I'd do anything to fit in!

As my social skills and confidence grew a bit, I found myself getting in with the other lads easily, with us getting into our fair share of troubles. Wherever and whenever there was something dodgy going on, you'd find me and my mates. The teachers didn't like our little group and probably for good reason.

As I said, my dad had issues with both his physical and mental health. It was tragic, really. His first major mental breakdown that I knew of came in 1983. By this time, I was already acting out big time at school. Mum was getting called up there on a regular basis to see various teachers that I'd upset. They all said the same thing: 'Mark is an intelligent boy but far too easily distracted.' I got loads of de-merits and was put on report cards every week to monitor my behaviour. I think some of it was because I found learning pretty easy, and in some ways, the pace of the classes was too slow for me. When the other kids couldn't keep up with me, I would just get bored and mess about. I was easily distracted, although, with hindsight, the comedy and messing about was probably in part me trying to distract myself and forget my troubles.

By the time I was 13 back in 1983, I was putting up with going to school because I had to, but at the weekends, I started to find my own fun. My best mate from school invited me to go to another Chelsea game with him and a load of friends from Hampton and Hanworth. I was well up for it. As I've said, I'd been before when I was much younger, but that was with a friend of my parents, so the second time going to Chelsea with the lads from school was when I really got into the atmosphere of a big night game at Stamford Bridge. I was barely a teen-ager, and I was hooked. It was the crowd and the mixture of passion and aggression which I loved. From then on, blue is, was, and always will be, the colour.

With all the lads, I started following Chelsea home and away. I remember bunking off school to go to midweek away games. We once went all the way to Walsall, and another time to York. We got on the train from Euston and Kings Cross, respectively. Honestly, what were we thinking? We were 14 years of age and leaving school straight after the afternoon registration, getting the bus, then taking the underground up to London, getting onto the InterCity train, arriving in time for the 7.45pm evening kick-off, and then getting the train back after the game and ending up back into a deserted Central London at 1 or 2am, sometimes even later, then waiting for the night bus home and getting on with some very strange people, finally getting back in at 3 or 4am! I'd told my mum I was staying at a friend's house whose parents didn't seem to worry (or care) as much as my mum. We'd stroll back into school mid-morning the next day and not really care about the lessons we'd missed. Somehow, we got away with this on more than one occasion.

In 1994, Chelsea got into their first European competition in more than 20 years, playing against Viktoria Zizkov in Prague (well, somewhere near Prague anyway). The Czech authorities moved the game 100 miles away to a small town called Jablonec, as they thought they could control the influx of excited but ticketless Chelsea fans better in that location. It was an adventure for us getting across Europe, dodging the authorities on trains, planes, and automobiles, and then trying to find a ticket, and eventually getting into the game anyway!

Supporting Chelsea continues to be an adventure for me, and it led me to be at the 2008 UEFA Champions League Final in Moscow on a momentous night when John Terry slipped and missed 'that' penalty, and we ended up losing to Manchester United. I remember seeing grown men cry that night and thinking, come on lads, it's only a game! It didn't matter either, as we won it in 2012 in Munich, beating Bayern in their own backyard. The travel, crowds, excitement, people, camaraderie, fun – all of these experiences run subconsciously through many areas of my life.

When I was 14, I was given my first sip of alcohol by an adult at a party. I remember straight away feeling a bit lightheaded. I remember liking it, though, and soon after, we started to buy our own alcohol and head over to the local park to get drunk. There would always be at least eight to ten of us, and one of us always managed to get served in the local off-license (liquor store). It was usually me that got served as I was the tallest! I hadn't even started shaving, and yet there I was getting served a load of alcohol. It was the mid-1980s, and no one checked IDs. Times were very different back then!

We used to drink every weekend, and I discovered (probably due to my size) compared to others, I had quite a high tolerance to alcohol, although every now and then, I could tip over the edge and lose all sense of dignity. The worst time that I can remember is after the 1985 FA Cup Final. This is back when there were only about four football matches a year on TV! It was Liverpool vs Everton, and some of my mates were Liverpool fans (despite never having been there). Anyway, I got so drunk I fell almost unconscious on my mate's parents' gravel driveway, which in my altered state seemed like the most comfortable thing I'd ever laid down on! The only way the lads could get me home was to stand me up, then let me fall backwards into a Sainsbury's shopping trolley and proceed to wheel me home whilst I fell out numerous times, much to their amusement. I was horribly ill all over myself and was then left unceremoniously at the front door of my house, trolley and all. My mates rang the doorbell and ran away before my mum opened the door to the sight of her firstborn in a very poor state, much to my brother's amusement! I have since apologised many times, of course, and I spent a few days in bed with alcohol poisoning after that one.

The school leaving disco was also quite a moment. At 16 and very drunk, I grabbed the microphone from the DJ and proceeded to belt out the Steve Walsh part of the Fatback Band's 'I found lovin', tell me what have you found? I found love'.

All these adventures outside of my home were exciting and (mostly) made me feel good. They were definitely a distraction from myself and my lack of confidence but also an escape from everything. And then, just to add another layer to it as I got a little bit older, I went and discovered nightclubs where all of my growing passions were rolled into one – music, alcohol, girls, and the allure of love, all right there in nightclubs – what a result!

Adding to the football buzz as a teenager, I'd been to a few under-18 discos, but it was when I was around 15 or 16 that I started going to proper gigs and nightclubs in and around London. My mates and I all shared the love of music. The sound for us back then was 1980s soul and hip hop. I attended packed concerts at Hammersmith Odeon (Fatback Band, Melissa Morgan, Alexander O'Neal, Public Enemy, LL Cool J, and Run DMC) and Wembley Arena (Cameo and Luther Vandross), plus we went to the Radio London Soul Nights Out and various Hip-Hop Jams. All of these were great nights.

I always got in easily to these venues because I was tall; however, the Hip-Hop Jams were quite dangerous for a tall, glasses-wearing white kid from the suburbs, and we got robbed on more than one occasion. I remember once having to run down Charing Cross Road away from the Astoria on a Sunday afternoon after we tried to get into a 'Time Radio Jam' (party), and we got jumped (attacked) in the street by a gang just for our tickets!

It was a couple of years later that I went back to the Astoria for a Saturday night out, and I walked straight into a room full of people dancing, smiling, sweating, and cuddling each other. It was no wonder I became hooked to that positive energy, everyone dancing to the four-to-the-floor drum beat of house music in Central London. Right then and there, I had landed in the middle of the Summer of Love in London.

What to Do With My Life

Stepping back again, I had left school at 16 without much direction and only a couple of 'O' (Ordinary) Levels to my name. I knew I didn't want to carry on studying at school or going on to college. I wanted to get out there, earn my own money, and continue the adventure I'd started in the world. I really had no idea what to do job-wise, though. Mum said, 'Get a job in a bank as you'll get decent mortgage rates.' I didn't have a better idea, so I strolled into the interview and accidentally got a job working in a bank in Twickenham. In just six months, I was promoted to a team leader and was quickly on my way to a management trainee course.

Like at school, I made some good friends in the bank, but I knew fairly quickly that I didn't want to stay working there for the rest of my life. It was a real-life classic comedy moment when I handed in my notice, exactly like the Ricky Gervais and David Brent sketch from *The Office* when Tim wants to leave Wernham Hogg. I had one of the bosses of the bank trying to convince me to stay. I was 18, and he was in his mid-thirties. Bless him, he was overweight, bald, and had a bit of a case of halitosis when he sat opposite of me and came out with the classic line, 'Mark, I don't think you should leave the bank. You have so much potential. In ten years' time, let's be honest here – you could be me.' Hmm. Let me have a think about that for a minute. It really wasn't for me.

By the time I reached my 17th birthday, my dad was in hospital non-stop. He'd been in and out for the last eight years, but I was young and had to do something to get away from this tragedy. I was drinking a lot and began to experiment with 'soft' drugs.

On my 18th birthday, which I'll never forget was on a Wednesday, I celebrated the whole week from the Saturday before right through to the Saturday after attending huge raves. However, on the Wednesday birthday itself, we all went out to the local pub where I got absolutely smashed on pints of lager with Southern Comfort and lemonade chasers. To this day, I still can't even smell Southern Comfort without reliving that night. There were 30 of us in the pub, and every one of them bought me a drink. By the time I'd drunk all that and smoked some hash in the pub garden, one of the lads thought it would be a good idea to get me half a pint of every shot from around the top of the bar and then give me 18 bumps plus one for luck, dropping me from a great height and giving me a bit of kicking when I was on the floor. Imagine what they'd do to one of the kids they didn't like! I got driven back to one of the flats afterwards, and needless to say, shortly after, I was sick as a dog and felt rotten, absolutely rotten. As a result, I had alcohol poisoning (again) and didn't crawl out of bed until the following Saturday, just about ready for the next party!

Shortly after that last episode, unsurprisingly, I started to move away from alcohol, and I didn't go back to it for a good few years. However, I wasn't finished there, oh no, not by a long shot. I looked for a new buzz, a new escape, but what could it be?

Finding My Passion (Tales of a Professional Idiot)

DISCLAIMER

What you're about to read are the actions of that professional idiot!
(I was young, so it can be my only excuse!)

So, these are my own personal experiences with recreational drugs.

Some of these experiences were so uplifting they are
hard to put into words, and others were so dark, I'd really
rather not have experienced them at all.

So, please, anyone, if you think it might be glamourous or cool or
are even thinking about getting involved in any such similar
behaviour, you need to know about the reality of these ups and
downs. You also need to fully understand that the examples

contained in this book have been known to cause some
immediate serious mental and physical harm to people as
well as some longer-term effects.

I was lucky I eventually wised up when I did.

As such, this book provides content related to physical and mental
health issues, and the reading of this book implies your
acceptance of this disclaimer.

Thank you for reading all that. Now let's get back to it!

IT WAS THE SUMMER OF 1989, and I was standing in a barn on
the outskirts of Windsor with 1,000 other young people. In the dead of
night, we'd parked our cars, jumped a few fences, trekked across some
fields, dodged a couple of cows (hopefully not slipping in the dark in
cow shit) before we heard the distant boom boom boom of the music.
As we got nearer to the barn, you could gradually hear the music clearer
and clearer. You could start to see the lights and lasers moving in the
night sky, and we all began to feel the buzz and excitement getting
closer to a rave. I'm sure some of you reading this will have your own
similar stories!

I was there with a group of friends. By now, there were at least 40 of
us, both boys and girls, partying together as we were all from the local
areas of Hampton and Hounslow. So once again, I'd found another
social group to be a part of, only this one got together in the evenings
and included plenty of girls. We all laughed, smiled, talked, and danced
late into the night! All great fun for a young lad.

The DJ was playing some warm-up tunes, and the atmosphere was
building up to be really good. I was thinking to myself what a great
night this is going to be. I'd always enjoyed music and had started
going to clubs when I was much younger, but this was a different level.
First up, it was illegal. It was also exciting and atmospheric. The music
was rocking and so loud, the lighting was amazing, the décor on the
walls was well designed and memorable, and the energy was high,
really high. People were mostly my age or up to ten years older than me,
and we were all in this together. Instead of fighting and the previous
aggression of football matches and the football hooliganism of the

time, everyone was dancing, making friends, raising their arms in the air, and cheering to banging house music.

That night someone said to me, 'Have you tried E? You know, ecstasy?' Being on the scene, I'd heard plenty about it, and some of my mates had done it, plus I knew loads of people around me were getting on it that night, but I answered truthfully, 'No, mate.' 'Here you go then' was the reply, and like always, the first one is free. I didn't think – I just took it.

To be honest, I pretty much forgot about it for about 30 minutes. I carried on chatting with my mates and then, all of a sudden, this feeling started to hit me. I remember it began in my feet. Weirdly, my heels felt like they had springs attached to them. I started laughing, and I mean really laughing, loudly! My best mate was there and asked, 'Wilks, what's going on? What are you laughing about? How does it feel?' The only thing I could think of saying between my laughter was, 'Mate, you see that picture up there on the wall?' (It was a line drawing of a woman's head, which was the logo of the night we were at called 'Respect', I think.) 'Well, that is the single greatest thing I've ever seen, mate!' He cracked up, laughing, and thought I'd lost it. He was probably right.

After that, I was gone. I was in ecstasy, dancing and dancing and dancing, floating around the room and chatting to everyone, people I didn't know. I was smiling like I'd never smiled before. I was sweating like crazy and hugging people, but it didn't matter as we all were. But let me tell you this too: it was a feeling of pure unadulterated joy; all my young inhibitions were gone in a second, it was incredible, it was euphoric, it was ecstasy. What a hit, what an explosion of joy, just... WOW!

Back then, ecstasy played a role in a lot of people's late teens, twenties, and thirties. I even found a way to create a life based around my addiction to pleasure, which enabled me to continue the party for over 15 years. Looking back now, I can see my mental health wasn't right. I wasn't well balanced, and I certainly wasn't making good choices. I became a functioning addict but massively resilient. I could drink more alcohol than most and take more of anything else than most others too. I'd still be standing at the end of the night, where some others weren't.

The Gateway is Wide Open

The gateway to my addictions was when I'd started drinking at 14, followed by smoking cannabis. After the alcohol-fuelled highs (laughing and acting stupid) and lows (fighting and puking), I found smoking cannabis a lot more mellow. I'd tried smoking cigarettes on and off for a while since I was 14, so the smoking wasn't an issue for me, and as I said, the feelings of cannabis were much more relaxed. There was still plenty of laughing and stupid chat but no aggression, which suited my people-friendly personality just fine.

I started with roughly one-eighth of an ounce (3.5 grams) of cannabis. We had all sorts of names for it (pot, dope, hash, ganja), and we'd sit around in big groups in a friend's flat smoking and laughing at stupid films. In fact, thinking back, we were the real-life Beavis and Butthead's well before they were ever thought of on MTV!

George Michael famously said, 'Don't smoke pot until you've achieved all your dreams,' and although I found it relaxing and fun, something inside me wasn't going to settle for just sitting about and talking rubbish all day and night. Quite quickly, I felt I was wasting my life, and thankfully I clearly had more drive and ambition than that.

I've mentioned that I was tall but lacking confidence as a teenager. However, I had some chat and always seemed to socialise easily, but mostly it was a mask to my true inner self. The louder and more confident I would be, the more people would want me around. But I wanted and needed them to like me. Sometimes that need can still come up from time to time; however, I'm a lot less bothered about it these days, thankfully. I tend to stand back and observe it and understand where it is coming from. Back then, though, I really enjoyed the front that I had created to protect myself, and it did lead me to get to know more and more people, which meant my access to many pleasures of the DJ life got easier.

After alcohol and cannabis, I graduated from there up to weed, grass, and then skunk. However, it really wasn't the drugs that were the problem here. It was my rebellious and addictive personality and the lack of strong male guidance in my life that seemed to drive my poor choices and actions.

Once that became the norm for me, I was ready for another new buzz. One of the lads said he could get me some acid. The first time they were little microdots that didn't do much. The second time they were blotters that were little squares of blotting paper soaked in acid. One evening I took one in my house to test it, which, as it turned out, was a *terrible* idea. It was super strong. The walls of my bedroom started moving and pulsating, and I began laughing loudly while watching boxing on TV! It was a real *Trainspotting* movie moment, especially when my now elderly dad walked into my room to see what was going on. He took one look at the state of me, shook his head, and walked straight back out! I was rotten the next day too. I hadn't slept a wink, and my body felt like it was itching all over. I was sitting at the counter of the bank facing customers. I said I was ill, and I was, just very stupidly all self-inflicted. My eyes were playing football with my nose!

Obviously, our first trip away in a group had to be to the fun capital of Europe, Amsterdam, later in 1988. We had a mad time in the Dutch city for a week. About 20 of us went, and we all slept in a dorm where I learned that *whatever you do, DO NOT be the first one to fall asleep.* One of the lads kept dropping off, and he had his eyebrows shaved and all sorts of bathroom products and cigarette butts stuck in his hair and smeared all over him.

And then came the big nights out in and around London. I started going to all the cool nightclubs in town: Shoom, Spectrum, The Trip, Made on Earth, Limelight & Busby's, and then out into the M4 corridor to Yikes at Slough Centre (Saturday night), Queens in Coln-brook (Sunday afternoon), and Passion at Valbonnes in Maidenhead (Sunday night).

And then there was that unforgettable life-changing moment in the barn in Windsor when that first hit got me. In 30 minutes, I went from a young, tall, inwardly nervous, awkward teenager who felt out of place a lot of the time (in my own mind anyway) into a completely uninhibited, confident, funny, outgoing socialiser who could dance from 10pm to 6am (or longer) and chat up and connect with lots of women easily. At the time, I loved every second of that. And again, I speak from personal experience here. I am acutely aware that it wasn't the same experience for everyone, so please do go back and read the disclaimer again if you need to. Big love. Thank you.

My Non-Stop Raving Years

So this was it, the start of my non-stop raving years. It was all music, dancing, friends, girls, parties, all-nighters, and all-dayers. All we did was eat, sleep, rave, repeat as a Fatboy Slim track famously once said. In those days, it was 5-6-7 nights a week and all day at the weekends, every weekend. It was all across London and the South East, along the M4 corridor and around the M25 for raves. It was a non-stop high, and it lasted for years. I was hooked on pleasure.

Massive parties were being put on by big promoters, and thousands of young kids like me were running around the UK looking for them. The first that sticks out in my memory is the 'Boy's Own' Summer party in East Grinstead. Boy's Own had the best DJs, which meant the best music, plus the coolest crowd, bar none. I felt privileged to get a ticket and to be part of it. This East Grinstead night was a legendary one held in a field by a beautiful lake. When we arrived, the moon was bright, and as the night wore on, we saw the moon disappear and the sun rise into a glorious sunny morning. Some of the pictures are amazing, and the music was Boy's Own cool. If you were there, it was truly unforgettable.

Another incredible night was 'Respect' at Didcot Railway Museum. It was a Magical Mystery Tour. We bought a ticket and got on buses at Queens Reservoir in Colnbrook with no idea where we were going. We were driven down the M4 to Didcot as the promoters had managed to hire the old steam train museum for the night. It was another incredible night into morning with young clubbers like me climbing all over the old steam trains and sitting on a replica station platform. There was even a waiting room, and as the sun came up, a surreal moment happened when the DJ made an announcement that there had been noise complaints from the neighbours. They turned the music down really low for ten minutes (which felt like an age and a bit of disaster for a hyped-up crowd), during which two fully uniformed policemen walked in. People were throwing things away and making for the exits when both policemen stood on the podium in the middle of the dance floor. The DJ pumped the music back up to full volume, and the 'policemen' knocked off their helmets with their truncheons and started dancing wildly! It was a joke which a lot of people thought was amazing. I admit I was cracking up; however, I heard a few of the more serious guys didn't think it was at all funny! These were not the type of people you wanted to annoy either.

Boy's Own then somehow managed to get access to a stately home near Milton Keynes and put a huge marquee outside. I remember Andy Weatherall, Terry Farley, and Paul Oakenfold all played, plus it was the first time I heard the new K-Klass – Rhythm is a Mystery track. When I heard it, I was so high I honestly felt like I was floating above the crowd. Those springs were back in my feet, and I was off! I couldn't stop listening to that track for weeks and months afterwards (as soon as I'd tracked it down on vinyl from a local record shop, that is).

Boy's Own did weekenders at Butlins too. They were classic. Loads of us piled down there for 48 hours of non-stop music, with little or no sleep, and then taking most of the next week to recover! No wonder that most of the late 1980s and early 1990s are a bit of a blur. We lived for it.

I Got My Name Out There

I loved music. I'd bought myself a pair of record decks, got involved in everything, made myself known on the club scene, and got my name out there with the DJ mix tapes. So the next natural progression was to start 'playing out' as a real DJ to a crowd of people. It started by taking all my equipment to friends' parties to play my tunes. I was a crowd pleaser and played records that people knew or ones I knew they'd like, so I was popular.

My first paid gig was at Reflex in Putney for £50. That was followed by another mate asking me to become resident DJ at his new Saturday night Toad in the Hole at Valbonnes in Maidenhead. Shave Yer Tongue in Bracknell was a big night for me, too, every Sunday. The nightclub was named after how your tongue would feel after a weekend of partying.

It was a disgusting analogy, but a great party! I loved playing my up-lifting tunes there! I wasn't always the industry favourite, and other DJs didn't always love me because I was such a crowd-pleaser. I wasn't a DJ's DJ, and that did bug me a bit as I would have liked everyone to love me, but I did my best not to care. I just continued to enjoy people dancing to the same tunes that I loved.

One night in Maidenhead, one of the guys from Flying Records in Kensington Market in London was booked at my residency there. He loved what I did when I played after him so much that in the blink of an eye, he'd got me working with him and the rest of the DJ squad in the record shop.

So now it's all happening. I'd found the way to get paid regular money for working in music and nightclubs. I attracted it all without being conscious of what I was doing. Although my gig ratio went up working in a cool London record shop with some other amazing DJs and record producers, it's fair to say I rarely earned any money from the shop itself because most of my wages were spent on buying the latest vinyl records. Think of an alcoholic working in a pub, and you'd be close. I earned the majority of my living money when I DJ'd.

That First International Gig in Paris

So, my first international DJ gig in Paris mentioned earlier was an interesting one. They booked and paid for my flight (no Eurotunnel back then). When I arrived on Friday night, I was whisked around Paris to a couple of venues for dinner and drinks and ended up in a full-on gay club (for the first time). There was hardcore gay porn being played on a few TV screens, and the place was full of guys dancing with their tops off, gyrating to the beats. I went on and did my thing playing my tunes, and they loved it, but as a 20-year-old straight lad, it was a bit of an eye-opener for the young me. I'd never experienced the energy of a gay crowd enjoying music. I'd also never seen two men kissing before. All of it was new. On Saturday night for the main gig in a large theatre in Central Paris, Rocky and his DJ partner joined me. They were Boy's Own DJs, and Rocky and I worked together in the Flying Records shop. We all DJ'd, and the night was going well until the promoter came to the booth looking all sheepish. He nervously asked me if we could stop now, so his dealer from Amsterdam could play instead!

So, just to get this straight, this guy had turned up with a pocket full of drugs and a huge plastic crate of techno vinyl, and he very quickly proceeded to clear the club with his really awful tunes. I must've decided to take the edges off the night myself and thought, *Oh well, if you can't beat them, join them*, so I got involved. At one point, I started to feel a bit weird, so I got outside for some fresh air. It was 6am and the height of summer, so we all sat outside a coffee shop. The next thing we saw, the doors of the club burst open, and the promoter came flying out, screaming and shouting. He turned and legged it full pelt up the road as fast as he could, chased by a really huge bouncer! We looked at each other and laughed. 'Did that really just happen?'

Worse still was to come, as we were meant to be sleeping in the promoter's apartment! When we did eventually somehow find our way back there, it must have been about 9am, and we were all exhausted. Luckily the promoter had survived the bouncer chase and possible beating. He proceeded to give us three teeny-tiny little airline pillows and an equally tiny little blanket between the three of us and said, 'You're sleeping over there on the floor, lads!' It was at this moment, laying on the cold, uncomfortable wooden floor of a Paris apartment, wide awake with no chance of sleep when one of us uttered the now-classic line, 'Where's all the glamour they promised us now, eh?!' We all laughed – good job, really, as we could have just as easily cried!

Week In, Week Out

I'm pleased to say that particular Paris experience didn't become the norm. As the years rolled by, more people got to know of me, and I played in more and more glamourous venues across the UK and worldwide. I loved playing at Kinky Disco in Shaftesbury's, situated in the middle of Shaftesbury Lane in London. It was buzzing every Friday night right through until 6am. I pursued that residency for a few months until they signed me up.

Week in, week out, I was playing a gig somewhere in London, across the UK, or internationally. Wherever I was, I'd receive VIP treatment.

The VIP treatment would mean getting looked after, never queuing up for anything, getting whatever I wanted when I wanted it, and getting paid for all of it! All this for the joy of DJing, the joy of playing those amazing records to an appreciative crowd, the joy of the crowd cheering for more at the end of the night, the joy of travelling the world and being looked after wherever I went was all wonderful. And the more I enjoyed it, the more successful I became. I remember one promoter saying to me, 'Mark, if you're happy, then I'm happy.' I was flattered, but I didn't really realise how good my life was at the time.

My most exotic gig in those early days was a week in Hong Kong in 1994 with a gig in a club called Westworld. From memory, it was on the 7th floor of the New Harbour Hotel situated on the waterfront. It was two years before the infamous Sun newspaper scoop of the England football players drinking in the China Jump just before Euro '96. It was a mad trip. It started with my getting on the plane and being squeezed into an economy seat, and then a guy twice my size sat down next to me. He decided to tell me he was a very nervous flyer and proceeded to take a Valium and fall asleep leaning against me! It was a 14-hour flight with a 7-hour time difference (ahead), so I arrived 21 hours after we took off, without a wink of sleep! I was disorientated at best when the promoters took me straight to the club.

I was three or four double vodkas in when someone suggested a 'Flaming Lamborghini' in the 'Dentist's Chair'. I had no idea what was happening when three people gathered around me, and two poured alcohol down my throat while the other set fire to it! Wow! I stood up and felt my neck muscles give way, and I thought, *I'm in trouble here.* My only desire was to get outside for a breath of fresh air. In Hong Kong in May, it's 30 degrees and 90% humidity. I got outside, my glasses steamed up, and I passed out on the pavement. Good times!

Going to work in the record shop on a Saturday after a Friday night out at Kinky Disco with less than two hours of sleep was always an interesting one. We all covered for each other in the shop, which was great as after a particularly late night or heavy weekend, we'd all be known to have a little sleep on the padded record bags and jackets out in the back office whilst all the others kept working! Even the loudest banging music became hypnotic and soothing when you needed to have a little siesta.

That isn't the funniest sleep story, though. That one goes to one of the lads who was trying to get home on the Northern Line after a night out once. The only problem was that he kept falling asleep and waking every couple of hours at the north and south ends of the line. He was on there for seven hours back and forth before he was finally awake for his stop! Classic.

After a while of proving myself as a good worker, I built my days up in the shop and managed to work my way up to five days a week, and then I'd be DJing and partying somewhere in the world at the weekends.

With my usual commitment and passion for everything I got involved in, I used to plan my adventures well. When I was out DJing at a nightclub in the UK, they'd usually close around 2 or 3am and then with a one, two, or three-hour drive from wherever I was back into London, I'd go to Ministry of Sound (MoS) in Elephant and Castle, arriving there at 5-6am. I'd save my last burst of energy for when I got there just before CJ Mackintosh went on in the main room. CJ was ex-DMC World Mixing Champion and usually played the last set from 6-9am. He became a bit of a hero to many for his smooth mixing and wonderful soulful vocal songs in amongst killer dubs. We'd dance until the lights came on and until we got kicked out every week.

Ministry of Sound had opened in London in 1991, and the club itself didn't even open until midnight. To start with, it didn't have a licence to sell alcohol and it closed at 9am. Therefore, the nights were based around its huge main room sound system, which was modelled on the systems in Paradise Garage and the Sound Factory in NYC. The DJs were playing vinyl on the rotary mixer, and on that sound system, it sounded wonderful, really warm, and bass-driven with incredible up-lifting vocals. The sound had a clarity that you just didn't get on any other sound system in the UK. It's a bit like wearing a pair of stereo headphones and standing in the middle of a club dance floor – a beautiful sound. I've always said you can tell when a club is owned by someone who loves music as the sound system is great, and equally, you can tell when the owner loves alcohol or money as they don't typically invest in the best sound system.

Problem Kids Were Born

After a few years of living this way, I decided I wanted to extend myself further. I was well known in the scene as 'Mark Wilkinson from Flying Records', but up to this point, I hadn't produced any of my own records. I'd seen the joy other DJs had experienced from making records and also how they'd catapulted themselves into huge DJ gigs and an amazing career from just one hit record. I wanted some of that for myself, so I knew it was time to get involved in making music.

Rocky was already established as a Boy's Own DJ and, despite the Paris experience that I'd arranged, had become a good friend. He was already producing some music as X-Press 2 and had some great dance floor success with a couple of excellent tracks on Junior Boys Own record label, Muzik Xpress and London Xpress. So I thought I'd ask him first. I thought he'd probably say 'No', but I asked anyway (if you don't ask, you don't get, and all that): 'Do you fancy making some tunes together, mate?' and without hesitation, he said 'Yes' (thanks, Rocky), and Problem Kids were born.

To be fair, it took us a few studio sessions and a few released tracks before we were dubbed Problem Kids, but I enjoyed every minute of the creative process. I'm no singer, and I gave up the piano when I was 12 because it wasn't cool (a decision my mum said I'd live to regret, and she was right), but I learned quickly how to become a music producer, how to work with others to create the sound I wanted. As a DJ, I already knew what worked on my dance floors, so making music I could play out was always my goal in the studio. We got dubbed Problem Kids after Rocky has seen a documentary the night before on children in care. The following day we were acting like idiots and messing about in the recording studio when a friend turned around and half-jokingly said, 'You two are a right couple of problem kids.' And that was that. We liked it, it stuck, and a new production moniker was born.

Shortly after that, a good friend who had hung out with me for a few years was suddenly promoted to booking the DJs for Rulin' (which was the US House Saturday night at Ministry of Sound). He had said to me for a while that as soon as he got the opportunity, he'd get me playing at the club. He'd travelled around UK gigs with me and loved my DJ sets, so it seemed a natural progression. However, I never put any pressure on him for that. He was good to his word, and I was presented with an amazing chance to become one of the resident DJs at the Ministry of Sound in London (I still love the sound of that!) and, of course, I jumped at the chance!

This opportunity meant I could leave the full-time record shop job and get more gigs worldwide, more recognition, more everything! I'm sure you get the picture by now. However, due to my (still) somewhat lacking confidence in myself and my own abilities, I suggested Rocky join me in the residency as Problem Kids. He was up for it, so we started playing most weeks in the club. We were on MoS tours every other weekend. We did a photo shoot, and we even had our own MoS manager to take care of everything for us. I'd made it!

When we travelled to another city or abroad, the promoter would take care of everything for us, from booking and sorting out our travel to picking us up at the airport, taking us to the hotel, taking us out for dinner, and making sure we had everything we wanted or desired, which could sometimes be a bit dangerous for an enthusiastic young man with an unconscious addictive personality like me. One of the weirdest gig weekends I had was a Thursday night when I got to play in an open-air club in Sao Paolo in Brazil (amazing) and then flew straight back for a Saturday gig in Milton Keynes! I'm being a bit flippant here as the MK gig was 'Ultra Vegas' and was actually a really great night, but you get the picture.

Things were going amazingly well, and I was living my dream. I'd created it, and I was loving it, but then things took a bit of a turn for the worse. Rocky had some personal issues in a relationship, and things changed quickly. It ended up that Problem Kids were no longer residents at the club. I really don't blame him, though. Rocky was only doing what he thought was right at the time, and I'd have probably done the same. From my point of view, though, and at that moment, I was gutted.

There was life after Ministry of Sound, though, and over the next few years, Rocky and I as Problem Kids released music on Junior Boys Own and made two albums with one of Manchester's finest record labels, Paper Recordings. We played more UK and international DJ gigs than ever. We played festivals and had some funny moments. I remember once when a journalist asked us how our festival warm-up set had gone. Rocky answered, 'Yeah, it was good, thanks. They were laying down at first, but we had them sitting up in the end.'

We also managed an Australian and New Zealand Tour in 1999. That was loads of fun apart from the fact that this was before the internet, and I had wrongly assumed that Australia was always as roasting hot as it looked on *Neighbours* every evening on BBC1. However, we went in June, and I only packed t-shirts, shorts, and flip flops. It was a rude awakening when we landed 24 hours after take-off in the drizzle and relative cold of winter in Sydney. It was dark by 4.30pm as well! A proper winter in Oz? Who knew? A few million Australians, obviously, just not me. A swift trip to the shops to get some jeans, sweatshirts, and some thicker socks, and I was back on track.

After a few years of great times, Rocky couldn't commit fully to the Problem Kids anymore as he had more X-Press 2 records to make. They went on to have a huge hit with 'Lazy' featuring David Byrne from Talking Heads on the vocals. So, I decided to start my own Kidsound record label (later morphing into Kidology Records and Kidology London). I also got to remix some big recording artists myself, from Kylie to David Guetta, from TLC to JB from JLS, and Abs from the boy band Five! Remember them?

I also started promoting my own Kidsound night at Velvet Rooms on Tottenham Court Road. It was a small club for 300 people with a huge sound system. We were there every Friday night in London with a stellar DJ line-up from around the world. We had the slogan *Rock Your Fridays and Wreck Your Saturdays* – how right we were.

Throughout this whole time – and we'll call this the early part of my life – I'd been into hedonism, pleasure, and instant gratification. I wasn't living in the present. I had a habit of always blaming others for my problems. I'd look back in anger or worry fearfully about the future. How was I going to survive in the music biz long term? I'd also be jealous about the fact I wasn't getting as many gigs or as much success as I thought I deserved, so I ended up doing all sorts to try and escape my thoughts, getting literally out of my head, out of my thoughts, laughing a lot, and having some admittedly good times. But ultimately, the guy behind the decks DJing or in the middle of the dance floor off his head, heavily addicted to everything and was masking plenty of unhappiness. The brutal truth was, I didn't really like myself.

· · · · · ·

CHAPTER 2 – REMIX OPPORTUNITIES

- What's your story? Are you blaming someone else or taking responsibility?
- What's your relationship like with your parents?
- Have you left home emotionally?
- Do you still spend time thinking about your parents' opinions?
- Are you thinking and deciding everything for yourself or being influenced by everyone else?
- Are you running away from something, someone, or even your own emotions?
- Are you self-medicating with anything (including alcohol)?
- To live your dream life, you must commit fully.

DJing at a Kidology night at The Cross, London.

For more photos from Chapter 2, go to www.markwilkinsonofficial.com/life-remixed.

CHAPTER 3

LOST IN MUSIC

Comparison is the thief of joy.

– Tony Robbins

Real love is hard to come by, so you learn to cope without it.

– Elton John

Pain is temporary. It may last a minute, or an hour, or a day, or a year, but eventually it will subside and something else will take its place. If I quit, however, it lasts forever.

– Lance Armstrong

BEFORE I CONTINUE, if you're wondering why I've added the Lance Armstrong quote above, especially after his drug abuse, cheating, and being stripped of his seven Tour de France titles, let me explain. You see, I think it's terrible. Just think about what he achieved, winning all those races whilst on drugs? Let me tell you something. When I was on drugs, I couldn't even find my bike! (I promise I'm joking.)

So moving on, most people know that throughout music history, certain drugs and music have gone hand in hand. The taking of drugs to different types of music has heightened the pleasure and the experience for the listener. And for some musicians, drugs have even heightened their creativity when they're writing songs.

Here are a few musicians who may possibly have been influenced:

• Jimi Hendrix: 'Purple Haze'

• The Stranglers: 'Golden Brown'

• The Shamen: 'Ebeneezer Goode' (where Mr C stood on Top of the Pops singing 'Eezer good')

• Lou Reed: 'Perfect Day'

• The Verve: 'The Drugs Don't Work'

• NERD: 'Am I high?'

• Gorillaz: 'Dare'

Acid rock in the 1960s and 1970s would never have happened without LSD. House music could have remained a niche musical taste if it wasn't for the wide availability of MDMA (ecstasy) in the 1980s and 1990s.

Here are a couple of little-known facts: Did you know that country music songs make more references to drugs than any other genre of popular music, and that includes hip hop?[i] Did you know that Eminem has made a career total of 305 drug references in his songs to date?[ii]

Listening to music is rewarding and can have numerous positive effects on all of us. It can reduce stress (depending on the type of music listened to), it can change your mood, and it can even improve feelings of belonging to a social group (think of Woodstock in the late 1960s, Punk in the 1970s, and the 1980s UK rave culture that I got swept up in).

Certain styles of music match the effects of certain drugs. Amphetamine, for example, is often matched with fast, repetitive music, which enables people to dance quickly. MDMA's (ecstasy's) tendency to produce repetitive movement and feelings of pleasure through movement and dance is also well known (remember the springs in my heels!).

Although it's important not to be casual and overstate the links between some musical genres and different types of drug use, information about drugs of choice around certain types of music can be useful in potential interventions. These days there are harm reduction initiatives at music festivals that have helped many a festival goer from not poisoning themselves.

I've also researched some interesting trials happening in the US that began in 2020. One trial is the FDA's MDMA-Assisted Psychotherapy Studies.[iii] Here is the description from their website:

MAPS (Multidisciplinary Association for Psychedelic Studies) are sponsoring the Food and Drug Administration (FDA) drug development research into MDMA-assisted psychotherapy for the treatment of post-traumatic stress disorder (PTSD). FDA has designated MDMA-assisted psychotherapy for PTSD a Breakthrough Therapy and has come to agreement with MAPS on Phase 3 protocol designs after a rigorous Special Protocol Assessment (SPA) process. MAPS' goal is to develop MDMA-assisted psychotherapy for PTSD into an FDA-approved prescription treatment by the end of 2021.

We are studying whether MDMA-assisted psychotherapy can help heal the psychological and emotional damage caused by sexual assault, war, violent crime, and other traumas. We also sponsored completed studies of MDMA-assisted psychotherapy for autistic adults with social anxiety, and MDMA-assisted psychotherapy for anxiety related to life-threatening illnesses.

These tests are going on right now to determine whether MDMA is actually a useful and healing treatment for PTSD! It is possible that there may come a time when we change our perceptions of some currently illegal drugs. In the coming years, there may be further opportunities to use some of these substances in therapies. We only need to think about the current rise and acceptance of CBD oils for treating chronic pain and illness. There's also CBD versus THC (the psychedelic compound currently illegal in the UK that gets you stoned) and the ongoing discussions on the legalisation of cannabis (following the lead of the Netherlands and Canada).

However, legalisation would be a huge subject for humanity to decide on. My personal feeling is that it isn't the drugs that are the problem. They are the effect. We are the cause. We first need to offer treatment for people's mental health and addictive behavioural issues. Then the drug problems would be minimised over time as people wouldn't feel the need to take them. We'll talk more about personal responsibility as we go through the *Life Remixed*™ experience.

It's also important to point out that not everyone becomes an addict. Some people can try alcohol, cigarettes, or anything 'addictive' once or twice and then simply put them down and never touch them again. So, is the substance really the problem here? For me, it was an addictive personality that was the problem. I could get addicted to anything and everything, pretty much everything that I tried and enjoyed!

As I've found out now, for the better, committing to something or someone positive in your life is great, and addiction to self-destruction makes for a very painful existence.

Understanding all this is not an attempt to explain away my younger self's behaviour in any way. However, what it does show is how easy it became to get 'lost in music' over a 25-year period. I found an artificial way to extend my fun, to stay up all night long, to smile and laugh a lot, and to dance the night away with all my friends doing the same. In my reality, it really did feel like everyone was doing it, despite the fact it was only a small number of people in the grand scheme of things! I was so committed to the life that I found a way to earn money from my passion in the music scene. My entrepreneurial spirit was burning away inside me all along. I didn't want to work for anyone else, and I achieved it for years. However, like so many things in my life, it took a long while for me to understand how to control and channel my energies into the more positive side of life. We'll cover more on all that as we progress together.

I told you already that I was 19 when my dad died, and to be honest, it's not easy to write or admit this; however, back then, it was almost a relief when he passed away as he'd had such a long period of ill health. Since I was nine in 1979, he had suffered a decade of awful physical pain and mental health issues. I learned more about his history as I grew up. Both of his brothers were killed in World War II (think *Saving Private Ryan*, without the heroic team sent to get him out). When he returned to the UK, I believe he must have been suffering from undiagnosed PTSD, and unfortunately, for the rest of his life, he wasn't strong enough to deal with everything that life threw at him. He (and then we) suffered a lot of fear, anxiety, and pain because of it all. I'll explain more as I began to understand what was happening. At the time, however, I was young and acting out to escape what I was feeling.

Those MDMA tests happening on PTSD now are interesting to me because I suppose you could say that I'd carried out my own personal experiment from 1989 onwards. I'd inherited so much fear of life from my parents, teachers, other kids (and society in general) that I took to my addictions to block it all out. To be honest, it worked pretty well for a while. Perhaps I was even ahead of my time! (Again, please know I am joking here!)

Mum and Dad had divorced back when I was 14. However, Mum always needed a man to love her. We've discussed this since, and she admitted to me that she never really loved herself back then. So after the divorce, she got straight into another relationship.

What was traumatic for me was that although mum had a boyfriend, my dad continued to stay at our house and sleep in the box room. Dad was 25 years older than Mum, and Mum said she didn't want to kick him out at 64 as he wouldn't be able to look after himself. I know that she came from a good place of caring for her ex-husband, but in my young mind, I couldn't see it. Nowadays, I understand they were all doing their best, but back then, I remember feeling angry. How could we live like this? How could Dad allow this to happen? Was he that defenceless? Did he have no pride?

Nowadays, I'm grateful these things happened in my life as I realise I am a product of it all. The fact that I wanted to be out of the house as much as possible because of these issues led me to the life I have created today. Back then, I was confused, as other people's parents didn't do such odd things. All in all, sometimes it felt like we were a strange little family.

The Escape – My Life in Music

With the backdrop of all of this fear and anger within me, I managed to create my escape through music. My life in music meant everything to me. It meant I could be free, so I put my heart and soul into it. I loved my own journey so much that I lived it to the detriment of everything else. My family suffered, and all of my early relationships with girls would be sacrificed for my music and DJing. The better my life in music got, the more I was buzzing with what I'd created.

It didn't take long before I was playing, making, and selling music. I created my dream life from my passion and enthusiasm. Music was the thing I had enjoyed the most since I was six years old. Through all the challenges of Dad's various illnesses and all the family troubles, I had kept the end in mind and established myself in the fledgling DJ and house music business. By 1990, I was free.

I'm sure by now you understand I'm not trying to make excuses for myself or glamourise anything. I'm sharing my early experiences and the feelings attached to those experiences here so I can connect the dots right through to the major life challenges I faced and on to my happy and successful life today. Let's keep going!

I did get to quit my nine to five. I was DJing more and travelling worldwide. Thankfully, I've kept some wonderful photos from that 20-year period, as well as a box of flyers with my name all over them. Here's where you can see them:

- We've got a gallery at www.markwilkinsonofficial.com/photo-gallery.
- We're running an Instagram page for you to see them all @liferemixedbook (www.instagram.com/liferemixedbook), so please do check them out.
- Connect with us on any of our other social media too:
  - Facebook: www.facebook.com/markwilkinsonliferemixed
  - Twitter: www.twitter.com/djmarkwilkinson
  - LinkedIn: www.linkedin.com/in/markwilkinson14
  - YouTube: www.youtube.com/c/MarkWilkinsonOfficial

The memories are all such a haze and can roll into one, so I'm glad I collected plenty of pictures throughout that time. I probably saved them all just to prove to myself that it did all actually happen! I played huge gigs in Hong Kong, Singapore, Thailand, Shanghai, across Russia from Kaliningrad to Vladivostok, Dubai, Brazil, Miami, all over Europe, and across every continent. Rocky and I rocked the 2000 Millennium

New Year's Eve at Shine in Belfast, which was a great night with 1,000+ clubbers celebrating the turn of the century. I started to be offered more gigs in Ibiza, which was perfect as it allowed me to spend the summers there. I've always preferred the warmer weather. Shorts and flip flops all year round is lovely.

Even while I was a young DJ, the universe gave me a dose of the truth, though. Deep down, I knew it wasn't being big or clever doing the things I did, so most of the time, I hid it pretty well from my mum and family. However, one morning I took a call while working in Flying Records. I was 25 by now and building a decent career as a DJ.

When I answered the phone, the caller said, 'Hi, this is Claire, and I'm a researcher at the BBC on the Robert Kilroy-Silk show.' This was a mid-morning 1990s audience-led chat show, a bit like Jerry Springer and Jeremy Kyle, just not quite as punchy. 'We'd really like you to come onto our show to give your side of the story on house music culture. We're really interested in your angle on what hundreds of thousands of young people are doing every weekend in the UK.'

For a split second, my ego got the better of me. I thought, *Yeah, I'll do that, be on TV, great.* And then Claire said, 'We've also got bereaved parents who have lost children to drugs on the show.'

A dose of reality hit me square in the face, my heart sank, and I knew there was no way I could do it. Recently, a beautiful young girl had lost her life after taking ecstasy in a nightclub that I had played in on many occasions in Basildon. Her awful experience had been publicly played out on the front page of the papers, and her parents must have been in utter despair. How could I possibly go on TV and talk about the lifestyle after what had just happened to her? I actually feel terrible even thinking about it now, plus I couldn't imagine my own mum talking to her family and friends about it. 'Oh yes, Mark was on TV the other day, on BBC1 with Kilroy-Silk, talking about music and drugs to some recently bereaved parents.' Terrible. I'd have been hammered on the show, and my mum would have been gutted. I knew the right thing to do. The BBC even tried to persuade me with a chauffeur-driven limo full of champagne to come and pick me up, but I knew I had to say no to the temptation.

On the face of it, I was a normal, slightly loud, cheeky, happy-go-lucky chap, but within, I was still hugely lacking in confidence. I fell in love a number of times in my youth. I was always looking for a woman to love me, to complete me, and to make me feel good.

Underneath it all, I was misguided. My dad just wasn't able to do it as he was older and had his own problems, as I've explained. I know he would have liked to help me, but tragically, both physically and mentally, he just wasn't up to it. My mum gave my brother and me her very best and tried to be both parents to us, but it just wasn't possible for her to be both masculine and feminine guides for us.

To my mum's huge credit, however, I did learn a lot about feminine emotions and how to be and act around women, so I do thank my mum for that and much more. I had a head start on most lads who didn't get that from their upbringing. I felt very comfortable talking with and being around women from an early age (every cloud and all that). However, the truth was that I was still carrying a lot of anger about how things had happened to me growing up, and I was full of fear that I wasn't good enough.

Operating from my perception of my upbringing, holding onto a lot of fear and anger, knowing a bit about women, and going to clubs fuelled with extra energy – I got what my ego needed by being the front man. I was the DJ, the man responsible for controlling the night, loved and adored for playing great music. I started to discover and enjoy women too. I loved them adoring me, putting me on a pedestal. They looked up to me in the DJ booth, and that carried on into relationships. I'm sorry to say that I wasn't the best man to be around at that time. My behaviour set a trend in my young life that led to a lot of pain and many broken hearts (including my own).

My first true love blew me away, and we were together for two years. We were in our early twenties, and we fell madly in love. Everything was amazing. We were young and reckless and had a lot of fun. However, after two years together, it became clear I just wasn't mature enough to deal with the woman that she was. It was hugely painful when we broke up. Even though I thought the music and DJ life was my everything, I still managed to end up with a severely broken heart. The next few years were spent trying to get over the loss I felt.

During this time, I'm ashamed to say I went out with a lot of women to get over the pain. None came close to helping, though, so I left them all in turn. Right here, right now, I need to say that I'm really very sorry to all the women who I hurt emotionally. In hindsight, I had a fear of rejection and being on my own, and yet that is what I kept creating for myself over and over again. Food for thought right there. Our thoughts become things!

To get over the pain, I threw myself headlong into music and became more and more successful. My diary was always busy up to three months in advance, which gave me some level of comfort and security. It was not enough to rid me of all my anxiety but enough to be able to enjoy the gigs while I was playing them. I wasn't as busy as some DJs, but I was doing well. There were times in the year when gigs went a bit quiet, and I had to up my game by calling more promoters, going out to more clubs where I wanted to play, meeting the people making the bookings, and partying late into the night so I could get to know them, and then following up with a call. And, lo and behold, I'd fill up my diary again.

I realised a lot of the time I was sacrificing a lot for the music. My friends would be all together on a Saturday night out, calling me to find out where I was. I would be sitting alone in a hotel in the back of beyond, waiting to be picked up for my gig. It certainly wasn't all glamour.

I always had a girlfriend around me to help me feel good, though. It's been said by a girlfriend that I only go out with 'the sorts', by which she meant the slim, good-looking girls. And she'd be right. On my arm, they made me feel good for sure. However, the music was always my top priority. The feeling of being in front of up to 2,000 people all dancing, singing, cheering, and screaming to the music that I had chosen was what I was alive for. Any amount of sex couldn't uplift me as much as when I'd stand up there playing my favourite songs to a huge crowd. I'd take a deep breath and take it all in, feeling the music and the beats so deeply that it's difficult to put into words. The incredible feeling of joy and happiness in all the noise and flashing lights took me to a very special place. I remember doing that a lot, for many years.

I never saw myself as successful enough, though. Others used to tell me that they did, but I couldn't see it myself. I was full of self-doubt, always comparing myself to others in a negative way. I always thought that I wouldn't be as good a DJ or as confident without the alcohol. I was also self-conscious about my glasses and my slightly chubby body, and I felt I wasn't as cool or successful as the other DJs.

I went from gig to gig, week to week, month to month, year to year, and I was happy enough that I was surviving and managing to dodge the drudgery of the 9 to 5. Looking back, though, I just wasn't grateful enough for any of it. We're all taught as children to say 'thank you', but it's mostly lip service at that age. I certainly didn't understand the importance of gratitude, which we'll talk about in more detail later. Looking back now, I wish I had understood gratitude more as I'd have been so full of love and appreciation for every opportunity and experience that I ever had as a DJ and would have enjoyed it all so much more. Even when all was well, what was going on just didn't feel good enough for me. I was never satisfied, and I had a deep feeling of never being good enough either.

When I was young, my family would say in a negative way that I 'was never satisfied and always wanted more', and I remember my grandad called me 'greedy' once at his house. However, I've since learned there are two sides to every story, and it's all down to our own personal perceptions. Although I acknowledge that my fears were driving me to act this way at that time, these days, I am able to see certain types of dissatisfaction as positives that actually keep me driven consistently towards my goals.

The girlfriends kept coming and going, and I did my best and 'loved' them all for a while. I suppose it was mostly lust at the time, and it always felt good for a few months, or sometimes even up to a couple of years. Ultimately, it wasn't their fault that they couldn't give me what I was looking for. As it turns out, no one could. Later on, we'll find out more about the journey of studying relationships in detail to understand why I couldn't keep one! I now know that all the breakups were almost all my responsibility through a basic lack of understanding of the masculine and feminine in all of us and how it plays out in relationships.

After many ups and downs, I met another woman who blew me away again. I thought, *this is it*. By now, I was 31, and everything that

I'd looked for during the last ten years had come back to me. We were in love, and in my mind, we'd be together forever. However, once again, through my own fear, self-doubt, and a general lack of understanding of relationships, I managed to blow it. I was beside myself. How had this happened again? I didn't understand. But happen it did, and I was now at a massive mental low. Yes, I'd made it into a drama myself, but I really didn't want that. I wanted to be with her and for us to be happy. I thought I could get her back, but it wasn't going to happen. I was completely devastated. How could this have happened yet again? I was crying a lot and in a real mess.

Where Do We Go When We're Unhappy?

After Problem Kids with Rocky, I'd teamed up professionally with another excellent DJ and producer to create a new production outfit. We started to produce some tunes, remix in the studio, and also DJ together at gigs worldwide. Where I had sometimes felt in Rocky's shadow, in this working partnership, we really bonded together on the same level. It was a laugh a minute, and we'd crack up non-stop. Aside from working well together, we had a good rapport musically too.

As I was going through this most recent heartbreak, my friend made a valid point when he said, 'When we're sick, we go to the doctors, but when we're unhappy and feeling bad, where do we go?' He went on to tell me about a mate of his who regularly saw a therapist. It was around this time that I was also watching the early seasons of *The Sopranos*. I said to myself, '*If it's good enough for Tony Soprano, then it's good enough for me!*'

I did need some answers as the pain in all areas of my life had been getting gradually worse. I wasn't healthy, wealthy, or happy. I was unhappy, sick, and broke most of the time.

I signed up for a course of therapy. The therapist was a really cool guy. He was mellow and came to London from Chicago. He played the guitar and loved music, too, so we bonded on that. Over the weeks and months, he gave me some great guidance on how to recover from this latest heartbreak. We worked through a lot of issues about my growing up and my parents.

There were a lot of tears from me regarding my lack of confidence, my broken relationships, and my lack of perceived success. What I found was that once I'd talked about it or cried it out, the issue pretty much went away. I describe it like an old pressure cooker. Once I'd talked about the issue, the steam could come out of my ears (not literally!), and then I could relax, forget about it, and move on.

The First Signs of Pain

Let's go back to when I was 26 and shortly after I became resident DJ at Ministry of Sound. I set up my own recording studios in Hammersmith (Care Studios, where all Problem Kids end up). I was DJing all over London, the UK, and worldwide, but my health had really started to suffer.

It started with some stabbing stomach pains, just a sharp pain to start with that lasted 20 to 30 minutes, but slowly the pain began to get more regular and more serious. At times during the day, the pain became so bad that I simply had to stop everything I was doing and lay down somewhere and hope it would pass. I'd also wake up at night in pain. The pain could strike at almost any time, which made life very difficult. I went to the doctor for some help. In my young mind, doctors could fix everything. However, every doctor or therapist I saw around this time insisted on asking me what sort of pain it was. My answer was, 'I don't know Doc, it just really hurts!'

For a time, our family doctor was our next-door neighbour and therefore a family friend, so I was sure he'd be able to help me. However, when I explained my symptoms, it was the first time in my life I heard a doctor say he couldn't help me. I was shocked and thought he was joking at first, but then he diagnosed me with Irritable Bowel Syndrome (IBS) and said there was little he could do about it. He told me to eat healthily and go to bed early. Just how exactly was I going to do that, Doc?

Financially, I was living hand to mouth as it was, so I wasn't willing or able to go to bed early as my livelihood depended on working late. Motorway service stations at 3am (or indeed anytime) weren't the healthiest of places to eat! It felt like everything depended on my late-night lifestyle, so there had to be another solution, except that short term, there wasn't one. The pains got worse, more and more debilitating, and I was getting desperate.

I was with a big group of friends in Ibiza for a few weeks enjoying the island and the best clubs in the world. We were partying hard every night and recovering in the sun every day. We were on a speedboat from Ibiza town cruising over to Formentera for lunch one day when I mentioned to the group that I was struggling with stomach pains. (I remember on the same boat trip, a friend cracked me up when we were talking about my girlfriend situations, and she came out with a smile and the unforgettable line, 'So many women… only one Wilkie'.) Anyway, this friend suggested I see a nutritionist who had helped her recover from similar issues. Handily, the nutritionist was based on the same street in Hammersmith as my recording studio (watch out for those little miracles in life!), so I had nothing to lose. I had to do something to try and stop this pain, so I made an appointment. This was the beginning of a healing path that I'm still on today.

Through a series of appointments, the nutritionist helped me regulate my diet and start to control the stress I was under. She helped me get more regular sleep patterns in the week by limiting alcohol and caffeine intake and taking melatonin periodically to regulate sleep. She also sorted out my hay fever and savagely blocked nose, which had also been worsening over the years. I did this by cutting out wheat, sugar, and alcohol. I used to drink alcohol every day and every evening and then not be able to sleep properly. I struggled to breathe with a blocked nose. I'd sneeze a lot and could barely take a breath. I'd wake up from a disjointed night's sleep in a tired state feeling grim and then not be able to deliver in the recording studio. My mum used to suffer a lot from hay fever, so I just assumed it was hereditary. However, I found by cutting out the alcohol, wheat, caffeine, and sugar, I got rid of the majority of my health problems at that time, and my improving health allowed me to start to enjoy a more normal life again, at least for a while.

The therapy and the nutritionist were working well for my mind and body, but let's be honest here, I'd probably made myself more sensitive with everything I'd put in my body over the last decade. So, my nutritionist recommended I go for a full-on juice fast, a five-day detox with her friends up in Berwick-upon-Tweed, just over the English border into Scotland.

Along with the therapist, the nutritionist was hugely credible in my eyes for helping me improve my life where doctors couldn't, so I booked and went up for a detox. I didn't know what to expect with the program, especially the colonic irrigation. To be honest, I wasn't keen because as far as I was concerned, it was a one-way street, if you know what I mean. I needed to sort myself out and to clean up my act, though, so I was motivated to give it a go.

Coveyheugh House was a lovely and relaxing place, and the detox experience included juices, a broth in the evening, massages, ear candles, kinesiology, and of course, the interesting daily colonics. I really wasn't keen on the tube up the bum, and my nutritionist in London and I had mutually agreed that we 'didn't have that sort of relationship', so she didn't want to get involved in that area! That was probably another reason she sent me to Berwick in the first place. Fair enough, really.

I had 'enjoyed' a couple of test runs in London with Princess Diana's (no less!) colonic hydrotherapist in Marylebone before I went up to Berwick, which, to be honest, wasn't too bad. So with that experience in the bag, I headed up on the train, ready to be cured of my pain or at least be flushed out from all angles! It was a weird experience having warm, then cooler water inserted into my colon. When you feel the water filling you up as it travels around your colon, you then give the hydrotherapist the 'I'm full' signal, so she stops putting the water in. Then my instruction was to let go, and all the unwanted stuff flies out and down a little pipe. I'll be honest; it's not a sight you see every day when a load disappears down a tube. However, it was an interesting watch and better out than in, I reasoned.

Being flushed out like that in front of an attractive therapist is an experience I won't soon forget. However, after a few days, the clean feeling both inside and out meant that going for detox was clearly good for me. I ended up going up to Coveyheugh House in Berwick for a week on three or four different occasions. I even got a group of mates to go up with me once or twice. If you think 'Five Go Colonicing', you won't be far off. Brian and Anne-Lise Miller of Body Management helped me beyond measure on the detoxes as will become clear. I was always secretly happy that Brian wasn't inserting the tube up the bum, though. That could possibly have been a step too far!

However, when I wasn't detoxing, making music, or DJing, the lifestyle that went along with it was still part of my life. The force of habit meant that once my body had stopped complaining, I went back to the behaviour I knew, every time thinking this time, it would be OK. I went to the gym a couple of times a week but without enough conviction for it to really make much of a difference. I did feel that I might have balanced out my life enough to recover from my now 'only at the weekend' habits. However, it was the pull of my uncontrolled addictions that meant I went back to my learned behaviour and kept on partying all night somewhere in the world every weekend.

I Needed a Real Change

As part of the pain of that second big break up, I needed a real change. I decided to sell the house I'd bought near Heathrow, and I moved into the basement flat my friend was vacating in Marylebone. I wanted the Central London DJ experience. I wanted to really live that dream. I didn't want £50 plus cab rides back to the suburbs. I didn't want to have to drive home after a club shut. I wanted full-on party time, close to all my favourite pastimes. I wanted to have it large, meet lots of women, host them in my central London flat, and generally live the bachelor DJ life.

Looking back, I'm happy that I lived that Central London life at that time. It was amazing for a DJ in his early thirties to be up there. London was still rocking with a new wave of clubbers who were into house music, and I was playing at all the top nights. There was everything available, and I have to say I enjoyed it.

Embarrassing Moments and Disaster Averted

So many things happened during those years when I was lost in music. I'd play out with my DJ partners at different times. I enjoyed the gigs, although there were some hair-raising and embarrassing moments in there too, and a few moments that could have ended life-long friendships for good!

Here's one. Rocky and I were booked for a festival in Ireland. We started drinking as soon as we arrived at the airport, so we were already on our way by the time we arrived in Dublin at 11am. By the time we were due to play at 5pm, we were absolutely flying. We played terribly; I mean awful. Half the time, it sounded like someone was falling down the stairs. We forgot smooth mixing, and we were all over the place, like someone banging on pots and pans, the lot. As soon as we finished playing, we forgot all about it and carried on partying. It was a long day and night from leaving Heathrow at 9am, getting to the event at noon, and going right through until 2am the next day. In a crowd of 20,000 people, unsurprisingly, we ended up getting lost from one another.

Time was flying past, and it felt as if from nowhere, the promoter was shouting at me to grab my stuff and get to the car park as there was a taxi waiting there for me. He warned me that if we didn't get this taxi, we'd be stuck out there in the middle of nowhere as there would be about 20,000 people trying to get taxis in the next hour when the festival ended. So along with a couple of the guys from Slam in Glasgow, we grabbed all our stuff, including all our record boxes and coats, everything, and made our way to the taxi.

At the time, I thought I was doing Rocky a favour by taking all his stuff too. I remember trying to keep up carrying a tonne of stuff (four record bags, two overnight bags, two large coats), but we managed to get to the car park and to the waiting taxi. It must have taken 20 minutes to get through the crowds, and by the time we got to the car park, I was absolutely shattered. We opened the boot and threw everything in. We got back to the hotel in Dublin, unloaded everything, and got it all upstairs.

In my altered state, I stood there looking confused. I was looking at all the record boxes. Everyone else's were there, mine too, but where were Rocky's? In my very confused state, my brain struggled with the scenario. I was absolutely positive I had carried everything from the DJ booth to the taxi as I was completely done in when I got there, and then I put everything in the boot of the cab, so I must have left them in the boot. I was convinced, but one of the lads said he'd emptied the boot of its contents, and they weren't in there. Oh no. Reality hits. I've only gone and lost all Rocky's stuff, his records, rare stuff, promos, even acetates (pre-promo records that you could only play a limited number of times before they'd wear out). I'd gone and lost the lot. What a good friend I was!

I went downstairs and sat in the bar with my head in my hands. Loads of other artists from the festival who'd got back to the hotel before us were in there too. I asked everyone, but no one had seen Rocky. I was feeling devastated that I'd lost his stuff. Everyone kept saying, 'It's not your fault, mate' and 'He's a good lad, he'll be OK.' Except I knew it was my fault and that he probably wouldn't be OK! I worried that he wouldn't forgive me for this one and that this could be a proper friendship and business partnership ender. Or would he see the funny side? If it was me, would I?

Mobile phones were just starting to be used. I kept trying to call him, but the network was down as there were so many people all in one field in Ireland. It was also cold by now and pissing down with rain, and I'd gone and taken his coat as well! Oh, God. This was a disaster.

It went on for a couple of hours when suddenly my mobile lit up, and it showed 'Rocky' on the screen. 'It's Rocky,' I shouted, and the whole bar went silent. At least 50 people were listening. I said, 'Hi Rock, you OK? Listen, mate, you know your records...' and then he cut in and said, 'Yeah, I've got them.' 'What? What do you mean you've got them?'. The whole bar went into an uproar. It was like I'd scored a goal. Oh the joy, oh the relief!

Rocky said, 'Yeah, they're in the boot of the cab with my coat. We're on our way back to the hotel now.'

It turns out that at the end of the festival, when the music stopped, he'd gone back to get his stuff from the DJ booth and found it had all gone. He thought it might have been nicked and tried to call me loads of times, but due to the poor phone signal couldn't get through. So he made his way back in the driving rain with no coat to the car park. He said he was cursing his luck the whole way (still hoping I'd taken them, of course). As he wandered around the pitch-black car park looking for a cab, he suddenly tripped over something. He looked down and said, 'Hang on, oh result, here's my coat!' followed quickly by 'Result, here's my records.'

He's since told me that he assumed I'd actually left them there for him, which is even funnier when you think about it. Can you imagine how lucky that was (for us both!)? What are the chances of that happening, especially with 20,000 people wandering around at the end of the festival? I'd been sitting in the hotel bar at 3am imagining some Irish kid making off with his designer coat and some very, very cool tunes!

The Time I Started a Riot

Everything around these times was a rollercoaster. I remember many ups and downs, and sometimes not being able to keep up the mask of my usually happy smiling self. Believe it or not, I once ended up starting a riot in a club in Sarajevo!

I went there to DJ for a friend a couple of years after the Balkan War had finished. I was well paid for it – danger money as it turned out. The DJ booth was on a stage right in the middle of the club, and I'd been left to finish off the night and was ready to go back to the hotel. The club owner was going to drop me back there. I had no local currency on me and didn't speak the language, and it was one of the few places I'd been where no one spoke English well.

At the end of the night, the lights went up, and a few people, including a group of guys, waited by the DJ stage to speak with me. A couple of girls asked for 'one more tune' and were flirting and laughing when out of nowhere, one of the guys threw what was left of his pint in my face. Hindsight is a wonderful thing. What I could have done was just accepted it and moved on, but stupidly I reacted and threw the rest of my bottle of water at him. Well, that was it, a massive fight started between every male in the club!

During the melee, I saw someone pick up my record bag from the stage and whisk it away! That was bad enough; however, on this partic- ular night, I'd been paid in cash, plus I had my passport and all my other valuables in the front pocket of my record bag as well! I remember my heart pounding out of my chest at this point. I'd lost the lot! And some guy from Sarajevo was getting away with all my music, money, and my passport home!

I quickly put my glasses in my pocket and dived full length off the stage into the crowd, with fists flying everywhere to try and get my life back! I fought for my stuff in that crowd and managed to retrieve my record bag from the back of the club as the security waded in and cleared everyone away. What a drama. I got home with a battered and bruised face and reflected that it did seem that these kinds of dramas were following me around more and more.

Back to the Music – Dab Hands

I created another production moniker called Dab Hands along with two new production partners. When asked in an interview what we were like in the studio, one of the chaps described us as the team from the *Cannonball Run*, with me as Burt Reynolds! I had to laugh as my brother and I loved those films when we were kids. Dab Hands was a reference to being really good at something like 'a dab hand' and also a thinly veiled drug reference.

We created some cool tracks, and with my background with Junior Boys Own and Paper Recordings, as well as both of the other chaps being very talented and well connected, people again started taking notice of us. We were asked to do a remix of Lou Reed's 'Satellite of Love' by the manager of another production outfit, and we thought, why not? David Bowie was on the backing vocals too, so I knew it would be good to do. I'm glad we did it, as we absolutely nailed that remix. As soon as we finished the Dab Hands remix, we gave it to the label, and it was on Chris Moyles Radio 1 Breakfast Show the next morning. He loved it and played it over and over. Later that day, it went straight onto Pete Tong's evening show and shortly after into the UK Top 10.

The sad part about it is 'where there's a hit, there's a writ' – and that turned out to be true as we ended up in a disagreement with the other production outfit, mainly because our mix was perceived to be more popular than theirs. Ours was the A-side, and our mix was played all over the daytime radio playlists. It was a shame as it all got a bit heated unnecessarily. We could have just all agreed to split everything 50/50 and continued to work together, but that's life.

Now I just look back and smile at the experience. So much has happened since then that it really is nonsense to focus on any negatives. Through my various health challenges, Dab Hands had still managed to produce a track that went Top 10 in the UK. I also DJ'd out that summer as Mark 'Satellite of Love' Wilkinson, which paid a few more bills. We followed it up with a track called 'DYOT' (Do Your Own Thing) featuring Steve Edwards on the vocals. We made a video for that track where I'm DJing in a flat at a party. It's on the following YouTube link and worth a watch. Steve knocks the vocal out of the park.

www.youtube.com/c/MarkWilkinsonOfficial

After My Physical Collapse

After the collapse described in Chapter 1, which happened around the same time as all this, I had to try my best to keep DJing and making music through the pain. I was motivated to keep going as it was all I knew and my only source of income. Of course, the love of music and friends and all the great feelings involved, from playing and making music to an appreciative crowd, helped too. But the pain got worse and worse, and I disintegrated over the next 18 months, so it got more and more difficult to work. I couldn't live without the huge amounts of painkillers.

Added to this, the internet had just recently launched in the early 2000s, and people were starting to realise its potential in connecting the world. To be honest, it was to have a life-changing effect on me and my music career. Up to that point, I'd dedicated my whole life to music and had found a way to earn enough money to live by DJing at the weekends and producing and remixing music during the week. I had always made decent money and enjoyed the life (before the physical pain arrived). However, when music started to be available on MP3 and downloaded from the internet for free, my income from the studio went from £5,000 a month to £500 a month, and then down to nothing, all inside two years! Thankfully I still had the live DJ gigs and live events to fall back on. I managed to keep the cash flowing enough to still make a living.

However, after the physical collapse, then getting more and more pain in my body, it was getting more and more difficult to move around. As I said, I lost a lot of weight really quickly too. I also had no strength at all. During the week, I sat around the house and played video games whilst sinking into the sofa. I couldn't physically do anything else.

My life was slowly becoming unbearable. I had those suicidal thoughts that I mentioned as I knew I wasn't adding anything of value to anyone's life, least of all mine. In fact, I was feeling like a complete waste of space. I felt like a drain on everyone around me, sometimes thinking that perhaps one day it would be better if I just took a load of pills and didn't wake up or went and jumped off a tall building or in front of a train. Although I wanted to survive, I really did struggle mentally without the physical health I had taken for granted for so long.

No one could understand what was happening, so I went to see yet another doctor, this time in Knightsbridge. I sat there for a 30-minute appointment and went through everything yet again. He spoke of various tests and possibilities as we sat through the appointment, and just as I was about to leave the room, the doctor really dropped the bomb. He said, 'Now listen, Mark, I do know of other male patients with similar symptoms such as yourself who've left stressful situations, and their symptoms have gone away.' I thought, *Wait, what? Me? Stressed?*

There was absolutely no way what the doctor had said could possibly be true! Was there?

Life went on, and I went for another detox up in Scotland. By this time, my body had really deteriorated, and I had almost nothing left to give. When Brian and Anne-Lise saw me, they were both shocked at the state I was in. They did their best to look after me in the week that I was up there, but as per my usual form, I was looking for a quick fix. However, that wasn't going to happen.

Brian had a DVD of a brand-new film called *The Secret* that had just come out. He urged me to watch it. I was indifferent but said, 'Sure, OK, why not.' I had the time while I was up there, so I watched it and gave it back to him. Brian smiled and shook his head. 'No, son, now go and watch it again.' I don't think I'd ever watched a film twice in one day, but he was so certain about it that I did as he had suggested. Afterwards, I tried to give it back to him again, and again he refused. He said, 'Now go and watch it 100 times,' and he made me promise to get my own copy when I got home, which I did. Brian knew what I needed, even though I couldn't see it myself.

Without realising it, I was slowly starting to listen and become aware of what was actually going on in my life, in my body, and with my thinking and feelings, which *The Secret* said were creating my current reality. I was in serious pain and needed to do something. As it turns out, Brian giving me The Secret was my saviour moment and my entry level into a new way of life. I was ready.

The 18 months that followed after the initial collapse in Chapter 1 to when I finally went to see a new NHS general practitioner (GP) was total agony. I had just moved from Marylebone W1 and bought a flat in Clerkenwell EC1. I felt more settled there and had signed up with a new doctor. This female NHS GP took one look at my state and said, 'I don't know how you've gone on for this long.' I was so grateful a doctor was finally listening to me and could see the pain I was in. She seemed to know what to do and said I needed to see a rheumatologist urgently.

This was the first time anyone had suggested a rheumatologist. None of the expensive private doctors had ever mentioned it, so six weeks later, I got my emergency appointment at University College London (UCL) hospital on Euston Road. The rheumatologist listened to my tale of woe and how bad my life had got and diagnosed me immediately with an incurable disease called ankylosing spondylitis (AS). He gave me a leaflet and said to read it. It described all the symptoms of AS, and I basically could have written that booklet myself. He went on to say that it was in my genes and that I was always going to get it. He gave me some medication, which he said would help my recovery from the acute situation I was in, and then he sent me on my way. Literally, a few hours later, once the medication had kicked in, I was almost pain-free and able to stand up and move around quite easily! My first thought? I could be ready to party again! Would I never learn?

Once diagnosed by the NHS, I went for a second opinion to see a private rheumatologist. I explained my lifestyle and the potential predicament of taking prescribed medications for the rest of my life whilst drinking and partying. He advised me that I could still do that as long as I was careful and didn't mix too many things in my system at any one time! I'll be honest here, that is up there as one of the worst pieces of advice I've ever received! However, it was probably what I wanted to hear at that moment and why I went to see him in the first place. So, what did I do? You know already. I went straight back to the DJing and clubbing life full-on as if this episode had never happened. It was all I knew, and all my life was based upon.

I realise the stupidity of that now, but thankfully something had started to change within me. When I continued to watch *The Secret* on repeat, again and again, my awareness of what was happening started to grow. There was a section on health in the film which, after my diagnosis, I watched with heightened interest. There was a huge 'a-ha' moment for me when Bob Proctor uttered these life-changing words: 'A disease is actually two words. You must hyphenate it. It's a dis-ease, and you cannot have a dis-ease if you're at ease. If your mind and body are in a healthy emotional state, you won't have a dis-ease.' This was life-changing information for me.

But hang on a minute. Doctors had told me I had an incurable dis-ease because of my genes, and I was predisposed to get it. And then Bob Proctor said it's a 'dis-ease', so if I've got a dis-ease, then I'm not at ease? I'd never thought about it like that. In my mind, I was OK. But my body was telling me something very, very different.

I also had a strong feeling that one day I must thank Bob personally for what he had said in *The Secret*. It woke me up. It's powerful stuff.

However, back at that time, and as you can imagine, I had so many questions. Two really stood out straight away: Why have I never heard any of this before? And really, *really*, just what exactly is going on here?

· · · · · ·

CHAPTER 3 – REMIX OPPORTUNITIES

- Choose hugs, not drugs.

- Music is the sound of emotions.

- Both masculine and feminine positive energies and guidance are important for a young child. (I'll explain more on masculine and feminine energy within each of us and also more on relationships in Chapter 13.)

- When the student is ready, the teacher will come.

DJing to thousands.

For more photos from Chapter 3, go to www.markwilkinsonofficial.com/life-remixed.

CHAPTER 4

GOT TO GIVE IT UP

If you're going through hell, keep going.
– Winston Churchill

Your way isn't working, try mine.
– Bob Proctor

*To make profound changes in your life,
you need either inspiration or desperation.*
– Tony Robbins

We come with a basic program; it's called self-healing.
– Dr Ben Johnson (*The Secret*)

Dis-ease cannot exist in a body in a healthy emotional state.
– Bob Proctor

*As humans, we're the only beings on the planet (that we know of) that
have been given a choice to have a thinking mind. We can create or
disintegrate. We have a choice to create or destroy. Every day on every
subject, we choose either with conscious awareness or unconsciously,
but either way, we choose to create or destroy.*

– Mark Wilkinson

Things are changing, life's rearranging.

– Danny Tenaglia (Hard & Soul)

Calm down, speed up.

– Bob Proctor

IF YOU'RE FACING, OR HAVE BEEN THROUGH, or can see any sort of crisis on your horizon, or you just feel a bit 'meh' and need some motivation, it's time to face up to it and remix your own life. As you've read, I've had a few challenges and made some mistakes along the way, so right now, please keep reading further into this book to find the solutions that worked for me and will work for you. Ask yourself, 'What's the next chapter of my life going to be like?'

Are you happy with who and what you are and with what you have right now? Or are you worrying? Would you like to create something new, something different, something better? Is life happening to you or for you? Do you know and understand right now that you are the creator of everything in your life? Do you know what the destination of your life looks like? Or are you simply feeling helpless, directionless in life, like a boat bobbing about on the ocean without a destination, compass, or a rudder?

We're going to go into all this and more so you can learn to feel great about life's coming attractions. Believe me when I say this: in every crisis, there is an opportunity.

Going forward with your own life remix, get a pen or a highlighter and make your own notes and highlights in the book. You can highlight or underline any quotes or words that resonate with you and that you'd like to come back to and read again. Make notes on any parts of the book or in a notebook that you feel will help you in remixing your own life, anything that will help you to achieve your goals, or indeed anything that you would like to speak to me about in person.

On the face of it, you may not want to totally accept every single idea that I put out there, and that's fine. All I ask is for you to read through everything first with an open mind, and when something does resonate with you, just take it in, and then try it out for yourself by putting it into practice. Try it in your own thoughts, feelings, and actions, and then when it works for you, just keep moving forward with a new awareness.

When I was facing these huge crises in my life, I heard a great piece of advice from Bob Proctor that resonated with me. He said, 'Your way isn't working, try mine.' To be honest, when I heard that, I literally had nothing left to lose. I thought, OK then, Bob, let's see what happens.

I was coming to realise that I had grown up with this addictive personality. From 14, I was drinking alcohol, and it carried on from there. I'd first tried smoking cigarettes when I was 10 or 11, and thankfully I didn't particularly love smoking. Also, my mum had the nose of a bloodhound, so she was on to me like a flash when she could smell smoke on or around me, so I didn't pursue that again until I was well out of the house.

I tried smoking again when I was about 18 after being given a cigarette in a nightclub. Smoking that particular cigarette at that particular moment felt amazing. So, as usual, I ended up going full-on with them for a while. I'd be taking three packs of 20 cigarettes to a rave and giving loads out, but smoking a lot myself too. My fingers would turn yellow on those nights I was having so many – my typical all-or-nothing rebellious addictive behaviour evident at its worst!

My parents had been religious, especially my dad. He loved the Salvation Army, but I had rebelled against him and religion, so I started behaving badly at school, and then I was out into my own teenage freedom and a life of music, nightclubs, and addiction.

So, there I was smoking like a chimney in Valbonnes in Maidenhead one Sunday evening. The music was loud, and there were a thousand other kids all around me dancing like crazy. Suddenly I was overcome with a deep and ominous feeling that I was going to throw up. I'd had problems in that area with alcohol but rarely otherwise, so this was a very strange feeling. My head was spinning and I thought I was going to pass out, so I made my way as quickly as possible through the human traffic to the bathroom and grabbed hold of the taps. I was splashing my face with water and trying not to be sick. People were slapping me on the back saying, 'Get it together mate' and 'One too many, eh?' and other things like that, but I was white (whiter than usual!), shaking, and in bits.

I stayed there for what felt like half an hour until the feeling subsided. I managed to regain my composure and walked unsteadily back outside into the mass of people and the throbbing loud music, smoke, and lasers. Clearly, the party was still in full swing without me. I was feeling nauseous, so I handed over all the cigarettes that I had left to the other smokers who stood around me, and I'm so pleased to say I've never had or even craved another one since! I know that story can make any smoker who would like to give up feel especially envious as they keep trying to stop. For me, it was easy, as I associated smoking with that awful feeling of almost throwing up. Every experience has a message. Job done.

I was already DJing and working full time in Flying Records in Kensington Market and later in the West End of London, Soho. I loved working up in Soho; I met amazingly talented people every day, with most of them clubbing, drinking, and partying people like me.

The problem was that when I got into anything I enjoyed, it was all too easy to get addicted. In my young, uncontrolled, and rebellious mind, I would end up focusing on one thing at the expense of all others. These were always the things that brought me quick and easy pleasure, whether they were creative or destructive things.

I think nowadays, for young people with addictive tendencies, things must be even more difficult! For instance, I'm thinking about the access to everything online, the constant swiping right on phones and tablets of dating apps. My young addictions would have been even more rampant with a smartphone in my hand! Could it easily take over a young mind and lead to unwanted issues nowadays? Quite possibly.

Speaking from my younger relationship experiences, when the girls put me on a pedestal, I could be happy with them for a while. In hindsight, I think I needed the attention because I wasn't especially confident in myself, and I didn't really love myself. I didn't realise that I wasn't at ease with myself and was using these wonderful women to distract myself from that fact. I needed them to like and love me as

I didn't like or love myself. When they did, I thought I must be OK then. As I've learned, that is not the basis for a successful relationship. Chapter 13 discusses relationships and how I fixed this issue.

My Body's Descent into Dis-ease

My body had started to complain through the hay fever and IBS that I've already told you about. As a young chap, I also had three violent episodes of a food allergy reaction to kiwi fruit (yep!) that took me down on three separate occasions. There are only three people I've ever known with a kiwi fruit allergy - that's me, a record producer friend of ours who came into the Flying Records shop as a vinyl distributor, and Ross from *Friends*. Seriously, it's in one of the early seasons when Ross has to go to hospital to get an adrenalin shot as Monica had made him a kiwi lime pie, and he's as allergic as me!

Anyway, I used to eat kiwi out of Mum's fridge all the time when I was younger, and then one day out of nowhere, I had a violent allergic reaction (both ends). Hours later, when I'd half recovered, Mum asked me what I'd just eaten. I told her, and she said I should stay off it from now on, so I took her advice.

About five years later, on a very hot summer's day at Flying Records in Soho, my mate and manager of the record shop Lofty got a punnet of strawberries all covered in slices of kiwi. It looked tempting, and I thought to myself that it can't have been the kiwi, can it? So, I went and got the same thing he just had. I ate it and, within seconds, felt the same allergic reaction as my throat started itching and closing up. I managed to get the words out, asking him to cover for me as I went and collapsed in the back office near the rotten old toilet for the next six hours of mayhem! He even closed the shop and went to Boots to get me a bottle of Pepto Bismol! He's a top fella. I staggered home about 8pm that day.

The third reaction was probably the worst. After the gym with my brother, we somehow got the smoothies mixed up and I drank one full of kiwi. I felt the reaction coming on again almost immediately. I managed to drive us home before I passed out on the bed. I was violently ill, and then my nasal airways started to close up. I asked Dan to ring Mum and get her round urgently, and bless her, she came over in double-quick time. Good job she did as I became acutely aware that if I was sick again and my throat closed up, then that would be the end! With both airways closed, I would have been a goner! Mum drove me as quickly as she could to Teddington Hospital five minutes down the road, and they rushed me in and gave me a number of treatments and injections to get me stable again. That one was a shock to all of us. Obviously, I now have EpiPens in various locations around me, especially as I had another near miss once with an orange and kiwi juice!

However, although now I've made the connection between all the things I did to my younger self and the clear hypersensitivity of my reactions, back then, I still wasn't really listening to my body. The truth is that I started acting like an idiot in 1984, and I just forgot to stop. My habit of not liking myself very much was to carry on every weekend and then try to recover enough in the week to produce some music and pay the bills. That got more and more difficult as most days I was in the studio, I was doubled over with severe stomach cramps. I'd be in the middle of making a track and then end up asking my studio engineer to change something in the track whilst I was crying out in pain on the sofa!

Then, of course, came the physical collapse you read about in Chapter 1. My body was so full of inflammation by then it just closed down. It stopped working. I was in total shut down mode. It had had enough, so it stopped supporting me, and that was when I hit the floor. It was after that dark moment and during the following 18 months of increasingly savage pain, and when the rheumatologist finally diagnosed me with an incurable disease, that I finally became aware of a few things that were going on around me, and more importantly, within me.

Thoughts Become Things

To this day, I still love the 2006 film The Secret. It's on Netflix now, and I recommend everyone watch it. I feel that it provides excellent entry-level information about universal laws, and the law of attraction in particular. With the new understanding I gained from the film, I began to understand the power of my thoughts and feelings. As I've mentioned, the part that resonated with me the most at first was Bob Procter saying, 'You cannot have a dis-ease if you're at ease.' On the first watch, I had not understood that at all. However, as I started to open my mind to the possibilities that my old way of thinking and feeling – all learned from a young age – had contributed to everything that happened in my life up until that moment, things became clearer.

I slowly started to join the dots, and everything began to make more sense to me. After I first started to change my thinking, I followed some good advice to look for the little miracles happening every day in life. I started to become more aware of positive outcomes from the way I was choosing to think. Slowly, slowly at first, and then much quicker, my life started changing. I noticed that when we take care of our thoughts and feelings, our actions change, and we can and will have the life we desire.

Although it's clear that *The Secret* was a massive worldwide success as a book and a film in raising awareness of the law of attraction, it clearly hasn't worked perfectly for everyone, and there are reasons for that. However, the film woke me up and made me aware enough to want to find out more, and through the application of the knowledge and further learning and understanding, The Secret has continued to work for me ever since. Let me explain how.

As I started to see little miracles begin to happen in my life (I'd think of something small, and it would turn up for me), I became quite fascinated with self-development and manifestation. I feel that when you see instruction from a film, a book, a coach, or a mentor actually manifest and come into your own reality, it's a very powerful thing. When Brian Miller said to me after the first time I'd watched *The Secret*, 'Now go and watch the film again, watch it 100 times', he knew what had to happen for me. He knew what was going on in my body was a direct reflection of what was going on in my mind, and he also knew that it is the repetition of the right information that ensures we program our subconscious minds. Repetition is mastery.

To be honest, I wasn't even aware that I had a subconscious mind at that moment, so of course, I wouldn't have understood anything about it. I was just so low, in so much pain and despair, that I took Brian's word for it and went with it. I would have done almost anything to get rid of the pain, so maybe it could work.

I found out that *The Secret* is based on an amazing book written by Wallace Wattles in 1910 called *The Science of Getting Rich*, which I read shortly afterwards. Wattles explains in simple, straightforward language how anyone, regardless of their background or circumstances, can attract wealth into their lives. Anyone can have happiness, health, and wealth. There is a simple start point in Chapter 7 of his book that is dedicated entirely to the subject of *gratitude*.

As a youth, I was completely unaware that I could actually be in control of my thinking and feeling. I thought I was one of those people who life just happened to. I bemoaned things not being how I wanted them to be. I'd think that I wasn't successful enough in my chosen music career, that I wasn't good enough, that I wasn't worthy, that I couldn't afford it. But what I didn't realise is that my predominant thoughts and feelings were all negative and about all the things that I didn't want, and they then turned up consistently in my life! The bad habits and addictions just took that pain away.

I started to understand that my *thoughts actually became things*, that the thoughts we choose cause our feelings, and feelings make our day, week, month, year, and eventually life, either good or bad, happy or sad, positive or negative. I realised that all the experiences I had ever gone through I had thought about in advance. They had come true and actually manifested, and eventually, I came to the harsh realisation that it was all my major fears that had come true.

I started to understand that I am a transmission tower that attracts what I am thinking (and feeling) about. So if you're feeling not good enough or unworthy right now, like a magnet, you'll continue to attract more of that, and eventually, it will become your whole life experience. The same thing goes with the positives. If you're feeling confident, happy, and joyful, you'll experience more of that. As a young chap, I remember thinking every time something good happened that it wouldn't last, and something bad would always follow it, and guess what? Just like clockwork, it did. A wise saying tells us, 'The most important decision a human being has to make is whether we live in a friendly or hostile universe.'

I remember being full of fear about my chosen career in music and that maybe it wouldn't last. While I was DJing, I was fine, but in between gigs, I'd experience anxiety. I didn't have any reality to back that up as my diary was usually busy. However, my doubts, fears, and worries started to get the better of me until I collapsed into that oblivion. I was choosing to live in an unfriendly universe: Everyone else was better than me. Everyone else was doing better than me. I wasn't good enough. It won't last forever. How will I survive? And that became my reality.

I knew about the universal law of gravity as we'd been taught that one at school, but *The Secret* taught me about the law of attraction – that *like* attracts *like* – so I studied more and more of the universal laws after that and understood that just like gravity they work for every person every time.

Understanding and then accepting these laws can be a challenge, and sometimes harsh realities might have to be learned and understood along the way. When we finally understand and take responsibility for all of our results, life can really begin. Everything can be magical when we know how to apply the universal laws. I remember Bob Proctor said, 'Life can be phenomenal, and it should be, and it will be for you when you take responsibility for your thoughts, feelings, and actions.'

I've added explanations of other universal laws in Chapter 11 for you to study and try out for yourselves. Something to look forward to.

However, one other important universal law that people can miss is that *force negates*.

Just think about it. Anytime you've tried to force yourself or anyone else to do something or to change, or even when someone has tried to force you to change, it's ended up being negative. Interestingly, I've seen many people after watching *The Secret* trying to force themselves to be happy and attract positive things into their life rather than accepting what their current position is and then reprogramming and rebuilding from there. That may be one reason why *The Secret* hasn't worked for everyone. If you're trying to force the law of attraction, it simply won't work for you.

Another mistake people can make with *The Secret* is they fail to take action towards their goals. So remember to ask, believe, take action, and then receive.

Time for a Big Decision

One day on another detox in Scotland, I had a kinesiology and visualisation session with Brian. By this time, my body was so stiff I could barely get out of the chair on that particular day, but he kept challenging me to get up. He was raising his voice and almost shouting at me, pushing me to get up, get up, get up, but I was struggling, so he asked me to stop and to stay sitting where I was. He asked me to close my eyes and then to carefully imagine myself getting up out of the chair, imagine being completely pain-free, walking normally, feeling fit, strong, happy, and enjoying life. I struggled to clear my mind at first, but I focused and managed to do it. Once I had the picture clear in my mind, he asked me to begin to slowly get myself up out of the chair. Slowly I pushed myself up and stood there, still very weak.

Without me realising it at the time, Brian had anchored me to that vision by asking me a very simple question: 'What are you wearing? In your imagination, when you are fit and strong, what are you wearing.' I answered, 'A yellow t-shirt.' Brian smiled. Please make sure you remember that yellow top. A quote I've heard since is, *the imagination is the greatest nation on earth*. There will be more on the power of this visualisation and imagination session later on, so stay tuned as it's a game-changer.

Another big moment during that detox in Scotland was the day I decided it was time to give up alcohol completely.

It was during another therapy session with Brian that we discussed my party lifestyle. I remember I'd had a big weekend DJing in London before going up for the detox. I'd been partying all weekend, then got straight onto the train at Kings Cross and up to Berwick for the week. I was in bits, taking loads of painkillers and prescribed medication just to get through the day when I sat with Brian. We'd had conversations before, but this one was different. For a start, we were on our own. I'd never really bonded with him up to that point. I always got on better with the feminine energy of his wife. He asked me an important question that day: 'Why do you drink, Mark?' I felt uncomfortable, actually really very uncomfortable. I started squirming in my seat, basically because I didn't have an answer! I'd never thought about it before. I'd drunk alcohol for 20 years, and I didn't know why. That's weird.

I sat there racking my brains for a while and kept saying, 'I don't know, I don't know. Because everybody does?' After a while, Brian had enough of listening to me fumbling around for an answer. I didn't know it then, but he had been an alcoholic in his time and also suffered from the same incurable rheumatic condition as me! So, as I continued to make excuses for my drinking, he stopped me, looked me dead in the eye, and almost shouted, 'Bullshit!'

I'd never heard Brian swear or raise his voice angrily like that before. He was kind of like Buddha most of the time, so you can imagine my surprise! I was taken aback! It was exactly what I needed, though – some masculine authority that I respected basically calling me out for talking crap!

We got deep into it then. I blabbered loads of words that didn't really mean much and managed to come up with, 'Well, when people offer to buy me drinks, it would be rude if I said no, right?' Brian laughed and put me straight. 'Yes, when you're the DJ, you're the focal point. Yes, you're responsible for the music and the whole party, the whole atmosphere, the whole night, but you don't need to partake in all this other crap to do it, do you?' Then he asked, 'Why do you think they offer it?' Again, I didn't really have an answer.

About now, I started to listen and really think, after all, 'Your way isn't working, try mine.' With Brian's help, I came to the realisation that, in my position on the London club scene, and by me accepting what other people were giving me without question, it was actually validating their behaviour. Tragically over a period of years, these decisions and actions had also brought me down to a place where I was in terrible pain and suffering.

The following weekend I was back in the club detoxed but still heavily on pain and prescribed medications when people tried to get me involved. But by then, I had decided. I simply and politely said, 'No, thank you.' I was worried that most people would call me names or say, 'What's up with you?' or use other ways to try to get me involved, but something really strange happened. About 95% of people said, 'What? You're not drinking anymore? Wow, that's amazing. I wish I could do that!' I was gobsmacked, truly amazed.

Months later, I used the 'Why do you drink?' line on a very good friend of mine when he needed some help. I was clean and sober by now, but he was absolutely smashed this particular night when I saw him. So, I let him get over the pain for a few days afterwards, and when he called me days later, still moaning about his hangover, I asked him the question. Bless him, he came up with loads of random answers too. I remember one was, 'I don't know what else to order when I get to the bar!'

Over the coming weeks, he tried a few more times to find an answer, and in the end, he admitted to me that he simply didn't know why he drank alcohol either! His dad was a big drinker, so perhaps he was just following the learned behaviour? Anyway, because he couldn't answer my question, he decided to give up as well. Amazing. I love having a positive effect on other people. We're still great friends. He doesn't drink alcohol excessively anymore, and he's now got a wonderful partner and three lovely children. Plus, he's happy, healthy, and wealthy.

At this point, you may decide to ask yourself the question, why would you spend your well-earned money on buying and drinking alcohol to excess? At best, you'll hopefully be having a good laugh for an hour or two and then end up feeling awful for a day or two. And that recovery time gets longer and longer if your body gets more and more toxic as you age. Have a think on it. Too much of anything over a lifetime can be destructive.

With growing my basic understanding and cleaning up my life and diet, I started to feel really good. Stopping drinking alcohol was massive. I woke up every day feeling good, with no hangovers and loads more time to create good things. I also heard that people tend to stop growing emotionally when they start dependency. This meant that by now, I was 37 going on 14! It was the end of 2007, and I was making these changes to recover my health and recover my life. Things were starting to move in the right direction, so I was hopeful of recovery.

Along Came Financial Stress and Shock

I continued to struggle with stress in my work and life situations. The music business had taken a massive hit in the early 2000s when people had worked out that music could be downloaded for free. I went from earning well for my tracks and remixes to earning £0, nothing, nada. 'Can you do this one for free? It'll be good for your profile!' became a common request.

Even some professional DJs were DJing in clubs with free low-quality music from their computer. Some didn't seem to realise that the sound quality was awful in comparison to vinyl or CDs. Some did it because file-sharing was new, available, and free, so they thought they were saving money. But it actually meant a huge drop in revenues in the music business.

All these changes happening quickly were quite a shock. However, thankfully I still had enough live events and DJ gigs to sustain me, and we created a style and look for my record label Kidology Records. I'd always had a group of girls hang around the DJ booth when I was playing, and my mates used to jokingly call them 'the Wilkettes', so when we restyled Kidology Records, we expanded that idea and came up with the name of the group of girls dancing at the party: The Kidology Kidettes. It turned out to be a great idea for the times, and many promoters and club owners loved it. We did tours all over, and things were growing well.

Then in 2008, we decided to uplift the business with some outside investment and started taking on larger capacity clubs at what turned out to be exactly the wrong time. We were putting on big London club nights that cost a lot of money with all the production and people involved, with budgets stretched even when the nights were full. I learned around this time that it's not a good thing to have all your eggs in one basket!

As 2008 progressed, each month, DJ gigs were getting harder to come by. Then, all of a sudden, out of nowhere, there was something called the 'credit crunch'. I didn't really understand money much back then, but I noticed two things: clubs weren't as full as they had been, and money was getting tighter. As I mentioned, we'd been on tight budgets already, so as soon as people stopped spending on nights out, we were in trouble. Going out is understandably one of the first things people stop spending money on when things get tight.

We were sinking, and all this was happening at exactly the same time as my close relationships and friendships were failing. I was, of course, in the middle of all this, trying to recover my physical health, but at the same time, everything else (stress, anxiety, and my mental health) was going downhill. At the time of the credit crunch, we had been running these large-scale parties. We were doing well at first, and then in one very quick year, we had gone from 1,000 revellers a night to below 400, with our break-even point set at 600–700 for each party. You can see where the profit margin went. It only took about six months of this for us to be in serious financial trouble.

Of course, I became hugely stressed by all of this, and despite my newfound understanding of certain aspects of life, it was really difficult for me to handle. One of Bob Proctor's coaches said to me at the time, *it always gets dark before the light comes.* I understood what he meant.

I also knew I had to continue to clean up my act, to get healthy. It would mean a complete lifestyle change, lots of early nights, and looking after myself to recover my health. However, as I was changing so much, it put too much strain on many of my friendships and relationships. 'You'll never be able to do it,' was something I heard at one point. That was a massive moment for me. There and then, I realised that my whole social circle and life would have to change. I smiled with both sadness and disappointment when I realised.

I was changing, and I needed and wanted other people to support and help me get over my negative addictions. It was really difficult when it clearly wasn't going to be forthcoming. I knew I had to move on. It was OK. I forgave everyone, including myself, on the spot as I understood by then that this was the best thing for me to do for my own mental health. Unfortunately, not everyone could forgive me as I withdrew from the lifestyle, so things really began to unravel. It took a few months to happen, but I knew I couldn't force anything to make others change with me as I knew force negates.

Looking back, I can fully understand that my changes at the time didn't fit in with others' lifestyle plans, so I simply couldn't stay in that social circle. I realised that the timing was off. That circle of friends' lives were based around late nights and partying, and I wanted – no, actually I needed – to change. Physically, I was no longer able to keep living that way.

Eckhart Tolle says in his book *The Power of Now* that when someone changes or becomes enlightened, as he puts it, one of two things will happen. You'll either grow together with people around you and all enjoy the journey together, or you will separate like oil and water. By now, I'm sure I don't have to tell you which one happened here.

As the wheels were coming off my life, one day, I packed my bags and drove up to Scotland in my soon to be repossessed car for another detox, for more tubes up the bum, and mental breakthroughs, an interesting combination! I was clearly choosing to commit to continued learning and growth.

When I got back to London, I had arranged to move in with a friend just off Clapham Common. I needed the space from the previous party lifestyle, and thankfully he was a cool and sensible chap. I also needed time to think about what I was going to do next. The last six months of changes had coincided around the summer of 2008 when the world, including my business, was starting to go off a financial cliff. But by then, largely, I felt relieved to be free from the environment I had been in. However, all the inevitable money troubles previously mentioned started to catch up with me, eventually leading to bankruptcy.

Thankfully though, I still had a couple of gigs left a month, and doing those meant I had some money to live off. I could pay the rent at my friend's house, and I could live as a single chap in his large house sleeping in the spare room. Sadly, when my company eventually did crash, I let some people down when I couldn't pay every invoice or all the money back to shareholders. It was the worst feeling of my life, and I am so very sorry to each and every one of them. I know I've made good to many by paying most of them back in lots of ways over the years, and its an ongoing process which I am committed to. I also completely believe in Karma, what you give out is what you get back, so I've always done my best to get everything sorted with anyone who got burnt at that time. Everything just happened all at once, and I was swamped, overwhelmed with no solutions or way out. I was trying to run a business based on live events during the credit crunch (one of the worst financial crises in history) when the majority of people decided to stay at home. Business went bad, and mentally I got in some really dark places. My thirties were very, very tough.

I Needed Peace and Recovery

Here's the thing, though. Every time I detoxed, I would try to come off the AS medication, but every time I did, within two days, I was crippled with pain again. So I had to keep taking the pills. I had heard Dr John DeMartini in *The Secret* say, 'Incurable just means curable from within.' I began to look around, more aware than I had ever been. Restarting with a healthy diet and recently single, I realised that the majority of my stresses were gone. I was chilling. I had those few DJ gigs left to pay my rent and eat. I'd left the previous circle of people I was hanging out in. I'd had a lot of therapy in my life to try and understand why I couldn't make relationships work, and my therapist said I was 'very brave' to move on in this way, although I honestly didn't feel like that at the time. It was just the healthiest thing to do! So I was relaxing, sleeping a lot, and trying to regain my mental and physical health.

I woke up in Clapham Common one day after I had just moved in. It was a crisp autumn morning, and I was laying in my room. All I could hear was the birds in the tree singing outside the window. Having lived in the city for a few years, it made a pleasant change from the noise of traffic and bars emptying old beer bottles into metal bins at 7am. Actually, it reminded me of living in the suburbs when I was a kid. I'd enjoyed parts of the last few years of living in the city, but now that rollercoaster ride had come to an end. London had eaten me up and spat me back out. I was knackered. I needed some peace and recovery time, and this was the start of it.

It was inevitable that my now small income was never going to cover the money I owed from the failed business. I had really tried my best for everyone. Still, ultimately, I had failed, and let me tell you, from the heights of where I thought I was as an international DJ and record producer, that was a huge and bitter pill to swallow. I wasn't prepared for failure at all when it became clear that one day I was going to have to go bankrupt.

With all this going on, though, something really strange happened to my health. Listening to those birds singing when I woke up that day, I remembered what that doctor had said about people leaving stressful situations and their symptoms going away. As I said, I had tried to give up the prescribed medication a number of times, but all to no avail. Even though I was detoxing nutritionally, the pain, the agony, still came back within a day or two and ravaged my body.

During that time, I thought that I would have to make my peace with what the majority of doctors had told me, as it must be true. This pain all over my body is simply incurable, and I'm just going to have to deal with it for the rest of my life. You might say this was another bitter pill to swallow, but at least on the medication I could hope to have a reasonably liveable life.

After a few days more of rest and relaxation, waking up in leafy Clapham Common every day and enjoying the clean and no stress living, I looked at the bottle of pills that the doctor had given me and thought, 'Let's just try coming off the pills one more time, for a couple of days to start with.' I suspected I'd be back in agony again soon enough without them, but I reasoned with myself, if you don't try, you won't know. This is where things got really interesting, and I had what you might call my next health epiphany, or miracle, if you'd prefer.

Basically, all the pain had gone, and it didn't come back for 1-2-3 days at first. I remember thinking that this is weird, but then it carried on for 1-2-3 weeks, and then 4-5-6 weeks, then months. I was amazed. The pain I had been in for years had left my body completely. After detoxing my life, leaving the emotional pain of the failed business, and leaving the old circle of people behind, the pain was gone and I could move freely again. I could sleep well and relax and enjoy life again.

THIS FELT INCREDIBLE.

Now let's be clear. This isn't anything to do with anyone or anything else external to me. It has everything to do with me and with my inability to deal close up with certain situations.

I was suddenly able to move around like a normal person in their late thirties again. So even though I'd done all the diet and clean-up work previously, it took moving to a low-stress life for all my pain to go away. This was amazing information for me to process. I swore to myself that day that I'd be so careful about any future friendships, relationships, and social circles that I got into. I decided that in the future, my circle of friends must be calm and loving with plenty of happiness and self-care to go around. Most importantly, I realised that I had to become this person first to attract other like-minded people. Like attracts like.

Admittedly at the end of 2008, at 38 years of age, I had no money, no assets, and was facing bankruptcy. But my phone was very quiet, my stress levels were balancing out, and my health was coming back, so I was able to deal with this and take it in my stride. In fact, any other problem I was experiencing seemed manageable in comparison to previously collapsing and then not being able to walk.

When I was faced with these challenges, these were the moments when I learned the most about myself. During these times, I basically had two choices: One would've been to go and jump off a bridge or a tall building. The other was to decide that I was better than this, to dust myself off and start again with the same enthusiasm I'd always had in the music business, but this time with the added personal development skills I'd been learning for the last few years. I just knew I had to reinvent myself and come back stronger. The rest of this book, and indeed my life, are dedicated to exactly that.

During the Christmas break in 2008, I was chatting with my mate on Facebook to see if he wanted to meet up in January. He said he'd like to but typed, 'I can't drink alcohol though. I'm running the London Marathon in April.' My mind started whirring. I was feeling really good, no aches, no pains, almost fully recovered, but I'd never run anywhere before, except maybe once or twice for a bus!

I remember the moment well when I sat there looking at my laptop and thought to myself that I'd been pain-free for the last two or three months and hadn't drunk any alcohol since April. I'm feeling good. Maybe, I could run the London Marathon. I had read that former

Monty Python comedian Michael Palin had said that everyone should run the London Marathon at least once in their lives, and I thought to myself: *This could be an interesting story, right?* Being an international DJ, then unable to walk and my joints frozen, being stuck to the sofa, living the life I had, collapsing and having suicidal thoughts, and now facing bankruptcy. Life had been a real rollercoaster, but I felt I was slowly turning a corner. Maybe I could do it, maybe I could run the London Marathon, and maybe I could share my story and help some other people too. I began to visualise crossing the finish line.

The thing is, in my mind, I thought, *running, me, really?* If you've met me, you know I'm six feet four inches and carry a few extra pounds here and there, so running had *never* been my strong point. In fact, sports themselves had largely passed me by as a participant. I was a trier, and I did get a 'man of the match' award once playing right back for Third Hampton Hill Cub Scouts back in 1981. It's also the stuff of legend that's still talked about to this day over the bar at Hampton Hill Cricket Club when I smashed my maiden 'not out 11' to save the under 16's cricket team from a certain defeat one summer's evening. But that was about it. Running was definitely not my thing. I might have even tried to take a few shortcuts when we did the old cross country run in the school PE lessons. I never actually had the audacity to jump on the bus to get there quicker, but trust me, I thought about it.

So, if you had told 14-year-old Mark when he started on his first sips of alcohol that before he was forty, he would run the London Marathon, he would've fallen over laughing at you, but here I was giving serious consideration to going for it.

However, the new man that I was – clean of any toxins, no work, low stress, no money, plenty of time on my hands, understanding my thinking and feelings better – wanted to recreate myself after a period of my life so painful that I thought I might never walk properly again. I thought that this would be a great story if I could actually achieve it. From being unable to walk to then running a marathon! Let's sort out the mind-over-matter debate for myself once and for all. If I can set my mind to this and achieve it, I knew for the rest of my life that I could 100% do anything that I set my mind to.

And so, with absolutely no running experience, I made the decision to go for it. I contacted the Microphthalmia Anophthalmia Coloboma Support (MACS) charity to offer to represent them at the London Marathon. They are an amazing charity set up to support children born without eyes or with underdeveloped eyes. As I'd always had eye problems myself as a child (nothing like as serious as what these young people have to go through, though), it did make sense to me to represent them. I'm forever grateful to everyone at MACS for allowing me the opportunity to get a vest for the 2009 London Marathon and the opportunity to raise a few thousand pounds for them, which I knew they appreciated.

My energy was up, my health had recovered fully, and I had learned that if I remove all the stress from my life, then my body will heal itself. It was a lesson I learned from my many relationships and my music career, but I still didn't learn the lesson fully until a flare-up of my knees some years later, only the next time it was the stress of working in the corporate world. More on that later.

I kept visualising finishing the marathon, and on Christmas day, 2008, I put on the only trainers I had that were far too clumpy to run in, and I went out for a jog near Clapham Common. I managed a few minutes but cut it short. I was shattered, and I thought I must have done at least two to three miles. Later that day, at Christmas lunch, my mum gave me a pedometer, so I went out the next day and did the same circuit. I was shattered again, and by the time I got back to the house, I was exhausted. I looked at the pedometer, and it said 0.8 of a mile! Disaster.

At this point, I really did wonder how on earth am I going to run 25.4 more miles in only four months' time? I started to think I couldn't do it. That's what the mind can do to us, and if we decide to give in to that first negative thought, we'd never get anything done. I knew I needed a better plan.

I downloaded a beginner's training program from *Runner's World* magazine that said I could go from nothing to completing the marathon's 26.2 miles in 16 weeks. I looked at it, and it seemed OK. The first day said 'rest' so I thought, OK, I can do that! The rest of the plan looked like a week-on-week build-up of fitness and distance. As I didn't have a lot else to do, I thought to myself, *OK, let's have a go. I will do this. It's going to happen.*

I started training. I also kept training my mind to think positively, to think that I can do this, to continue to visualise myself crossing the finishing line of the London Marathon, running up The Mall on a sunny day in front of Buckingham Palace. I did that a couple of times a day. I lay on my bed with my eyes closed, picturing myself doing this. I lay there, and as I held the picture in my mind, it felt great – the law of attraction in action.

I wanted to prove to myself that if I visualised something, believed in it enough, and trained myself well enough, then I could achieve it. I wanted to prove to myself that everything I learned from *The Secret* really works. If I could cross that marathon finishing line in April 2009, aged 38, after being unable to walk for an extended period in my thirties, I would know, for a fact, that absolutely anything is indeed possible! Finishing that marathon would transform my thinking and my life, but could I actually do it?

All the while, I kept up my detox diet with no toxic foods or drink allowed in. My energy was higher than it had ever been! I rested well, slept well, and when I needed the energy for a long training run, my body had it. Having been a meat-eater, borderline alcoholic, and addict all my life up to that point, it was a massive revelation to me how good I felt.

I had started with that 0.8 of a mile, and then every few days, I'd build up a little more. The next two months saw me run 3, 5, 10, and then 12 miles in a day. I used Clapham Common, as well as Bushy Park and Richmond Park in South West London for training. Although admittedly, it was a bit cold at times in January, I soon warmed up, and I kept on training. I was feeling good. I also felt free, and we'll talk more about true freedom in later chapters. One of the most important things I took from running at that moment in my life was that I could still be successful at something even though I had nothing material to show for almost 20 years in music.

Now you could say I had replaced one addiction with another, and this may well have been true. However, at least this was a healthy addiction, a positive addiction if you like. It was making me feel good naturally. But was this more escapism? Pure Forrest Gump? You could be right. Run, Wilkie, run.

There will be more on the marathon journey and what else I learned while training coming up.

Learning from the Worst Moments in Life

In amongst the marathon training, I had to go to the High Court in February 2009 and go through the bankruptcy process. All the running probably gave me the strength to face it. I'd exhausted every avenue that I could trying to pay my debts, but they were overwhelming, and I didn't have a plan or a way out, or at least I couldn't see one at that time. I researched bankruptcy as an option since, by now, the DJ work had all but dried up, and materially I had little to nothing plus no assets or real qualifications to fall back on. I was basically done for financially. I've since learned to diversify a lot more with multiple sources of income, but back then, it was either go bankrupt, be made bankrupt, or spend a decade or more trying to pay back the money with a tonne of interest without an income. I couldn't see a way out. I decided to fall on my sword. I went to the High Court in London.

When I got to the court, and I hope you never find this out for yourself, I told them my sad story, and I listed all my debts and the fact that I had no real discernible income. They told me to write down all my debts on a sheet. They made me wait for a few hours, then the clerk came out and said, 'Mr Wilkinson, that will be £500, please.' Erm, excuse me, what? I couldn't believe it. I looked at him in amazement and said, 'Really?' He repeated his request for money, and I looked straight at him and said, 'I clearly haven't got any money. We've just been through this. I don't have access to anything. I'm maxed out in every area. I don't have £500. What do I do?' He said, 'Come back when you have £500.' I couldn't believe it. I went downstairs, and I think the reality of it all kicked in. I sat down and cried my eyes out.

There was no option, nothing I could do about this apart from ring my mum. My dear old mum had worked hard for her entire life and had a few quid left in her bank account each month, not much but just enough for her to be able to help me out on this awful day. Not my proudest moment.

I said, 'Mum, please can you give me £500 to go bankrupt so I can put this nightmare behind me?' She immediately said yes and told me to come round that evening to sort it out. I burst into tears again, and it wasn't just about this particular day. It was about everything that had happened over the last few years, the rollercoaster of pain and the incurable dis-ease diagnosis, my crazy music career disappearing before my eyes, the highs and lows of relationships with women who I thought I would marry, and now being faced with this horrible financial situation.

My tears were still flowing, but my feelings turned to a huge amount of gratitude to my mum that I'd never really felt before. I swore to myself that day that I would never let her down again. As a young man, you know I hadn't been the best son, to say the least. I remembered all the times I'd hurt her or made her cry, the time she'd lost her finger for me on a slide, all the times she had to come to the school when I was misbehaving, the time I got my ear pierced at 14 and she cried, the time I got a 50cc motorbike at 16 and she cried, the Sainsbury's shopping trolley incident, and then the anger and worry that I had put her through when she found out about my toxic habits. I mean, the list goes on and on.

For the last 25 years, I had worried her to bits. There were some moments that we both enjoyed, but there was also plenty of other times where I let her down badly. Right then, I said that's it, no more. I think it was the day at last that I became a man. I'd been a selfish little boy, chasing a music dream, chasing women, chasing highs. This was the day that I became an adult. So, I swore from that day, *9 February 2009*, that I'd do everything I could to make my mum's life the best it can be, and to this day, I continue to make that my goal.

There is a lovely side story to the commitment that I made that day. Understanding more and more the importance of goal setting and visualisation, I asked my mum to make a goals/bucket list. She put as her number one goal to ride a camel around the pyramids in Egypt. Last year, we achieved that, and I have the photos and videos to prove it. It was a fantastic moment with my family when I witnessed a huge smile on my mum's face as she rode a camel around that historical and mystical site just outside Cairo. It only happened because of my commitment that day that I would never let her down again.

So, even the worst moments of my life have actually been things that I have learned from. It's the things that we perceive as failures where we can learn the most, and they're only failures if we think them so in our perception. There is no good or bad unless we think it is so. In reality, everything just is. So what is the easiest solution for your own mental health? Forgive yourself and everyone else. Accept it. It is what it is. And start to feel gratitude for what you are, what you do, and what you have.

After this massive financial disaster, I found myself strangely tranquil. I think I'd had all my suicidal thoughts when I was seriously ill, so this was something I could handle and had to handle. I decided to follow what I'd learned in The Secret to change my thinking and feeling about money as well as health. I decided I'd use this massive failure to learn from and create a successful comeback.

It was around this time when I was committed to my own personal development that I heard two quotes that really helped me change and grow.

Comparison is the thief of joy.

What anyone else thinks of you is none of your business.

Let those sink in for a moment. Read them again.

These thoughts helped free me from the mental prison that I'd built up around myself. They relaxed and freed me to be my real self. Once I'd grasped them, it was amazing how much more free-thinking time I found to create good things!

As soon as the penny dropped with these two quotes, I realised how much time I had spent comparing myself unfavourably to other people and how unhappy it had made me. So I stopped that immediately! I also stopped wasting time trying to work out what other people were thinking about me. I mean, what is the point? I can't control other people's thinking, so why waste any of my time thinking or worrying about it? It's none of my business. I'd say after grasping the wisdom of these two quotes, I did something else that really rocket-fuelled my life. I calmed myself down, and I sped up!

I'd lost everything, materially at least. I was a 38-year-old, out-of-work DJ. I had no relationship, no money, no nothing. After the marathon, I even moved back into my mum's box room (where my dad had been side-lined after their divorce). As you can imagine, I wasn't happy with that, and trust me, this could have been the lowest of the lows for me. However, I did have my health, and considering I'd been in agony just a year or two earlier, I realised that I could use my transferrable skills to plot my comeback. I used the downtime well, and the motivation to get out of that box room put me right back on track.

So, I decided to follow all the instructions for setting goals. Bob Proctor said, 'Set a goal that seems so outlandish that when you achieve it, you'll know it's because of what you've learned.'

I was bankrupt and signing on for six months of unemployment benefits when I made a decision that I was going to achieve a salary of £400 a day, or £8,400 a month, which would equate to just over £100,000 a year. I didn't know how I would do it, but I chose to believe it would happen. I visualised and kept focused on my goal as I knew that would be my recovery. I had faith that I could get back to a real life again!

We're going to cover all of this in more detail in the coming chapters. However, these were the burning issues and questions I had to deal with:

- I had to take responsibility for everything I'd created in my life so far – the good, the bad, and the ugly. I was told that *responsibility is the key to freedom, and I badly needed freedom!*

- I had to ask myself, what was it about me that attracted the people and negative circumstances that stressed me out so much? That is possibly the hardest question I've ever had to ask myself. The answers came to me, and they were deep. Some things I didn't want to face, but I knew I had to so I could work on myself and move forward.

- I had to achieve acceptance of what is – again, another massive challenge. The breakdown of my ego from international touring DJ to bankrupt was tough. I dealt with this by adopting the following mantra: *Don't look back in anger, nor forward in fear, but around in awareness.*

So right now, ask yourself some questions.

Ask yourself, are you suffering any pain in your body? Or emotional pain? Are you feeling stressed? Do you reach for alcohol, junk food, sugar, or any other toxins when you feel stressed? Are you perceiving something in your life in a negative way that is causing stress in your mind?

The important takeaway from this chapter is that our bodies are a reflection of our minds. So, if you're feeling bad or in pain, it's time to look inside yourself and find out what is really going on within you. Life Remixed™ is all about helping you achieve a great life whilst being here on this planet by giving you the same tools I used and the understanding to do so.

We'll cover all these points and more in the coming chapters. My hope is to help you feel great, to help you realise there is always a way back from any perceived crisis, to help motivate you to be healthy, wealthy, and happy – as happy as I feel now.

By helping you do the above, I get to live to my own purpose, which I'll reveal in Chapter 7.

. . . . . .

CHAPTER 4 – REMIX OPPORTUNITIES

- Addiction (to anything self-destructive) is a dis-ease.

- Always listen to what your body is telling you.

- We attract what we think about and feel. We attract what we are.

- Set big goals, so big that you have no idea how you'll achieve them.

- Every morning and evening, close your eyes and imagine (visualise) that you've already achieved your goals. See your future self living exactly as you would like.

- You can literally bring anything you visualise into reality.

- Ask yourself, how good does this feel?

- Enjoy the process.

Marathon training.

For more photos from Chapter 4, go to www.markwilkinsonofficial.com/life-remixed.

CHAPTER 5

I WANT TO THANK YOU

*The entire process of mental adjustment and atonement
can be summed up in one word, gratitude.*

– Wallace Wattles, *The Science of Getting Rich*

Turn your wounds into wisdom.

– Oprah Winfrey

*If you aren't grateful for what you already have,
what makes you think you would be happy with more?*

– Roy T. Bennett

CAN YOU NAME TEN THINGS to be grateful for right now? This
could be family, friends, your house, your car, the fact you can read this
book, or something as simple and small as your morning cup of tea or
coffee. You get to decide! Go!

1. _____

2. _____

3. _____

4. _____

5. _____

6. _____

7. _____

8. _____

9. _____

10. _____

In *The Secret*, Lee Brower says it's important to have 'an attitude of gratitude', but up to a certain point in my own life, I don't think I'd been truly grateful for anything. At best, I'd been young, passionate, and misguided. At worst, I'd been young, negative, and self-destructive, meaning that life was never as enjoyable as it could've been.

Although I couldn't see it at the time, I was living in a self-imposed prison of negativity, pain, and sickness. The negative mentality that I'd grown up with had kept me trapped like a prisoner or like a mouse on its wheel, going round and round with no escape, no purpose, no growth, no major achievement.

Once I'd succeeded as a DJ, producer, remixer, and record label owner, I simply didn't learn, grow, or adapt any further. I just kept repeating the same pattern for years until, and eventually, it didn't work anymore. Staying in my comfort zone was the easy option, so I kept on doing it. Perhaps this will resonate with you?

However, during my commitment to completing the London Marathon and all the training that went with it, I'd moved massively outside of my previous nightlife comfort zone. I discovered a new sense of peace and calm. I literally went from inner turmoil to inner peace in the space of a few months. It was a wonderful thing to do for myself in every way. It aided my recovery from some very tough mental, physical, and material situations that could have seen me done for if I didn't possess the energy, will, and vision to bounce back.

When you start running for an hour or more, suddenly, almost naturally, you have to learn to breathe in a different kind of way. Rather than lots of shallow breaths into your chest, it becomes a deep breath into your gut. Once you master this way of breathing, you can pretty much run for as long as you want. That was an amazing discovery during my training, which meant that with the right set up and nutrition, I could do two to three laps of Bushy Park or Richmond Park at a time (18–21 miles). It felt great to be free and running after all I'd been through, and the added bonus was I lost a lot of weight, looked healthy, and felt great.

To put it into a movie context, one of my favourite films is *The Shawshank Redemption*. You may remember the ending (spoiler alert coming up) when Andy Duphrane escapes the hell of 30 years in prison by crawling through the sewer pipe. As he falls out into the freedom of the river, he opens his arms, and in the rain, he looks up at the night sky and smiles and laughs as it cleanses him, he's free. It's a dramatic cinematic moment and something I identify with totally. It felt like that as I came through all the self-imposed negatives that I'd experienced in my life and started to discover real inner peace, love for myself and others, true joy, happiness, and positivity. And, of course, the start point of all of this recovery is gratitude.

I learned about gratitude from several authors (Tony Robbins, Bob Proctor, Louise Hay, Wallace Wattles, Rhonda Byrne, to name just a few). You'll find a recommended reading section at the end of this book and on my website: www.markwilkinsonofficial.com/recommended-reading.

The Importance of a Family Unit

Once I'd learned about gratitude, as I said, I began to feel huge gratitude towards my mum for the first time in my life. She'd been through so much drama in her own life and managed to keep a roof over my and Dan's heads the whole time. And when I fell and needed her most, she was there for me, 100%, without question.

I had thought I knew best, and I'd gone out on my own for 15–20 years and eventually lost the lot. If it wasn't for her, I could've been sleeping under a bridge or couch surfing at friends' houses for years. As it was, at 39, I was warm and loved and living in the box room at the family home and getting £40 a week unemployment benefit, so I made sure that I was grateful for that love and care and every single penny of those benefits.

Most successful people have been through really hard times. I also hung onto the fact that many millionaires have been bankrupt in their thirties. Louise Hay shares her own personal story in a chapter of her book *You Can Heal Your Life*, which is on my recommended reading list. She said that between her two major careers, she had a year or two of 'quiet time', as she put it, where she worked on herself and her own personal development. During that quiet time, she kept calm and felt happy, grateful, and relaxed as she knew it wouldn't last forever, and she prepared herself for when things were going to get really busy again. I liked that a lot and trusted that my journey would be the same, so I enjoyed those quieter months while I rebuilt myself and my life.

I kept on feeling grateful for anything and everything. I was grateful for the air to breathe, the park to run in, the TV to watch in the warm house. I felt gratitude to the guy in the café in Hampton Hill High Street who made my lovely baked potato lunch most days. And mostly, I was grateful that all this had happened before I was 40. As my uncle said, 'You've still got time to turn it around, Mark.' Wise words.

Cleaning Up My Life

After the massive success of *The Secret* and my own use of the law of attraction to start to improve my life, I wanted to study and learn more. The genie was out of the bottle, and I started to study a lot with Bob Proctor. I learned to understand so much more about our subconscious mind (our emotional mind). He made a lot of good points regarding how we have to repetitively and consciously learn something (conscious thinking) before it seeps into our subconscious mind (feelings). We then take action automatically and live from that subconscious feeling. He used the examples of driving and learning a foreign language or a new skill as eventually, they become automatic.

This made sense to me, so I decided to dedicate myself to studying how successful people became successful, and to this day, I haven't stopped! I had the choice to keep repeating old patterns or to try something new. I decided that I could be better than what had happened to me so far, and I decided to commit the rest of my life to proving it. This book is the journey to success.

Finding the time was easy at this point. As you know, I was out of work, so I studied hard. I listened to anything I could on audiobooks, and I read Napoleon Hill's book *Think and Grow Rich* several times. Napoleon Hill had studied 500 millionaires over 25 years and found common ground in all of them. He then put what he'd learned in the book. I thought there would probably be a thing or two that I really needed to know in there, and I was right! I continue to read extracts from *Think and Grow Rich* even today and use them a lot in my coaching. My goal for *Life Remixed*™ is that reading this book will open your mind to the possibilities, and you'll become as hungry as I am for great information. Anything on my recommended reading list is a great place to go after you finish reading *Life Remixed*™.

I also signed up for an inexpensive online video course with Bob Proctor called 'Six Minutes to Success', and every morning, a video landed in my inbox for me to watch, learn, think about, and then act on throughout the day. I still get the emails today and log in every week for some added inspiration. I kept on running as well to maintain my fitness, and the more I kept fit, and the more I studied, the happier I felt. Healthy mind, body, and spirit.

I began to realise what had been happening in my life. I'd always been 100% committed to things, but always to things outside of myself, for instance, the feeling that I got from DJing or possessing material things. But I'd never paid much attention to my own self-image, self-care, or self-confidence. Then when rock bottom hit, I had suddenly learned the value of commitment to looking after myself – physically first, then mentally – to having a more creative and positive way of life, to feeling a deep gratitude for life, to feeling successful even though I didn't have anything at the time.

And now, with my life a blank slate, this time around, I could recreate it all very differently. I reasoned that if my thoughts had created all these things in my life thus far, then a change to my thinking and feelings could create better results. I chose to believe it could, and it was time to find out.

Everything started to change gradually at first. I was OK with that, to begin with. Rome wasn't built in a day and all that; however, I wasn't on that job.

I remembered I'd been very impatient as a child, and that impatience had carried on into adulthood. I learned from *Think and Grow Rich* that impatience is born out of fear. After all, we all have the same amount of time to work with, and when I decided to choose to have faith in myself and trust in the process, it became clear that there would always be enough time to achieve my goals.

I started to understand that I am responsible for all my results, and that I am the creator of it all. Tough as it was, I decided to choose to take responsibility for all the things that had happened up to now and for all the people I'd encountered and experiences I'd had that were good, not so good, and everything in between. I also learned to forgive everyone for everything, including myself. That was a tough one but so worth it. To forgive means 'to let go of completely'.

These were good decisions to make as it meant I was now free to create *what I really wanted*, to not look back in anger or forward in fear, but around myself in conscious awareness, and to encourage my creative mind to grow and take action. It felt like waking up to a new life.

As you know, at this point, I'm 38–39 years old, single, bankrupt, living in my mum's spare room, and an out of work DJ! I thought to myself, *Well, this really could have gone better, but through the decisions I'm making right now, the only way is up!* I got to thinking a lot and plotting my comeback. I noticed that the more gratitude I felt for every little thing that happened every day, opportunities started to open up again. I still DJ'd a few great gigs during this time and made the most of the skills I had despite my lack of cash or assets.

You can imagine over the years that I'd built up a huge network of people worldwide that I'd been friendly with, worked with, partied with, or entertained somehow with some great music. However, when I hit rock bottom and ended up with nothing at almost 40, the majority of the world turned their backs on me. It's a very weird concept, actually. Think about it. When you're bankrupt or even homeless, and you really need some assistance, the majority of the world ignores you and walks past. And when you're smashing it and really mega-successful, everyone wants to know you and to give you loads of free stuff, even though you don't really need it and could pay for it easily. Strange one that.

So as a professional socialiser and people person, this was a really difficult time for me to cope with. As I went through these changes (cleaning up my life and deciding to change my thoughts, feelings, and actions), my circle of friends completely changed. First, I had to go through about six months of real loneliness and hardly seeing anyone that I had previously known before I could start to cement some deep, meaningful lifelong friendships again. As this happened, I realised that most of the previous people that I'd called friends and had been spending time with over the last few years weren't close friends after all. These 'friendships' were based on the shallow things that I'd based my own life on previously. Again, like attracts like.

I heard a great quote that said, 'A true friend walks in when the rest of the world walks out.' That was very true for me. A handful of true friends stayed or came back into my life. (Special honourable mention to Paul for all the love and support he gave me at one of the most difficult times in my life. Thank you, mate.) Other than that, my social circle completely changed.

The Start of My Comeback

All of this was positive change, even if it didn't feel like it at first. I restarted a new Facebook profile and used it a lot to connect with new people, and I changed my old personal account into a different page. The new profile was for only people I knew or those with a similar mindset, and I started sharing a lot of self development quotes and initiated discussions to share and help other people, and to still feel connected myself.

As I was changing, there were moments that I can trace back to the start of my comeback. The start of my current success began in Phuket, Thailand. It happened because of my change of thoughts and feelings and because of me applying the law of attraction in actions as well as living with immense gratitude. So get ready to plot the start of a pretty miraculous journey.

Back in the Flying Record shop days, I made a Swiss friend. He used to buy a lot of vinyl, and we bonded and hung out when either one of us was DJing in London. He moved to Phuket in Thailand after leaving a bank well before the 2008 credit crunch and now lives there. After I started to move on from the incurable dis-ease and bankruptcy, he invited me to Thailand to stay with him for a couple of weeks. I've never liked the winter in the UK, so I jumped at the chance. I went over and discovered the south of the island of Phuket, Rawai, and Nai Harn Beach in particular, which have become two of my favourite places in the world to visit. It's an absolute paradise with golden beaches, a clear blue sea, and loads of great restaurants.

While I was there, I was put in touch with a friend of a friend. He'd had some recent health challenges, and we had a meeting to chat mainly about health and our use of *The Secret* to recover. We decided then to keep in touch. A while later, when I was back home, and we were catching up again online. I was feeling a bit down as a deal for me to be a resident in a club for the high season over there had just fallen through when he said, 'You know I'm a shareholder in an FM radio station here in Phuket, don't you? Would you be interested in coming over for a year to guest DJ on the station, play some cool dance tunes, and live here in the warm for a while?' 'Erm, Let me have a think about that for a minute!'

I thought, *Wow, this stuff is really working.* Things might not always work out *exactly* as you would like; however, as long as you remove the emotional attachment to the outcome, I know you'll attract things you'll enjoy. By now, I was only putting out happiness and positive vibes, and by the law of attraction, I'm only attracting the same back into my life, which is compounding my own happiness, meaning more happy results. I didn't have much money, but I always, always had enough to live off, plus I didn't have much going on in the UK. Here I was being offered the opportunity to go and live in the sun, play music on the radio and in the occasional club, go to the beach at the weekends, and just generally get the opportunity to recover and clear my head from what had gone before. I had the chance to learn to love life again, and I thank all involved for giving me the opportunity. I really needed the break from the UK for the dust to settle, so it was perfect timing all around. Some things are meant to be, and the universe provides for you when you have faith and trust in the process.

While I was over there, I made some ex-pat friends that we still keep in touch with when we visit. I also met Lisa Allen for the first time. Lisa is from Shepperton, near where I grew up in SW London, and we went to all the same clubs in and around London when we were kids. She said she knew who I was, but we'd never spoken. Mark, her husband, is from Brighton, and until recently, they'd lived together in Thailand for 20 years. Lisa joined me on the breakfast shows on the radio station, and we completed film reviews each week, which were a lot of fun!

So, there I am, working on the radio in Thailand, recovering from bankruptcy. Then Lisa tells me that two to three years before that, she and Mark were dive instructors living in a small place as they didn't have much money. Then she invites me over to use their pool! I rode up on my beaten up cheap little scooter to these large security gates! The guard lets me in, and I rode around into the Royal estate to their house. It was lovely, beautiful in fact, and I thought, *Wow, how have they done this?* And also, *I will own one of these.*

Now, at the time, I had no idea how I was going to do that. I just knew I would do it. That confident feeling around money is something that I have worked on. I practice every day by looking at whatever I would like to come into my life and saying with belief, 'I can afford that, I can afford that, I can afford that.' Over time this strategy has worked and continues to work. Losing everything changed my relationship with money, taking all my fear away. More on that later.

Anyway, I wondered how they'd gone from where they were into this wonderful house inside three years? Mark was away, but when he got back, he told me he'd studied Health, Safety and Environment (HSE) and now worked month on, month off on oil rigs. He told me there was a lot of psychology in HSE and how it played a role in workplace accidents. I loved the sound of that and thought it was something that I could do as I'd been studying myself and my own psychology for a few years by then. Also, he was getting paid a year's salary for only working six months of the year. *Result! I'll have some of that!* It would have worked perfectly with my DJ career at that time too. I would have time to make and play music amongst working away. It sounded great.

Up to that point, I'd dedicated my life to music. I'd put all my eggs in the music basket. Admittedly, I had lived and mostly enjoyed my passion for 20 years, but I never had a plan B. Plus, I didn't have any assets, so when the work dried up, it led to massive challenges. I also knew I had to change myself first, and then my results would change.

I'd also been studying myself and my own personal development for a few years by this time. I learned in a National Examination Board in Occupational Safety and Health (NEBOSH) health and safety qualification, there is a whole section on psychology and the prevention of accidents. I thought this is perfect for me right now. I listened to the universe and went with it, moving outside of my comfort zone every day.

People often ask me how I went from DJ and music producer to HSE manager. Well, there's the connection, plus it was in line with my newfound purpose, which I will talk about later. I still DJ'd now and then. I realised that the reason I DJ'd in the first place was that I wanted other people to feel good and to feel what I was feeling. When people celebrate a tune, it makes me feel amazing. So, I got into HSE because I would like people to have a great day at work, go home safely and in good health, and enjoy their quality time with their loved ones – a similar purpose, just a different way of achieving it.

Our entire lives can change in vital moments of decision, and I'd had a few by now. I knew the exact moment when it was time to leave the paradise island of Phuket. I was sitting on Nai Harn Beach reading books as I had done nearly every weekend for almost a year when I had this feeling of it's time to go home. I closed the amazing book I was reading, and I decided that was it. It was time to go. I was almost 40, and I still had many things to prove to myself.

Perhaps if I had been 70, I could've retired there, but I had a desire to make a financial comeback and also finish this *Life Remixed*™ book, to share my experiences from being unable to walk to running marathons, from bankrupt to financial freedom, to hold events that could help others recover and learn to enjoy their lives. That desire was strong in me, so I came back to London. I had a lot to prove.

I came to realise that being addicted to anything or anyone in a negative way can sap our energies. Being addicted means we are too focused on one thing, usually ourselves, and I was too wrapped up in myself and got into many things that made me feel pleasure for a short while, but after some years, they had a huge negative impact. However, I had worked steadily on healing the boy inside me, and it's only right then that the man finally appears. I have dedicated myself to this now and continue to grow daily. It's a non-stop process, and once you get started, you can't turn back.

I really like this list from the film *Heal* on Netflix of nine things that can help us grow towards living a happy and healthy life:

1. Radically change your diet.

2. Take control of your health.

3. Follow your intuition.

4. Use herbs and supplements.

5. Release suppressed emotions.

6. Increase positive emotions.

7. Embrace social support.

8. Deepen your spiritual connection.

9. Have a strong reason for living.

We'll discuss how you can progress with all these ideas as we go through *Life Remixed™*.

However, I suggest you take some time right now for your own self-analysis. Where are you now? Is there anything you would like to change?

Can you name anything you'd like to change about yourself or in your life right now? I've left space for five.

1. _____

2. _____

3. _____

4. _____

5. _____

One of the biggest challenges for us is to learn to be *grateful* for the things we'd like to be different, the very things we perceive as negative right now. That's a really strong exercise and may take some time to perfect. However, when you master it, you'll be happy and grateful that you decided and committed to doing it.

You can decide to grasp these ideas and make these changes to be happy right now in the present moment. So what, if anything, is stopping you?

I'll end this chapter by repeating those words on gratitude from Wallace Wattles in *The Science of Getting Rich*:

The entire process of mental adjustment and atonement
can be summed up in one word, gratitude.

Now, after reading that quote again, let's think again on ten things to be truly grateful for right now in the present moment. It's a gift, and that's why it's called the *present*.

Write your mantras (or affirmations) in the present tense. For example, start with 'I am so happy and grateful now that _____.' Also, as you progress with this practice, you can start to think of things to be grateful for that haven't happened yet, things that you would like to achieve in the future.

1. _____

2. _____

3. _____

4. _____

5. _____

6. _____

7. _____

8. _____

9. _____

10. _____

By using gratitude and the other strategies I'm about to share in this book, I sorted out my own suffering, so I've now committed to ending suffering for as many people as I possibly can for the rest of my life. I'll be explaining more as we go deeper into this book as well as through online and live events.

You can get in touch with me on all social media and also email me at hello@liferemixed.co.uk.

We'll talk more about gratitude, faith, and how to grow a successful, happy, healthy, and wealthy life as we progress.

What is the most important thing to end this chapter? Keep smiling and feeling thankful for every little moment that you get to experience on this planet, as trust me, we're really only here for a short while. Let's make it wonderful.

. . . . . .

CHAPTER 5 – REMIX OPPORTUNITIES

- Work on having a daily attitude of gratitude – on all subjects at all times!
- Read, listen, study, learn; the more you do, the more successful you'll become.
- Repetition is mastery.
- Believe in yourself – even when the rest of the world doesn't.
- What you give is what you receive.

Nai Harn Beach, Phuket, Thailand.

For more photos from Chapter 5, go to www.markwilkinsonofficial.com/life-remixed.

CHAPTER 6

YOU GOTTA BE

Be the change you want to see.

– Mahatma Gandhi

*It's the repetition of affirmations that leads to belief.
Once that belief becomes a deep conviction, things begin to happen.*

– Muhammad Ali

*Design your life, rise above mediocrity, become the
greatest version of you.*

– Mark Wilkinson

*Let us not look back in anger, nor forward in fear,
but around in awareness.*

– James Thurber

See things as you would have them be instead of as they are.

– Robert Collier

*When you are joyful, when you say yes to life, have fun and
project positivity all around you, you become a sun in the centre of
every constellation, and people want to be near you.*

– Shannon L. Alder

NOW IT'S TIME TO START APPLYING the strategies that I learned and for you to put them into practice in your own life.

Once the decision is made, you really can create your life exactly as you would like it to be. Everything starts with your decision to do it, so you must start from there. You can also begin at any moment in your life. If need be, you can start over from nothing (as that's where I found myself after the incurable dis-ease and bankruptcy). Only this time around, you must understand that you are the creator of all your experiences. I chose to believe that I am the creator of it all, and that choice continues to be very liberating. This is so much more powerful than being a helpless victim in life. When we can understand that life is happening *for* us, not *to* us, we are unstoppable!

As per the last chapter, let's start by creating everything with a deep feeling of gratitude for every moment we get to experience in this endless universe and for every little miracle that happens to us every day whilst on this planet. Waking up every morning in itself is a little miracle. Start by simply feeling grateful for that and for the air to breathe, and for your eyes to be able to read wise words from amazing authors from around the world. Feel grateful for your ears to be able to hear amazing videos and audiobooks (and music, of course!). Have gratitude for the marvellous mind that you have been gifted as a human being and for your ability to be able to accept or reject ideas. Be thankful for the fact that your body is working well enough for you to be able to enjoy your life. This list could go on and on. I'm sure you get the idea.

The Secret said, 'givers gain' and 'what you give, you receive'. I had heard from friends about the value of volunteering for Crisis at Christmas, which offers food, warmth, companionship, and vital services to homeless people over the Christmas period. I'd heard it said that you could really get a sense of perspective on what life would be like without the support of a family unit by volunteering, so I signed up to give some time to the homeless at Christmas. This was around the time when I thought I had nothing. Just by giving my time and energy at Christmas to those home-less people made me realise that actually, I still had everything. I had love from my family and friends. I had the basic human needs of food, clothing, and shelter. I learned to appreciate it even more by being there.

I was told that when I truly understood that responsibility is the key to freedom, I'd then be free to start living my own life.

That sounded great, but to begin with, I wasn't completely convinced. I had my story, which you've been reading, about why things hadn't worked out for me, poor me, the victim. It must have been someone else's fault, and I just got caught up in the middle of it all. As it turns out, all of those years of being the victim were really hard to let go of, especially at first, but I knew I had to do it in order to grow.

I understood by now that I had self-medicated with alcohol and who knows what else for many years and still managed to survive the self-destruction. However, I had avoided taking real responsibility for anything and had run away or tried to distract myself from my problems. In my own mind, I had never been truly successful, not in the grand scheme of things, when I compared myself to people 'living large' and doing better than me. As I said, I had all the reasons (or excuses) readily available to back it all up.

At this point, it will be interesting for you to think on this, to dig deep, and see what stories you might be using for the justification of your own way of life, or indeed for your own results. You can have results or excuses, not both. As you've read, I thought my story of not taking responsibility and blaming others somehow excused my behaviour. As like attracts like, it felt like everyone else around me was doing the same, so it must be OK, right? Amazing how we can justify things to ourselves when we want to.

Can you name any of your stories you'd like to let go of and move past? You can list them here:

1. _____
2. _____
3. _____
4. _____
5. _____

To move forward, right here and right now, the quickest way to achieve it is to start by forgiving everyone for everything. This may sound tough to begin with; however, please start with yourself. Forgive yourself for everything. Know that you were doing the best you could with the information you had at the time (as everyone is). Once you can learn to accept that, and it may take some practice, then you can move on much more easily to forgiving everyone else for everything. The forgiveness here is largely for you to be able to move on yourself. To forgive means to let go of completely. When you truly understand that everyone else is simply doing their best at that moment, forgiveness can come easier.

I also picked up some great advice from season one of *Ted Lasso* on Apple TV+. Do you know what the happiest animal on the planet is? A goldfish. Why? 10-second memory. Now go and be a goldfish. I love that! Imagine yourself with a 10-second memory. How happy would you be?

At the time, I have to say letting go of my own stories was just about the hardest thing in life for me to accept. I was so attached to them. The uncomfortable truth that every personal development author, mentor, and coach was already telling me is that *I am wholly responsible* for everything: for all the poor relationships in my life, those with my family and all the women that came into and out of my life, for manifesting an incurable dis-ease, for losing everything and the ensuing bankruptcy. All of that was very tough to even hear, much less to begin to accept. I really didn't want to. It would be so much easier to blame everyone else or put it down to bad luck or circumstances. I knew thinking that way would keep me stuck, though.

Then I read this quote attributed to Napoleon Bonaparte: 'Circumstances, what are circumstances? I create circumstances.' Those are wise words.

Val Van de Wall also said, 'Since you cannot change other people, blame is inappropriate. Blaming others causes a person to remain bound in a prison of their own making. When you take responsibility, blame is eliminated, and we are all free to grow.'

I kept on thinking this through. It hurt a lot to think it was *all my own fault, all my own responsibility,* especially the poor relationships and ill health! However, I kept studying various books with various teachers, and the same message kept coming through. I couldn't escape it – *responsibility is the key to your freedom.*

There is a saying that goes, 'When the student is ready, the teacher will come', and I have found it to be 100% true. Bob Proctor got through to me when he said, '*Your way isn't working, try mine.*'

Wow, that was as easy as it was the absolute truth. My way hadn't worked to the level I would have liked. I have also heard many times to 'find someone who is living the way you would like, and model or copy them', so I decided then and there to copy Bob. He openly says that a lot of his teachings are based on his reading of Napoleon Hill's book *Think and Grow Rich,* in which Napoleon Hill studied 500 millionaires for 25 years and put everything he learned in the book. Bob has read it hundreds of times over 50 years plus. Well, I'm about twelve years into it now, and I use what I've learned in my own businesses and coaching daily. It's also one of the reasons that this book you're reading has happened.

For a book that is written about thinking and getting rich, interestingly, there are precious few references to money contained in those pages. That's something to really think about in itself. I took from the book that true wealth and creativity were within me, and it didn't cost a thing. And if I develop my personality and character in line with the common principles from those 500 millionaires, surely, I would inevitably become wealthy myself.

Again, I acknowledge that I did have my doubts, but I kept studying, thinking, growing, and learning. I studied a lot on the subconscious mind – basically the feeling mind, more heart than head, more feelings than logic. It became clear to me that in my past, *before* I could even think and choose for myself (my first memory is around age four), that I had been programmed with the vibration of those around me. We only have to think in a loving and kind way of the vibrations that people close to us must have been in when we were first born, possible doubt, uncertainty, fear, and worry. Like the majority of people in the world, I had picked these vibrations up from my parents, the wider family, other children, teachers, TV, and from society.

Then, by not being aware enough to understand and change as I grew up, I had attracted all the negative issues that came into my life. We could get into the whole nature versus nurture debate here, but for my part, I feel there is some balance to both schools of thought. We are born with certain genes that make us look like our parents, and our subconscious mind is programmed by those around us before we can start to accept or reject things for ourselves. We then live our lives out blissfully unaware that we could make big changes if we really would like to.

After being at rock bottom, I began to understand that I could actually retrain myself. I could unlearn the things that didn't serve me and go in a different way. I could be in control of what I was thinking and feeling at all times. I observed that my innermost thoughts and feelings were creating my outer material world experiences. Once the penny dropped, I decided it was time to stop being a victim and to choose to take responsibility for all of it. The power is always in the decision. I understood that blaming others is for the weak, and when challenged, I knew I wasn't weak. I'd been through so much, and l knew I was stronger than the circumstances I had found myself in!

Once I accepted this, it was so freeing. Dusting myself off and going again with a new mindset was actually really exciting. I felt enthused and like a massive weight had been lifted from my shoulders. My next thought was: *So, if I've created all this crap unconsciously with negative thoughts, feelings, and actions, what would happen if I choose only positive thoughts?* Would this lead to only positive feelings and actions?

What if I chose to only live in the seven positive emotions identified in *Think and Grow Rich*? Those emotions are love, hope, desire, enthusiasm, romance, sex, and faith. Perhaps I would get everything I'd ever wanted? I had nothing to lose. Bob Proctor's words, 'Your way isn't working, try mine' were fresh in my head. Come on then, let's give it a go.

To move things along for you, let's name five things in your life right now that you're not completely happy with. These could be ideas, situations, relationships, colleagues, or your own thoughts and feelings that you'd like to be free of. I warn you here that this can be a tough self-analysis process, and it might take a while to get there, but once you accept that you can change things, I can testify that it is the most amazing, freeing, happiest thing you'll ever do. If you're hesitating, always ask yourself, 'How much would I like to change?' By asking yourself better questions, you'll always get better answers and, therefore, a better life.

1. _____

2. _____

3. _____

4. _____

5. _____

How do you feel after writing those down: mad, bad, sad, glad? Fearful? Angry?

Whatever you're feeling here is OK. My business coach, Kevin Green (who we'll talk about later when we get to money and business in Chapter 9), has a saying in life and business to 'always become the observer'. To me, that means, both as a successful businessperson and also with your own thoughts and emotions, start observing what happens when certain situations and emotions come up. Before you react without thinking, hit the pause button, take a moment, take a breather, and observe. Ask yourself, how do I feel? Take a genuine interest in how and why you're feeling this way. If you feel happy, then that's fine. Keep doing it. However, if you're feeling mad, bad, or sad, then it's time to think about making some changes.

This chapter is all about 'you gotta be', so now it's time to challenge another well-used phrase and set about creating yourself and what you would actually like. My belief is that with positive thinking and our creative, imaginative minds, we can manifest anything that we would like in our lives. After all, I had by now accepted that I created loads of 'bad' stuff through my own negative thinking, and I could see now that I was starting to have positive results through positive thinking.

So, this next challenge is around the phrase 'Seeing is believing' or 'I'll believe it when I see it'. This is a well-worn phrase, and it is misguided at best. At worst, it robs you of understanding the incredible part you play in the creative process.

I prefer 'believing is *seeing*' (see what I did there?). This is how we start reprogramming ourselves. Now, myself, I'm not one for long, drawn-out meditations. Whenever I get a minute or two to myself, I've found that short meditations really work for me. I simply close my eyes, clear my mind, and imagine exactly what I would like to create in my life, and choose to feel great about it. I also surround myself with vision boards containing images of the family, house, car, and money that I already have, and even better, things that I would still like to be, do, and have.

These practices and short meditation visualisation sessions continue to change my life and perspective daily. I can sit down to put my socks on and look at a £1 million pound note on the wall. (They're on Amazon, so I suggest you buy a few and put them around your house and office!) It drives me forward every day and reminds me of the reasons I am now doing what I'm doing.

Now, whenever a negative thought or doubt comes up (and they still do at times), I just observe it. I think *that's interesting*, and then I laugh it off or replace it with a positive and think of all my successes in life.

The real game-changers, as I came to discover, are *purpose, vision,* and *goals*. We'll cover purpose in the next chapter, how I found mine, and how you can find yours too. As a beginner to all this at the time, I found goal setting a great exercise. I realised that over the last 20 years in the music business, I rarely set any goals. The main one was just to be able to pay my bills and survive in the DJ lifestyle. However, as I changed, I got into regularly making a list of goals and putting the number of years I feel it will take me to achieve them (such as 1, 3, 5, or 10 years). A goal must be so big that you have no idea how you'll achieve it. Set goals that are so big they make you feel uncomfortable. Now you go!

GOAL   __ TIME IN YEARS (1, 3, 5, 10)

1. _____   _____

2. _____   _____

3. _____   _____

4. _____   _____

5. _____   _____

6. _____   _____

7. _____   _____

8. _____   _____

9. _____   _____

10. _____   _____

There is a lot more detail that we go into on goal setting during events and coaching. However, I'd just like you to make a start here. From the above list, start to break these goals into smaller goals to get you there. Break them down into goals you can achieve in 3, 6, 9, or 12 months. With commitment, you'll be amazed by what you can achieve in the next 90 days alone.

GOAL   __ TIME IN MONTHS (3, 6, 9, 12)

1. _____   _____

2. _____   _____

3. _____   _____

4. _____   _____

5. _____   _____

6. _____   _____

7. _____   _____

8. _____   _____

9. _____   _____

10. _____   _____

This is easy, simple, and fun. You've made your lists above, so now work on your 3-month goals every day with focus, enthusiasm, and a smile on your face to see your thoughts come to life. It's how I finished the London Marathon and continue to achieve goals daily.

However, I didn't start setting goals properly in my life until after the bankruptcy at age 39. I do sometimes think it would have been good to start earlier. However, there's no time to overthink things when you're as busy creating as I am nowadays!

As I said earlier, set goals that are so big that when you think about achieving them, they make you feel uncomfortable. And then get comfortable being uncomfortable. Some of these goals may seem a long way off at the moment. However, I can tell you that ten years goes quickly when you're loving life and achieving goals. The life I lead today is the life I visualised ten years ago when I had nothing. I found that when goals start to be achieved, you'll start to see more and more come to you. It's all about momentum! Once you get your pace and you get confident in the process, you can and will do more.

The real skill is to live in the present moment (using forgiveness, acceptance, and gratitude as your tools) and then, with laser-like focus, make your moves towards each goal in turn. I suggest you check your goal list regularly. Put them in your digital diary or print them out and stick them up where you'll see them every day. Once you've started and committed, you'll be surprised how many of them you achieve and how quickly! Feel free to let us know by sharing your story at hello@liferemixed.co.uk.

The next thing to commit to as you visualise your goal are your *mantras and affirmations*. These are statements that you frequently repeat to yourself, either in your mind or even better out loud. I've actually done a free giveaway of '21 Mantras to Change Your Life'. It's a PDF you can download by signing up for our free resources on the website: www.markwilkinsonofficial.com.

Like anything worth having in life, you have to commit for it to work. Start with yourself. You are worthy, and you are good enough. Expect to achieve your goals and then commit to your mantras and affirmations. Like going to the gym to create physical muscle, these are the only known ways to build your mind muscles! You must choose your own mantras and affirmations and work on them at least twice daily, morning and evening. I even use them in my mini-meditations throughout the day. It's even better to say them out loud to yourself. In all areas, repetition is mastery. How do they make you feel when you speak them? Really good, I hope!

Here are a few of mine:

I am so happy and grateful now that I am happy.

I am so happy and grateful now that I am loved and loving.

I am so happy and grateful now that I am healthy.

I am so happy and grateful now that I am confident.

I am so happy and grateful now that I live in a friendly universe.

I am so happy and grateful now that I am financially free.

I am so happy and grateful now that I have multiple sources of income.

I am so happy and grateful now that money works for me.

I am so happy and grateful now that I live in a world of opportunities.

The importance of these mantras being in the now, using 'I am' and 'I have', cannot be overstated. The more you can imprint the positives in the now upon your subconscious mind, the more emotionally involved you'll get in these wonderful positive outcomes, and the easier the steps will be to becoming what you would like to be, do, and have.

Along with your imagination, mantras and affirmations, as in the examples above, are the best-known ways of making positive changes in your life. The thoughts and feelings we hold on to become our reality, along with the words we speak. Change happens through the repro-gramming of our subconscious minds.

When I realised the power of this (through my own trial and error), I became very careful about the thoughts I allowed to stay in my mind for any length of time. I began to replace any negative thought quickly with a positive one. I also became a lot more careful with the words I was speaking. When we speak, we vibrate, and that vibration passes right through our entire body. When we think and then speak negatively, this can put us into a negative vibration. When we think and speak positively, the power of this puts us in a positive vibration. Then like vibration attracts like vibration.

In Buddhism, they say that it's a sin to waste words, and I understand that now. We must learn to speak only in positive ways to raise our vibration, build ourselves up, and be kind to ourselves. The law of attraction is part of the law of vibration, and we attract what we vibrate in harmony with. If you say the words that you're financially free enough times, then it will happen for you. Then, of course, do only positive things with the money you receive. Help others always.

A great saying is that small minds discuss people, average minds discuss events, and great minds discuss ideas. With this in mind, I decided I was going to focus on ideas as much as possible. These days we have multiple businesses with only positive ideas flowing through them daily! This isn't an accident, luck, or fate. With the creative power that I came to realise we all have, I've designed it this way. And you can too. Start with believing in yourself, observe your thinking, decide to make a change, and choose to think positively. Don't allow anyone else to knock you off course. This is your life, and your inner happiness is just beyond this decision.

Think about Muhammad Ali and his quote at the start of this chapter. Throughout his career, his mantra was 'I am the greatest', and he repeated it over and over. First, he believed it, and later everyone else did too. Clearly, he had the talent to back it up. However, his talent *would not have been enough without his belief.* There are a lot of highly talented people on the scrap heap of life by their own lack of belief. So, what sort of words do you use when you talk to and about yourself? What are your deeply held beliefs about yourself? Where did they come from? Are they serving you? Are they helping you grow? Think about it. Take time and really think about it.

The more positive the mantras and affirmations you use in your day-to-day life, the more successful you will become as 'fake it until you make it' is a real thing. Speak well of yourself, and your life will improve. Commit, build, grow, and be happy, healthy, and wealthy. Sounds easy when I write it. Having done it, I know it takes time and patient effort with full commitment. It's so worth it, though. Making these changes in my own mind got me off the floor and back up onto my feet and beyond. It is possible to get knocked off course from time to time if you lose focus, and that is where a good coach comes in. I've chosen a few amazing coaches to work with throughout this journey.

I only started making my changes when I hit rock bottom. The purpose of *Life Remixed™* is to help you start to make your changes well before you get all the way down to where I was! It isn't the place to be.

I wrote *Life Remixed™* to save others from having to go there. When you read these words and decide to make these positive changes, I'll be right there with you. You must also use your imagination and visualise your future. It works for every person every time. Remember, this is easy, this is simple, this is fun. However busy you are, you can take five minutes a day and imagine exactly what you would like to be, do, and have in your life. Please take time to enjoy the process of growth and become exactly who you would love to be. We all have the same amount of time in the day, so all this comes down to is your energy and attitude.

I heard a wise man once say, 'I only hire attitude as everything else I can train.' This is true. We can train ourselves, or retrain ourselves, to be the very best that we can be.

I learned the hard way that any thought (negative or positive) held on to for a period of time, long enough so that we become emotionally involved with it, will actually come to pass. Thoughts do become things. They literally become our reality.

Once I realised this, I clearly had some choices to make, so I made my decision to not only choose positive thoughts but to get emotionally involved with them. I'm happy to tell you that for the last 12 years since I started doing this, I now only experience a positive, happy life.

As MFSB (a classic track from 1974) told us, it's true that love is the message. There came a moment when I realised I'd been selfish for long enough. My early DJ and music career was all about me and my young ego. I loved the music, of course, and I found a way to play music for others and for it to make me feel amazing by sharing. This, in itself, was wonderful. However, I took it too far by adding in all my addictions.

It got to a point where I was using everything for my own benefit, for my own ego, for my own pleasure, to try and feel better about myself as I wasn't confident and didn't like myself. I also realised that my mum had been in a loveless relationship for many years and that she and my brother needed me. It was finally time for me to step up to help myself grow and to help my family improve all of our lives. We are all victims of victims until someone steps up and makes changes. I decided in my family it had to be me.

Through my own personal development, I decided to focus on love and asked myself more and more, what is love? If you ask yourself better questions, you'll get better answers. I've since asked many people this question, and most don't seem to be able to answer it. A lot of people will say it's a feeling, or that they can't explain it. I learned that if we can't explain or articulate something, we struggle to understand it. So I came up with a definition that I feel really explains love for me.

I thought deeply about a mother's love. Healthy mothers love their children, no matter what. From my own experience, no matter what I did, my mum still loved me. She might have had some anger and fear within her, but in the end, she completely accepted me and always loved me. The more I thought about it, it became really clear to me that my definition of love had to be total acceptance. The more I thought deeply about this, the more I liked it, and then when I started to practise total acceptance in my own life, everything started to become a lot easier.

I started with myself. I knew I had to. When you need oxygen on a plane, you must always start with yourself even before giving it to a child! This was a huge challenge for me as I didn't want to accept my mind, body, and previous actions that hadn't served myself or others. But I pressed on and used my thoughts, feelings, and actions to work on totally accepting myself and who I am now. I started to feel good, then great. I started to like and then love (totally accept) myself. It's a great feeling that I highly recommend you develop and hone through practice and self-encouragement. Go and look in the mirror now and totally accept yourself. Do it 100 times. Keep going. *You can do this.*

The next decision was to totally accept my family. We hadn't always got along as I felt we were so different. When I got myself into a place of total acceptance in my own life, it was much easier to accept every-one else. It didn't take long before everyone else's lives became a lot easier around me too. *Total acceptance* was the key to true love coming to and through me, and like ripples in a pond, everyone else started to feel it too.

Please, as you read, don't accept or reject these ideas immediately. Remember, whether you think you can or you think you can't – you're right. Henry Ford said that. Give these ideas some time to sink in, and then try them out for yourself in your own life. Please do feel free to email me at hello@liferemixed.co.uk and let me know the results!

Now, in order to live this way of total acceptance, I don't have to agree with every single thing that is happening in the world. However, in my own life and what I can influence, I practice total acceptance of what is, and I continue to commit to doing the inner work on myself. And, when any direct challenge comes up in my own experience, I can deal with it. I see too many of us wasting time on things we can't affect or control. If we all focus on getting our own experiences into a better place using total acceptance, our world could be a much happier place.

I also knew deep down that I had to fix my relationship with my mum to be able to have a successful relationship with any future wife that I would attract. I knew I wanted to get married and share my life with someone. So, after a while of working on improving myself to become a better person, I worked closely with my brother to free my mum from a failing relationship. I also worked on every aspect of my own life around her. I'm happy to say, to this day, we both continue to grow. I'm sure we can still wind each other up every now and then. However, I did ask her to make that goals list, and we've achieved a number of things from the list already. That has been a very rewarding experience and continues to be so.

Here are some examples of the power of my mum's goals list. She's always loved the Wimbledon Tennis Championships, and despite living locally and watching the first serve to the last winning shot for two weeks on TV every year, she'd never actually been there. Since making the goals list, we've managed to get tickets for five out of the last six years, and even one pair of tickets for the women's final! I shared earlier that the latest goal she achieved was riding a camel around the pyramids. At the age of 74, there she was on top of this camel. It was such a joyful moment for us all. The next goal is going on a safari. Do you need any more proof? Start improving your life today with purpose, vision, and goals, and start living the life you deserve.

Life is about energy and growth in all areas. I found out for myself that life will always be a struggle without a solid commitment to your own self-development. Do you want the best? Do you deserve the best for yourself and everyone else? The simple answer is yes.

Start now. You need to be the best you can be at all times! It really is up to you. With my personality type, I'd like to do it for you, but we both know that isn't possible. However, I'll tell you right now that you can do it, 100%. Start with yourself, and like those ripples in a pond, everything else will take shape. It works with every person every time. Let's keep going.

· · · · · ·

CHAPTER 6 – REMIX OPPORTUNITIES

- Gratitude is the start of all inner happiness.
- Responsibility is the key to freedom.
- Get into successful thinking.
- Study successful people.
- We make our own circumstances.
- Always become the observer.
- Believing is seeing.
- Fake it until you make it.

Big heart in Birmingham.

For more photos from Chapter 6, go to www.markwilkinsonofficial.com/life-remixed.

CHAPTER 7

SENSE OF PURPOSE

The purpose of life is a life of purpose.
– Robert Byrne

Know your purpose – best of all, you get to decide what it is.
– Neale Donald Walsch

Finding your purpose will ensure that you feel motivated and help you decide how to spend your time.
– Mark Wilkinson

THE TWO MOST IMPORTANT DAYS in your life are the day you were born and the day you decide why you were born.

Do you know your purpose? Do you know your reason for being here on this planet? What is your 'why'? Do you know the reason you get out of bed and turn up every morning? Have you ever thought about it? If you have, can you articulate it?

I've asked many people these questions over the last ten years, and very few can answer in a clear and concise way, if at all. Some will avoid the question altogether, look confused, or *um* and *er* a lot. As it turns out, most people haven't given their purpose in life much thought at all. It's almost as if they're getting up every day in a subconscious trance and are just doing what they've been told or trained to do by others.

When the failing business took the buzz of music and DJing away for me, the whole lifestyle started to feel very unfulfilling. I felt like I was lost. It was like sailing out into the rough open seas every day without knowing my destination, with no compass or even a rudder. Would you do that? I would hope not!

Some great teachers and mentors asked me the same question about my *purpose* or my *why* many times before I ever came up with an answer. I'd say things like, 'What do you mean?' or 'Oh, I don't know.' Then I'd crack a joke and try and move on. I didn't answer this question for quite some time. It kept coming up, though. Life wasn't going to let me off the hook. Why are you here? Why do you do what you do? Why music? Why a DJ? Again and again, I didn't have any decent answers.

The many authors, teachers, and mentors that I've already mentioned in this book had all said that *it was up to me to decide my purpose*. I knew what felt good to me. I just didn't have a way to articulate it.

Then one evening, out of nowhere, I connected all the dots and came up with the answer.

I was in my mid-thirties, and by now, not only a DJ but also a successful record producer and remixer. I had had a Top 10 hit and also ran my own record label when a friend of mine asked me to give a talk to 30 students in Manchester. I had already been through the first excruciating pain of AS and was medicating heavily so I could at least have a reasonably OK life again. I was ready to give back and talk about what I'd achieved in music. I also hoped to inspire these students to follow their dreams and make things happen for themselves using my early ideas and understanding of *The Secret* – strategies I was using practically in my own life.

It was a great session, and at the end, before I went off to my DJ gig for the evening, about ten students hung back at the end to thank me and say how much they'd enjoyed it. This was an important life-affecting moment for me as I suddenly realised I was getting a very familiar feeling. When I played to a crowd of people in a club who loved every track I put on, or when I played the last set at the end of a DJ gig, and the lights came on as the signal for everyone to go home, people would be cheering, stomping, and chanting for one more tune, one more tune.

At moments like this, when what I had done was making other people so happy, I would get an immense and overwhelming feeling of pure joy running through my entire body. It's difficult to explain unless you've felt it. Perhaps if you've done it yourself, or if you've scored an important goal for your favourite team to win a trophy, you'll know what I mean!

Whenever I felt that feeling, I knew I'd done something truly magical for the people on the dance floor that night. I'd get goose-bumps all over my body, and I'd breathe really deep. It felt a bit like the first time I heard Elvis or The Beatles on my mum's stereo. Sometimes hundreds (or even thousands) of people would be loving their night out because of the music I'd been playing. Just knowing that people were happy and grateful to me for making their night out really special was wonderful. I chose the music and created the atmosphere that kept them dancing all night.

Now, here I was in a small room in Manchester with these students appreciating my speech. Boom, lo and behold, I got exactly the same joyful feeling when they stayed back to thank me for my efforts.

Later that night, lying in a hotel bed in Manchester after the gig, the penny really dropped – the lightbulb moment. That's when I knew and understood my greater purpose, my reason for being on this planet. My life commitment is to bring joy to people. Joining the dots, it's what I was already doing professionally. DJing and music was just the vehicle. So, my younger self had chosen to bring joy using music. During the week, I used my chat and comedy to have as much fun as I could as often as possible. So, there it was, part one of my purpose. As I lay there, I thought to myself, as long as I'm bringing joy to other people, then I'm happy myself. Nailed it.

Once you can articulate something, then it's much easier to imagine, to fully understand, and act upon. And as I thought more about it, I realised there had to be more to my purpose than just bringing joy. I kept on thinking about what else do I like to do. What else helps me feel good in this life? What else have I got that helps other people? Once I had the initial joy part sorted out in my mind, it got a bit easier, and more things kept coming into my mind. I enjoyed learning and then sharing that knowledge. I got a buzz from inspiring myself and others, and I love creating things. I had mainly created music and parties up to that point, but now with my mind whirring, perhaps I could do more in other areas too?

Purpose and decision are so important, especially for our masculine side. So, I decided that my life's purpose is *to bring joy and knowledge, to inspire and create.* This was clearly the reason why I got up every morning. This is what I am alive for, and it felt good to be able to understand and articulate it. By describing mine, I'm hoping now that you will start to think about and decide upon your own life purpose.

Thinking even further into this, the way we use our language is so important. All I do now is create my life *on purpose.* Everything I do from the moment I wake up until the moment my head hits the pillow is on purpose.

I'll give you an example. If someone gets in touch and wants me to go to the pub, sit and complain about everything in the world and in our lives, be down and miserable, drink alcohol, or wallow in misery, then I would struggle to be there. That isn't part of my purpose. Now, please don't get me wrong here. If someone needs my help, I'll always do what I can to help them, inspire them, suggest other ideas, and create positive changes that could help to change their perspective on their problem to help reframe it. However, after a while, if I can't get through to them or help them to see the possibilities or make positive changes, then eventually, I'd have to excuse myself and get back to something more fitting for my own purpose.

Now, this may sound a little harsh or, to some, even selfish. Trust me that it really isn't. Each of us must put ourselves first, and we have to protect our own lives and our purpose. Fill yourself up first, then give to others. You can only give what you already have.

For me now, I have to protect my joy, my knowledge, my inspiration, and my creation. You must protect your own purpose to be able to live it so you can share and give to others. If you're not careful, especially when you are starting out, you can be knocked off course by other people or events. Resilience in this area is vital. Giving your power away to someone outside of yourself is not the recipe for your happy life. Everything you'll ever need is inside of you. Protect your inner peace and happiness with great self-love. Cultivate and improve yourself daily, and then share from a place of positive, loving gratitude.

When you can stay strong and live *on purpose*, the right people will respond to your sense of passion and direction. The law of attraction (aka the law of vibration) states 'like attracts like', so only people who resonate with you on a vibratory level and who are in line with your sense of purpose will want to be around you. Others will continue to congregate with and be attracted to people in similar vibrations to themselves. So, if you're looking around right now and you'd like to improve your vibration, have a look within yourself because the law states that you have a lot in common with the people closest to you. Could it be time to make some changes and raise your vibration to help others around you improve their lives, to attract happier people and situations into your life? Trust me, when you do, you'll soon find other people respond to your changes, or you'll attract a new crowd to be around you. We often hear when the student is ready, the teacher will come, and it is so true. Your job in this is self-awareness.

As you know, I only discovered personal development after I'd been to my own personal rock bottom. The agony and pain of ankylosing spondylitis and the bankruptcy that followed it in my thirties was such a personal low point, but thankfully I decided not to jump off a bridge or to end it all. I chose to think, *I'm going to dust myself off here and start again*. I realised that I could be better than the circumstances I found myself in, or actually created for myself, as my new learning was showing me. So, I chose to commit to personal development after finding my way in via The Secret. Finding my purpose for being on this planet was one of the wonderful outcomes that I can now live with and enjoy for the rest of my days.

I learned a lot about failure too. Failure is all about perspective. In my own case, I could have spent the rest of my life bemoaning what had happened to me. However, I chose to be motivated enough by these experiences of failure to reach out for some help. There are some very wise people in the world (*your way isn't working, try mine*). By watching *The Secret*, it woke me up and started me on the journey that, once you're on it, you can't (and don't want to) stop. You simply can't go back. Once you begin your own development journey, you get hungry to know more, to do more, to be more, and to have more.

There is a reading list at the back of this book. I'm so grateful to every author on that list for writing down their wisdom, and I urge you, once you complete *Life Remixed*™, to move on to their books. I became a student, eager to learn to improve my situation, and you can do the same. To put it simply, whatever it is you're feeling right now, there is an author somewhere in the world who has written about it and shared how they fixed it, so I know you can and will find the answers you're searching for in life. I guarantee it.

By reading *Life Remixed*™, joining us at an event, or being on one of our programs, you're not only investing in yourself and your own personal development. Like ripples in a pond, you'll be developing your families and growing significantly in all areas. You'll also realise that by default, you'll also be helping me to live my purpose, and for that, I send you my absolute deep love, joy, and gratitude. Thank you for picking up this book and reading it. Each of us living to our own life purpose is the most important thing we can ever do. I promise it is directly linked to your daily and lifetime inner happiness, and I know that you deserve to be happy.

James Allen wrote in his little book, *As A Man Thinketh*, 'Until thought is linked with purpose there is no intelligent accomplishment' and he's right. Know your purpose, think, and act on it, and intelligent accomplishment will follow as surely as night follows day.

When you align purpose, vision, and goals, you will be happy all your days. If you decide not to do this, you could continue to go round in circles your whole life or continue to repeat your learned and possibly self-destructive behaviour. You may end up in your rocking chair regretting not making more of yourself and your talents. Once you become aware of this, you'll realise that lack of knowledge, under-standing, and alignment has contributed to all of your unhappy times. Let me explain it like this:

Your **PURPOSE MUST** be **HUGE!**

Then, build your **VISION**, repeat mantras and affirmations, and use your imagination to visualise your future.

Finally, pick your **GOALS**, and add a time limit to achieve them.

Set 1, 3, 5, and 10-year goals, and then break them down into three monthly goals as described in Chapter 6.

Once you fully understand your purpose on this planet (and remember to make it as huge as possible), find quiet moments to close your eyes and keep building your vision. We think in pictures. If I asked you to imagine your front door, then you'd be able to picture it. You can see the colour of it in your mind. So, by imagining your perfect life in pictures, you're already working towards achieving it. I think about my vision daily, and my life continues to grow towards it.

The other thing you must commit to, like going to the gym to build muscle, is saying over and over the mantras and affirmations that state what you would like to be, do, or have. You'll find a list of 21 mantras that I regularly use at www.markwilkinsonofficial.com.

By committing to mantras and saying them out loud, they vibrate throughout your body and, in turn, reprogram your subconscious mind. Your subconscious mind then turns your thoughts and feelings into habits and actions and sets about delivering them for you almost on autopilot. Does this sound like fun? A bit of make-believe? Yes, it absolutely is. It is also easy, simple, and fun, and it WORKS! Think about watching a child when they make-believe something, and then it ends up becoming part of their life. We are exactly the same. As adults, through limiting thoughts and beliefs, we can lose the ability to imagine our most wonderful life.

I only discovered this by having a lot of fun in life, then having the huge crash, and then being blessed enough to start over. I'm really grateful now that it all happened, both the 'good' and the 'bad' as you may perceive it.

When you're feeling super confident, it's even better to share your goals with someone else, such as a coach, and let them hold you to account! That'll make sure you deliver. The importance of coaching in all areas you'd like to improve cannot be overstated.

The thing is that getting wealthy isn't really about money in the bank at all. It is being in the cycle of life, the flow. Money comes in and goes out. We'll talk more on this in the money chapter. For now, think about it like this. If you continually think to yourself that you want more money, then you're always going to want more money. If you say to yourself, 'I'll do this thing just to get money and get rich, but I won't really enjoy it,' then it probably won't work, or if it does, you won't be happy and satisfied with life.

The best way to gain, retain, and circulate wealth is to wake up every day and live your life on purpose. Do what you love and love what you do. You can then achieve true wealth. I guarantee you'll feel great while you're doing it. True wealth is being able to do what you like, when you like, with whom you like.

Once you've decided on your purpose, it can be lived in a multitude of ways. Music was originally my only tool for bringing joy, but then I expanded that into everything I do every minute of the day. Your main goals in life have to be to live to your purpose, be happy, and create multiple sources of income from living from your passions. This is where you will add value, give the best service, and create the wealthiest life. Then in line with the Chinese proverb, you really 'will never work another day in your life!'

People say to me, 'Don't you miss DJing and the music business?' They're surprised when I answer, 'Not at all.' I still DJ when I choose to, but how could I miss something when I still live the same purpose as before, just in a hundred other different ways? There's more on all this when we get to Chapter 9 on money.

Knowing your purpose (why), having a vision and strategy (how), setting goals and action steps to get there (what), and finding a coach to inspire you (who) will serve you perfectly in this life. It always works with every person, every time. I can testify to it.

However, if you still lack faith or feel confused about your purpose, don't feel overwhelmed or worry about it. Finding your purpose can end up being a bit like driving in the fog. Don't sit and wait for it to be absolutely clear. Take positive actions towards what you enjoy doing, and you'll find your way. Your intuition will fill in the gaps in the decision making. You may not have all the answers immediately. Just get started and keep going, and never give up on this. You'll find it, it will come to you, or you may stumble across it the way I did! I only found mine by moving out of my comfort zone and taking the action of talking with those wonderful students in Manchester.

Whatever you do, make the decision that you *will* find your purpose. Think on this. To get somewhere, you must define your end goal. When you start walking or get in the car, you already know where you're going, you know the destination, and you stick to the plan to get there. Sometimes, you might take a detour and still get back to the plan to reach the destination. Start with the end in mind, and I promise you'll get there.

The sooner you can define the end goal, the clearer everything else will become. A life without a purpose is a life without a destination.

What will your life look like when you sit in your rocking chair and reflect on it? What will you have achieved? Name your top five lifetime goals right here (have faith and think BIG!):

1. _____

2. _____

3. _____

4. _____

5. _____

Well done! Now make a plan and take steps every day towards these goals.

These days I'm so grateful to have been through all these experiences and failures and found my way back out of them. I defined my purpose and now live to it. Living my life *on purpose* feels great. From the moment I wake up to the moment I go to sleep, my life now is dedicated to bringing joy, knowledge, inspiration, and creation to every moment of the day to myself and everyone I interact with.

I won't say it's always easy, as I can be consistently challenged on this. For now, let's think of the previous scenario of not going to the pub with a friend in a negative mindset. Some would say I'm being selfish and not helping. I would completely disagree as I know I would always give my very best to the situation. However, as I've said, if I'm not being heard and not being effective, then I would have to move on. You can only help people who are willing to help themselves.

We only have a limited time on this planet, and I have to ensure that I am full of positive, joyful energy all the time. To be able to coach and give positive energy to others, we must have lots of positive energy ourselves. I have to be overflowing with the good stuff all the time for myself and my clients. I make sure to protect myself so that I'm in a position to give, give, give to everyone at all times. Remember, though, if someone doesn't want advice and guidance, then it's best for you not to try. Just wait for them to come to you before sharing your unique gift. And leave your family and friends alone, unless they ask for your advice and guidance, of course.

By living this way on purpose, I am so happy and grateful that I'm consistently happy and satisfied with life. The good news is, from the position I found myself in and from wherever you are right now, if I can do this, you can do this. Absolutely anyone can. It's all down to a decision, your own decision. All I did was listen to intelligent and successful people, combined with a strong sense of will power to get back on my feet. I practiced, practiced, practiced to arrive at writing this book.

. . . . . .

CHAPTER 7 – REMIX OPPORTUNITIES

- Decide what makes you happy.
- Pleasure is external; happiness is within.
- Decide on your life's purpose.
- Successful people make decisions quickly and stick to them.
- Live your life *on purpose.*
- There is no such thing as failure, only learning events.

London photoshoot.

For more photos from Chapter 7, go to www.markwilkinsonofficial.com/life-remixed.

CHAPTER 8

A NEW KIND OF MEDICINE

Let food be thy medicine.

– Hippocrates

If you don't make time for exercise, you'll probably have to make time for illness.

– Robin Sharma

Observation is power, judgement is weakness.

– Bob Proctor

BY THIS TIME, I was having breakthroughs left, right, and centre. You can see from the last few chapters that life was starting to get better and more balanced after the rollercoaster highs and lows of the party times. Because of the work I was doing on my mindset, the music life and my addictions were starting to fade. The terrible lows and darkness of dis-ease, suicidal thoughts, and bankruptcy had hit me hard. I'd sobbed my eyes out for a while, then started to dust myself off and try new ways of living. However, with the seeds of newfound information and perspective, ideas started to grow in my mind. I felt driven to learn more, to do more, and to be more.

As I said in the last chapter, once the top is off the personal development bottle, you can't just simply put it back on and pretend that it's never happened. If you tried to do that, you'd know you were going backwards, and you wouldn't feel good about it. Every healthy human being has some drive towards growth, so you must keep pushing on. However fast or slow doesn't matter. Find what works best for you. You have to keep learning and learning, growing and growing, more and more, onward and upward, at your own pace every single day.

When you bring in to play what some would call my previous addictive personality, and you learn to channel yourself into the more positive side of life using your thoughts, words, feelings, and actions, then the energy and enthusiasm simply flow out of you. This is when you're in the zone, and you can get on a real roll in life. If anything, I'm now addicted to happiness, love, and positivity. This is pleasure-seeking in a different, happier, healthier, and more positive way.

Around the same time that I heard Bob Proctor talking about dis-ease in *The Secret*, I'd also been gifted an audio program from Tony Robbins called *Living Health*.

Through my severe health challenges in my thirties, I had become aware that both mental and physical health truly is wealth. Without health, we have nothing; therefore, we must not take it for granted. I had been blessed with natural health when I was young, and then I lost it during and after I abused my body unconsciously for so long. Then thankfully, I found ways to start again.

The beginning of rediscovering good health again came through various mind and body awareness breakthroughs. I tried things out for myself and didn't just take other people's word for it. I tested out their theories and suggestions for myself in my own mind and body. I would always need to see if the things they suggested actually worked. When I found that they did work, then I kept using that particular strategy. On the rare occasion that something didn't work quite right for me or how I expected it to work, I would let it go, with no attachments or judgements. I just tried something else instead. So always test everything out for yourself as I did, and when you find what works, stick at it.

I was starting to get my head around the mind/body connection and the importance of a positive mindset and the impact on my body.

I was committed to positive thinking, positive feelings, and positive actions for true growth. In addition to all that, I discovered that the food (fuel) we put into our bodies is hugely important for optimum health. As a young guy, I had merely gone on taste, and then as I reflected, I got to thinking that as a touring international DJ, I probably hadn't been the healthiest of chaps, putting it bluntly. I don't think I'd seen a green vegetable for 20 years! I don't think I'd drunk enough water for 20 years either! Airports and motorway service stations weren't the greatest for healthy choices (although there are some slow improvements coming in now). So, I started to learn that good food and the right food and drink for us as individuals are actually great medicine for our bodies. Therefore, we must understand, know, and choose the right food and drink for us.

If I'd written this book ten years ago (I've been thinking about doing it for that long!), I'd be extolling the virtues of a 100% vegan diet, and here's the reason why. I was going through these changes using *The Secret* and *Living Health* when I stumbled across a book in a New York bookstore called *Skinny Bastard*. It was absolutely fascinating. It was written by Rory Freedman and Kim Barnouin, two female American nutritionists who studied with Tony Robbins as they backed up everything that he had said in the *Living Health* CDs that I had listened to.

After my nearly 20 years of mayhem and generally having huge highs and devastating lows, I decided – or rather my body was deciding for me – that I needed to do more to clean up my act and detox. Not just a wonderful week away in Scotland with the old tube up the bum, and then coming back into London Kings Cross and getting straight back on it, eating lots of crap (comfort) food to try and make myself feel OK. No, none of that, but to actually decide to change and commit to a 100% nonstop healthy lifestyle. I knew this would be a challenge for me, but also it was something that I had to do if I was going to look after my body and enjoy the rest of my life. I knew I had to go through these changes to choose life, and I really hoped to get lots of support from everyone around me.

I finished *Skinny Bastard* and went through another detox in Scotland when I decided to make a few concrete decisions that would help shape the rest of my life. This was the moment I mentioned earlier when I gave up alcohol completely.

I realised that alcohol was my first issue, the gateway problem for me if you like. It was the start point that, through my addictive weakness, led to all my other bad decisions. So, the pain in my body (otherwise known as nature's handbrake) made me wise up. I've since learned that all pain, mental or physical, has a message for us. My decision number one had to be to stop drinking, and therefore, surely, I would start to make better decisions. One of my conscious thoughts at the time was when a doctor tells you that you have an inflammatory dis-ease in your body, it's probably not the best decision to be putting in one of the most toxic inflammatory substances that we know of – alcohol.

I'd been following more and more of Tony Robbins' work and seeing videos of his interventions at seminars whilst detoxing up in Scotland. He calls alcohol 'the product of decay', which I found interesting, so I decided to go to his Unleash the Power Within (UPW) event. I noticed that Tony still uses part of this living health program in the UPW program. On that note, I highly recommend you attend his UPW weekend to help you on your journey (or at least take some time to watch the documentary *I Am Not Your Guru* on Netflix).

To detox completely, I gave up all toxic foods and habits. A non-exhaustive list of these would be meat, wheat, dairy, caffeine, smoking, alcohol, and drugs. I was empowered and needed to change, so I decided to give up the lot, all in one go. All or nothing as usual! It was a tough ask, but I had nothing to lose and much to gain. I had been in agony, and I was taking painkillers and prescription medication. I was unhealthy, unhappy, and broke most of the time. I was also in a career that I was beginning to doubt would sustain me and allow me to achieve my dreams of a long, happy, healthy, and wealthy life.

Tony said to ask yourself better questions, and you'll get better answers, and consequently, a better life. He also asked three questions:

How much of the planet is water?

How much of your body is water?

How much of your diet could be water or water-based foods in order to stay healthy?

The answer to each question is about 70%.

Another great set of questions on health, which really woke me up, were:

How long can you go without food? (about two weeks)

How long can you go without water? (about two days)

How long can you go without oxygen? (about two minutes)

So, by that rationale, what's the most important thing to have in your body every day? OK, oxygen, then water, and only then food. So, a 70% water-based diet, lots of vegetables and green foods, plus fruit could help me recover my health. OK, I'm listening. That seems practical and easy enough. I'll do it! In life, making decisions is key.

After learning from all these books and wise people (nutritionists, detoxes, Bob Proctor, and Tony Robbins' *Living Health* program), I knew I had to keep committing to being even healthier if I was going to have a positive and happy life again. I had to give up every toxin that I had been putting into my body on a daily basis for my adult life. I'll admit it was tough to detox, really tough, but I knew it had to be done. After numerous headaches and drinking a lot of water, the full-time detox started to feel great. This was the first time I had ever thought about the lack of quality in my diet, and for that matter, the Western diet overall.

Tough as it was to change my diet so completely, I kept going as I could feel it was working for me. The pain in my body was the turning point for me to start listening. It was time for me to start really loving myself, to start accepting myself completely as I am. Once I started to do that, it became easier to start looking after myself and to start nourishing myself properly, both mentally and physically. I was both desperate and inspired, a strong combination, as it turns out.

Something else that I learned almost by mistake whilst running my marathons was the power of deep (and I mean deep) breathing. I mentioned this earlier in Chapter 5, but it's so important. Every time I tried to run when I was younger, I always ended up out of breath very quickly, mainly as I was untrained and unfit and also that I was trying to breathe lightly through my chest. However, there was a moment when out marathon training, probably around when I passed three miles for the first time, that I simply stopped taking those shallow breaths through my nose and chest and naturally started taking huge deep breaths into my stomach.

As soon as this happened, I realised I could keep going for as long as my physical body, legs, knees, ankles could keep going. This was a great discovery as it meant even when I was running great distances, I would never actually be out of breath. It was only my overall fitness that might let me down, but I could work on that to improve it, so I became confident that I could get to that finishing line at 26.2 miles. It was so important to me to be able to prove to myself that I could make a decision, train for it, and finish something that seemed so difficult at the outset. It would mean that the rest of my life had hope. At times, it really felt like the rest of my life depended upon me finishing the 2009 London Marathon.

There are plenty of pictures of me during the time I was training. There are very few of when I was really sick. Whilst sick, I got stick thin at times, actually dramatically so. I just didn't want the camera on me when I felt, looked, and moved so badly. Thankfully, this was before smartphones with cameras, so I got away with it. To be honest, I just wanted to sink into the background when I was ill.

The pictures of me when I was marathon training show that I had lost about 4.5 kg (10 lb) of fat and gained plenty of muscle. There was even a photo taken of me at a season in Ibiza just after the marathon, and I had to do a double-take, simply because I was surprised that I looked so good, and it made me laugh. Is that really me?!

Completing the first London Marathon story back in 2009, my running top arrived from MACS a couple of weeks before the marathon itself in April. I wrote 'DJ Mark' all over it as I wanted people to cheer me on. One of the most amazing things about the London Marathon is the support. Londoners come out en masse to support all the runners, and at parts of the run, particularly in the early miles around South East London, it's actually more like Notting Hill Carnival. Every single pub has a massive sound system outside and is rocking some great tunes. It's quite an atmosphere. More than once, I fancied stopping off because, even though I don't drink alcohol anymore, I still enjoy the atmosphere of a good party!

That first marathon was my favourite. I went on to run three more after it. My total was three London marathons and one in Berlin. The second London one in 2010 was achieved with a group of friends running with me, which was wonderful, and each marathon I ran was in lovely sunny weather, thankfully. I've always preferred to be too warm than too cold!

That first time in 2009, I ran the last couple of miles along the embankment in London, through Parliament Square, and up past Buckingham Palace to the finishing line at the Mall. The feeling was pure elation, pure joy like I hadn't felt for years, joy that I hadn't felt since I was a child, a natural healthy joy, a joy without any toxins which had dominated my life for 20 years. My family and a few close friends were at the finishing line to see me get my medal, to have some photos taken, and to have a little lay-down! And once I'd recovered enough, we all went out for a lovely meal where I ate loads as I had probably burnt about 5,000 calories that day!

As I walked into the restaurant wearing my medal, everyone congratulated me. The love and joy that I felt during that marathon and crossing that finish line, plus the celebration of my photos on my social media, the congratulations and wonderful words of support from everyone, and the money that I had raised for MACS changed the course of my life forever. And of course, I hope it helped change some of those children's lives too. I know it also inspired some other friends of mine to try it, to clean up their own lives and move past some of the destructive things we did to ourselves as youngsters.

Whenever I mention the marathons, I find some people are obsessed with finishing times. I was really happy with my personal best of 4 hours, 39 minutes, and 10 seconds in that first London marathon. That will probably remain my best, as I'm not planning on running any others. Never say never, though.

And here is the most important lesson from the marathon. I didn't even realise this until a few weeks later. The official picture of me holding my medal standing at the end of the 2009 London Marathon was one of me smiling, looking fit, strong, healthy, and wearing *a bright yellow t-shirt.*

Do you remember my visualisation session with Brian Miller up in Scotland on a detox some years earlier? Brian had challenged me to picture the healthy, successful, strong, fit, and happy Mark, and I said I was wearing a yellow top!

Well, there it was, right in front of me. Almost exactly as I had imagined a few years earlier whilst in real pain and turmoil, it had actually come true! I found inner peace running the marathon, with the deep breathing, the joy and love and support, and giving to charity. And now, my own visualisation had come absolutely true in front of my eyes. Once I'd realised it, it blew my mind. I had visualised and predicted this moment years before! All I could say was, 'Wow, this is amazing.' I rang Brian immediately to share my revelation with him. A man of few words, he simply said, 'Now you know it works.'

After the call, my mind went straight to what else could I do now with this information?

With the knowledge and power of my imagination and visualisation, I had the proof and understanding that my thoughts really do create my life and achievements. It was so exciting and empowering, and I realised at that moment that I still had the time left on this planet to create my dream life. Bob Proctor has said, 'Everything you want is just the other side of your greatest fear.' Even after the marathon, I knew I had more fears to face. This was just the beginning. It was time to put more into practice, to get comfortable being uncomfortable.

So back to the new kind of medicine. The detox and vegan diet worked so well for me that I went from unable to walk to running a marathon in the space of only a few months, in itself an incredible transformation. It had also helped clear my mind, detox my body, and raise my energy so high that I felt on top of the world.

However, being bankrupt at this time, I started to think about how I was going to move forward now with the rest of my life. It was time to manifest the life I deserve. I started by setting some professional and relationship goals. As I mentioned before, by a wonderful use of the law of attraction, I had met a good friend when on holiday in Phuket. We had been chatting together about The Secret on a few different occasions, and that is how I ended up working on an FM radio station in Thailand.

I continued with the vegetarian diet as it was pretty easy whilst there. Thai food can be just as good without meat, so all during this time, the evidence of any ankylosing spondylitis had gone. I was living pain and medication free. I was enjoying my life again, living under little or no pressure or stress. I was learning that there was no dis-ease in my life because I was at ease in my mind and body.

This was a wonderful time after the nightmare that I'd been through, the agony, being unable to walk, and basically wondering if I'd ever be able to live a normal life again. I didn't have a lot of money, but I was healthy and able to enjoy music and life again.

I went to my favourite beach (Nai Harn) in the south of Phuket every weekend. It was here that I spent that time reading four of my favourite books on repeat. My friend gave me Louise Hay's *You Can Heal Your Life*. I also had The Secret, *Think and Grow Rich* by Napoleon Hill, and *The Way of the Superior Man* by David Deida. These four books and the actions that I took after reading them were to continue the changes in my life and move me into a fully positive way of thinking, feeling, and acting.

Remember you can also see the full reading list on my website: www.markwilkinsonofficial.com.

Hay's *You Can Heal Your Life* is about fully understanding the connection between the mind, the body, the emotions, and the dis-eases created in our bodies. *Think and Grow Rich* is about inner wealth, creativity, being in control of ourselves, and of course, earning money. *The Way of the Superior Man* showed me all the mistakes I'd made in my numerous previous relationships and then how to go about fixing them in the future. Each of these books, once I'd read them over and over (repetition is mastery) and then put into action their teachings, were to stand me in good stead as I continued to remix my own life.

One warm Sunday afternoon lying on my favourite beach on the paradise island of Phuket, I remember closing *The Way of the Superior Man* book and having 'a moment'. I thought to myself, *That's it. It's time to get back to London and make something important happen.* I also knew that my family needed me and that I'd been away long enough for the bankruptcy to clear. I'd cleared my mind and become certain of my life purpose, vision, and goals, so it was time to go home. I was sad to leave the paradise island of Phuket, but I knew I'd be back. I also knew it was time to share more of my life again, to give more service to more people, and to look after those closest to me. And meet a wife.

In an earlier chapter, I mentioned meeting Mark and Lisa Allen in Phuket. They inspired me to get back on track with a NEBOSH qualification, and I thought this sounded good. I needed something new to go back to the UK with. I knew I couldn't be a struggling DJ forever. As much as music was my passion, I wasn't prepared to be broke and struggling for the rest of my life. Seeing their life really opened my eyes to what could be possible with a few exams and a new start. I'm forever grateful to them for the time they took to talk me through everything. They're great friends, and I love catching up with them.

I hope you can see the correlation here. With my clear thinking and my clean diet, plus my use of the law of attraction, my life remix was well underway. I was feeling better than I had felt for years! My mind was open to new possibilities for growth.

I came back to the UK and followed the instructions I had been given to the letter. I didn't have the money to do the course to start with, but I kept it in my mind daily and knew something would happen. And here's a lesson for us all. A couple of days later, I received an email asking me to go and DJ on a boat party on the Nile in Egypt, and the fee was exactly what I needed to pay for the course. That is the law of attraction in action.

I completed the NEBOSH exam and then started to put feelers out. I was talking to friends on Facebook about my personal self-development as well as sharing a lot of quotes from the books that I'm sharing with you. What I found interesting was that even the people who read the same books as me sometimes had a completely different result. Some of them read the books, put them down, and never thought of them again. But because of my experiences, the highs, and especially the lows that I'd been through, I internalised all of the information and then began to act on it for myself. I was motivated for better results.

Everything we do in life is a decision. Doing nothing is also a decision. However, deciding to become successful through positive thoughts, feelings, and actions is the best decision you will ever make. It takes commitment, and it is open to every human being on this planet.

I'll speak more in the next chapter about money and how I bounced back fully and created my financial freedom. Suffice to say here that I shot up the corporate ladder quickly in the construction industry over the next few years. I still managed to keep up with my vegetarian diet even though it became more and more challenging when back in the UK, and especially around the construction canteens and then corporate canteens, where most people at that time genuinely thought I was a bit weird for being a vegetarian. As I write this now, I'm absolutely fascinated that veganism has caught on to the extent it has. Perhaps Tony Robbins' teachings and my commitment to veganism were way ahead of their time!

However, as time went by, I started to be tempted, and I slipped back into some old habits. I'm happy to say I've stayed strong and never gone back to alcohol or any serious toxins. However, the first to work its way back into my diet was sugar, followed by caffeine, and then bread and wheat, and lastly, meat. Looking back, I would say that allowing these things back into my diet became comfort food. After the bankruptcy, and to start my financial comeback, I had moved massively out of my comfort zone into a new area of construction, a world that was completely foreign to me. I'd certainly never been 'on the tools' like most of the other lads, so I had to work hard to gain my colleagues' respect. As I metaphorically climbed the ladder to the people in the boardroom, it became even more challenging. However, I was massively motivated to achieve and look after my family, despite putting myself under stress to do it.

Slowly but surely, over a few years, even though I was earning more money than I ever had from DJing and music, my physical health began to deteriorate again. The dis-ease was starting to come back into my life.

This time the focus was on my legs and especially around my knees, and as you'll see in some horrific photos that I have documented on my website and at the end of this chapter, the area above my knees was swollen almost beyond belief. Both legs were full of fluid and inflamed tissue, which collected above the knee, stopping the joint from working. It was almost impossible to walk – yet again! Getting up and down stairs wasn't happening without a lot of pain, and all my movement was very limited. It's hard to describe what it's like until you lose the use of a part of your body, and you really don't realise how much you rely on your knees until they don't work!

Normal painkillers didn't work this time, and whilst the rheuma-tology department of the hospital did the very best to relieve me of my pain every time I could get an appointment, they could only see me every three to six months, and my legs would be full of fluid every three days! I ended up spending a lot of money on private appointments simply because the fluid would come back so quickly the NHS couldn't cope with me. I had bucket loads of steroids injected into me on multiple occasions to try and stop the fluid from building back up. However, nothing seemed to stop the flow.

In the end, in desperation and having seen doctors do it hundreds of times, I bought everything I needed to be able to sit at home and drain the fluid out myself! It sounds disgusting, and it was. Sometimes I'd take over 750ml (25 ounces) out of each leg! Rank. I made sure I had all the correct alcohol wipes to keep the area clean before I put a needle in my leg. However, one day at work, just after starting a new job, I began sweating and shivering uncontrollably. I went home early, and within 36 hours, I was admitted to A&E at Kingston Hospital in Surrey.

It turned out I'd got an infection and given myself septic arthritis! This type of sepsis is a potentially life-threatening condition that started with an infection in my knee. Up to this point, apart from being born, I'd never really been in hospital. I'd had the odd short operation (hernia, toe, wisdom teeth) but had never stayed overnight, and here I was with the doctor telling me that my life could be in danger, and I was going to be in there for two to three weeks!

They had to perform three washout operations on my left knee. This was a real low as it became obvious that they weren't there to operate to try to solve the actual fluid knee problems that put me in there in the first place. This time was just for them to wash out this infected knee and, of course, saving me from this life-threatening infection. Fair enough, and of course, I was really grateful. I did have a bit of a sinking feeling when I realised that this hospital stay wasn't the solution to the huge build-up of fluid in my knees, and I would have a lot more to endure before I could fully recover.

What I found interesting this time around was that mentally this health crisis was nowhere near as bad as the first time around. I just took the lesson from my knees and looked for solutions. I knew I'd recovered once before by completely de-stressing my life, cleaning up my act, and making myself well. Of course, each time, I used modern medicine to assist my healing while I investigated the mind and body connection and the impact of stress and diet on my body. However, I knew deep down once again that it was still largely my own responsibility to get myself back to health – to be at ease.

Over five years, I ended up having seven knee operations, and I'm so grateful to all the medical professionals who did their best to help me through another challenging time. Losing my way nutritionally whilst in the corporate world and then not dealing with the stresses of being so far outside of my comfort zone in a new working environment was really challenging. Also, I knew that everything relied on my keeping that job and that the decision for that was not completely in my hands. If the boss didn't like me, we'd all have a problem. I felt like I had to suck it up to be able to bounce back and look after all my loved ones.

Rolling all of these issues into one had a huge impact on my mind and body and, therefore, on my mental and physical health. Perhaps this resonates with you. From my experiences, there is no doubt that mind and body are connected. The stress I felt at this time definitely came out in my body. I was exhausted and not performing to my best, but I felt like I had to keep going. I had to set everyone up in the family before it was time for me to move on and get back to a life that I knew I'd enjoy. I'll explain more in detail in Chapter 9 how I achieved this next level of freedom.

Since I left the last corporate job in 2018, I've been absolutely committed to getting my healthy and happy life back, making sure I'm eating right and enjoying everything I do, committing to being completely at ease. Now that I am living this way, without negative doubts, fears, and worries, the wealth and money side of my life is taking care of itself. I've set myself up with multiple businesses, which I will talk about in the next chapter. However, it doesn't matter how much money you've got. If you're not healthy and happy, then to me, it isn't success. Successful people are healthy, happy, enjoying life, and giving great energy in every moment. After all my studies and experiences, I knew I would thrive again in the right environment and circumstances. Remember, Napoleon said, 'Circumstances? I create them.' I knew he was right. It was time to create good things again.

I've learned now that the dis-ease could still be active in my body if I'm not careful with my thoughts, feelings, and actions. This includes the surroundings I'm in, the diet I'm eating, and the stress I'm under. So, I reached out to a nutritionist again to help me get back onto the correct path. And to be honest, I thought it most likely that he would push me to be vegan again as well as cut out sugar, caffeine, and any other toxins.

Alcohol will always be a 'no' for me. I think I'd have to be pretty self-destructive to be told I've got an inflammatory dis-ease and then put a solution in my body that creates more inflammation. So without the alcohol, I definitely will have more chance of being healthy. I knew my diet had suffered again for a few years, but I wasn't as aware of the stress I'd been under working for someone else, particularly with some who didn't appreciate my skills. So I set one of my goals for the rest of my life to do what I like, when I like, with who I like. I also wrote out 'my perfect day', which I'll share. Gratitude is vital in all areas, including business.

So, I was put in touch with another nutritionist, one who is more of a nutritional coach. He sent me for a few tests up in Harley Street that

I hadn't had before. These were blood tests, stool tests, and food allergy tests and were specifically ordered for me and my body. The results were fascinating.

He also really surprised me when he asked, 'Are you happy to eat meat again? Basically, you're going to have to eat meat to get well.' I had wrongly assumed that veganism would be the answer to my problems (as it worked for me 15 years before), but apparently, now, nearly all the vegan proteins I'd been consuming were causing inflammatory responses in my body. Along with reducing my sugar intake massively, these were the changes required.

This realisation is a massive turning point in this chapter because if anyone tells you that *you need to be vegan, or you need to eat meat to be big, strong, and healthy*, in all honesty, it's simply not true. It's not possible for anyone to know exactly what's right for you or your body unless you've had tests done on *your own body specifically*. Although veganism had worked for me once before, it clearly wasn't the solution this time around. I needed more balance.

I've come to realise that food is actually medicine, a new kind of medicine, or perhaps the oldest form of medicine that we know. I urge you to understand your own body and choose the best nutrition for it. Look after it as it's the only one you'll get. I have been following the food recommendations from my nutritional coach, and my body has recovered yet again.

I think it's fair to say that all dis-eases can be multi-faceted. In my own experience, it has come down to 80% stress and 20% poor diet.

I'm sure you understand now that I'm coming from a place where I can confidently say that I've recovered from an incurable dis-ease not once but twice. The point is to find the strategies and the diet that works for you and your body *specifically*, as what works for me might not work for you. Anyone who gives you a mass generalisation may think that they're working with your best interests at heart. However, until you've had personalised tests done on your body, cells, blood, and digestive system, then I don't think it's possible for anyone to tell you with any certainty exactly what will work for you in this moment of life.

God bless the NHS here in the UK (even more so as I write this during Covid-19). However, they don't have the time to run these kinds of tests for the 65 million-plus people in the UK. So, this one is down to you. It's your personal responsibility to find the solutions that work for you. Get yourself a nutritionist or a nutritional coach to run the right tests, find the answers about your body in detail, and keep yourself as healthy as possible so you can live as long as possible.

Both my knees continue to recover from the last operations. All I've done is to follow the dietary instructions from the tests on my body. I've also left all of the stress of working in the corporate world behind me now and only work with people that I choose and like.

During 2020 and the Covid-19 pandemic, things did start to get a bit challenging again. I was eating too much sugar and gained some weight again. A great doctor recommended that I read *The Obesity Code*, which I duly did. The book's main focus was intermittent fasting and eating healthy (so I cut out the sugar again). We also now order all our food from a fresh and organic food box service for excellent healthy meals. They take 30 minutes to prepare and have only 600 calories per meal. They have a great smoothie range too.

When I'm fasting, I only eat food between 12 noon and 8pm and drink fluids the other 16 hours a day. Since I've been doing this, I've shed 10 kg (22 lb) in the last three months, and I'm still going. I haven't looked back and will continue with this healthy life as it's working well.

Life is energy, and to be truly successful, we must have access to an unlimited energy supply!

. . . . . .

CHAPTER 8 – REMIX OPPORTUNITIES

- Breath deep – oxygen is more important than water and food.
- Drink plenty of water and only eat nutritious food.
- Look into intermittent fasting (read *The Obesity Code*).
- Great food is medicine.
- Any pain, physical or mental, has a message for you; make sure to listen.
- Once you start on this journey, you can't stop.
- You cannot have a dis-ease when you're at ease.
- Find out exactly what works for your body – specifically for you – and then apply the knowledge; your energy will be through the roof.
- For long term health, you must learn to remove all stress from your life.
- You are whole, perfect, and unique.

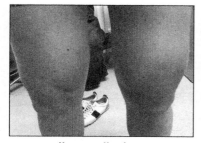

Huge swollen knees.

London Marathon finisher 2009.

For more photos from Chapter 8, go to www.markwilkinsonofficial.com/life-remixed.

CHAPTER 9

FOR THE LOVE OF MONEY

Money makes you more of what you already are.

– Bob Proctor

Love people and use money.

– Bob Proctor

Don't look at the price of the shovel when you're digging for gold.

– Kevin Green

SO HERE WE GO THEN – a chapter on money, the root of all evil as we may have been taught – or is it?

For over 15 years, every self-development book I read or video I watched all said to find someone who is already doing what you would like to do, then model or copy them. I then saw Kevin Green speak at Excel in London. It was a life-changing moment for me. I was actually there to see Tony Robbins speak live for the first time; however, I decided there and then that Kevin was a guy to follow and to learn from. He was based in the UK and teaching the strategies of the wealthy, which, when you decide to follow them, can only lead to you becoming wealthy yourself.

Before we start, would you like to know four basic ways to go broke?

Addictions

No dreams

Toxic relationships

Lack of discipline

Look at your current life carefully and then read on.

I was brought up in a world where we never had enough money. My parents didn't really have an opinion on whether money was good or bad as such, but I was always taught that we never had enough of it, and we kept to that script when we were growing up.

I'm sure you've heard of money described as 'evil' on many occasions. Much of society can teach us that the love of money can mess people up. However, what I've discovered by studying my own personal development and successful people over the last few years, the more I understand that money is a tool. Freedom is the goal. It has also become obvious to me that Bob Proctor is right in the quote at the beginning of this chapter: *Money makes you more of what you already are.*

So, if you're already a chaotic person and you make or win a huge amount of money, it can make you a tremendously chaotic person! I'm sure we can think of a few people who've gone off the rails spectacularly when a lot of money arrived unexpectedly in their lives.

However, on the flip side, if you're a calm, loving person and you make or win a huge amount of money, you can become a wonderfully calm and loving person and a great philanthropist if that is your calling. With more money, you can choose to extend your reach to help people far and wide, reaching way outside of yourself to use your own and others' efforts and actions to help more people. Put simply, when the penny dropped on this one, I decided to get really focused on how to add more value and give more service to earn more money. How could I do more to help others with the time I have left on this planet?

I decided to choose that money isn't good or bad. Money is the direct result of the service provided. The amount and quality of service and added value dictates the amount of money you will receive. However, it took me losing all my money and ending up bankrupt to come to these realisations!

Of course, my hope for you reading this book, coming to a Life Remixed™ event, or being coached is that you won't need to go through a difficult and emotionally challenging experience like bankruptcy to learn this valuable lesson.

Reading numerous books that discussed money and listening to many inspirational people talk about money, it became very clear to me that money comes to you when you give more service to as many people as possible. So the more professional and specialised service I can provide in all my businesses, the more money will come into my life. Simple when you think about it.

I've asked many people over the years, 'How do you earn money?'

The answer the majority of the time is, 'I go to work, I have a job, and I get paid.' And that's it. Occasionally, they might say they're looking for a promotion and a little bit of extra money, a small percentage of a raise, but that's all they've got to say on it.

I've often reflected how the salary that they are on right now is a direct result of the amount of service that they are currently providing. Some people are very sensitive about this and do not like to talk about it. Others take it as a real eye-opener and an inspirational moment. I often explain that money and wealth come from creativity and caring for others. It's great when people have these lightbulb moments, and I see their eyes open. They suddenly realise that they could provide more service to more people and earn more money than they currently are, and their mind starts whirring.

Seeing their joy as they make a plan to grow what they do is a buzz to me and aligns perfectly with my life's purpose.

I always like to help people achieve their purpose, vision, and goals.

When you've got a purpose, a vision, and a big goal, and you know what you're going to do with the money when it comes to you, it seems much easier to work at your passions and provide the service required to earn the money. Once you know what makes you happy and what you would like to do with your life, then spending time thinking of the positive things you will do with the money can be one of your biggest motivators.

To change my mindset around many things, including money, I decided once again to use the power of affirmations and mantras. Mantras describe what you would like to be, do, have, and achieve. Mantras put on repeat in your own mind are powerful. It's the repetition of the right information that makes the desired imprint on the subconscious mind and for the belief to become a habit. Over the years, I have written a huge number of mantras down and put them on continual reminder in my diary, so every morning and evening, I'm notified to read them out loud to myself. Remember, repetition is mastery.

These mantras can range from being fitter and stronger to being *happier, healthier, and wealthier.* I also have mantras about improving relationships and dealing with difficult people and situations. The beauty of this practice is that you can create your own reality in your thoughts and emotions before it becomes a reality in the material world. There have been numerous studies that show your mind can create pictures of upcoming attractions, and as long as you choose to believe and feel good as if it's already happened, your subconscious mind is unable to tell the difference. That is how we create, and it works for every person every time, whether you're aware of it or not.

I usually practice my affirmations and mantras when I'm alone, although sometimes I can bring them into conversations and coaching too. I also make sure that I am emotionally attached to the outcome in a positive way. I think and speak them, and I feel great. And what I've discovered over 15 years of repeating various mantras to myself is that they do become my reality – my achieved goals. Once they become my reality, I then move on to new ones.

That's not to say that absolutely every single mantra has come true bang on schedule. However, even when the timing is off slightly, the universe aligns me with something similar (and usually better) than my original goal. I make sure that each of my mantras is always in line with my greater purpose that I shared earlier and that every mantra and action I take on a daily basis always takes me closer to my desires.

Remember what I said earlier about please do not simply dismiss any ideas in this book. I'd ask you again to commit and try these ideas out for yourself. Start small over a couple of weeks to a couple of months. Think about what you'd really like and make sure it feels good for you. Then repeat over and over, morning and evening, and throughout your day: *I am healthy, wealthy, and happy* (repeat) or *I am financially free* (repeat) or whatever your mantras are to move you towards your development goals. Commit to the process. I know it will happen for you as it has for me, so make sure to let me know how you get on.

I didn't really start my goal setting until I was 39 years old. Up until that point, I was too busy trying to make a living to step up and make a fortune. I was lost in music, and music was my only income. I had all my eggs in that one basket, and that is something I've learned isn't the best thing to do, especially if you don't have any assets. If you're going to be wealthy and an entrepreneur working for yourself, I urge you to work on multiple sources of income and build assets that pay you income every month.

As examples, my first goals – set at 39 whilst I was recovering from an incurable dis-ease, bankrupt, single, and living in my mum's spare room – were:

3 months – get fit

1 year – run a marathon

3 years – earn £100,000 a year

5 years – get married

10 years – give great service to great people and become financially free

I've achieved every one of those goals.

So, what are your goals?

3 months – _____

1 year – _____

3 years – _____

5 years – _____

10 years – _____

No matter what your age is right now, you're going to be amazed at how all of these goals can and will develop in your life. It is never too late to make a change, as long as you're thinking positively and feeling great in your subconscious mind and as long as you have the desire. If you are really persistent that you simply *must* achieve, *then it will happen for you.* You can have as many goals as you want. There are no rules to this. I have loads of mantras and goals, and I always put a time limit on them so my mind knows exactly what I'm working for.

Remember that you have to be aligned with your purpose, your vision, and your goals for these things to materialise in your life. If you are off course in any way, your feelings will let you know, and all you have to do is listen to them. If you need to start to feel good again, then change course. We human beings have a way of making our lives over complicated. As a young chap, I was a master at it, and now from my experiences, I find the simpler we make life, the easier it is. The choice truly is yours. It's your life. You are the creator, so design it how you would like it.

Align your thoughts, feelings, and actions, and you will be unstoppable.

Having been bankrupt and losing all my money once before, it's no longer a fear to me. As I've said, many millionaires have been bankrupt in their thirties. I now choose to believe that I use my positive energy to attract only good things. I also know and understand the power of a negative thought, so I never entertain one now. This means I feel happy and confident in my positive thoughts and emotions. I now say confidently that I'll be happy and healthy for the rest of my days. You can decide this for yourself too. With the wealth that I am building today, I know I can do great things to help many people. 'Watch this space' because with the wealth I'm creating in the next 10, 15, 20 years, I will surpass anything that I'm doing today and be able to keep growing and keep giving.

Many self-development books have said 'money is energy', and I now understand and agree. I'd also say the more positive energy you use to create money, the more positive money will be for you. So if you sit in your house all day and watch TV, you're not giving out or using a lot of energy, and, therefore, you're not going to receive a lot of money.

These are simple equations, I know, and yet so many people don't use their energy to the best of their ability.

This is where a coach comes in to keep you on track. I have nutrition, life, personality diversity, business and wealth coaches, plus a personal trainer, and every one of them has helped move me forward. It's vitally important to have a supportive team around you.

As you've come this far in *Life Remixed*™, I congratulate you. For some people buying books is 'shelf-development', but not for you. I hope this book and our events motivate and inspire you to get a coach and read other books from my recommended reading and study list. These knowledgeable teachers and authors will give you further strategies towards your greater wealth and happiness.

Think about all the ways you give service already. Could you give more now? Could you give better service to humanity? Could you serve other people in other ways that you don't already? These are great questions to ask yourself, and although I do not live my life with any regret, I do sometimes wonder what I would've done with this information if it had been given to me at 20 years old rather than 35 and above.

One of the things I've really focused on is becoming the best in the world at what I do. I've committed time, money, and effort to get highly qualified in various disciplines as well as carrying on with some DJing and music production. Admittedly, music isn't 100% of my life anymore. However, it still has a special place in my heart when I hear a killer track. We're also live on Mixcloud every Saturday night during lockdowns with a vision of more live events to come.

There are so many great programs and qualifications that you can use to progress your ability to give great service to others. Look out into the world and find what it is that you want to achieve. Strangely, it was only when I had absolutely nothing that I made a decision to really start going for it, to start learning and developing in order to grow. I had to, as I had nothing, but now that I earn more money, I am in a position to help more people.

I have really committed to knowing my strengths and managing my potential limiters as part of my development. I'm a big picture guy and am not always brilliant at the detail. One of my development mantras is *I am great at the details*, and guess what? I've actually improved in that area, much better than I used to be. However, I'll readily admit there are people who are much better at the detail than me, so I'll quite happily let them get on with that.

As part of my commitment to growth and to identify my strength and potential limiters, I did an excellent online personality diversity indicator (PDI) assessment with a company called Equilibria. The E-Colors self-awareness system created by Lewis Senior for use in the energy business to improve safety and productivity on oil rigs is second to none. I'm most grateful to Lewis, his family, and his wonderful team for devising the E-Colors program as it showed me which areas of my personality that I needed to develop to become a more rounded individual, and at the time, to succeed in the work environment.

I also read Lewis Senior's book *At the End of the Day* when I was sitting at home as a bankrupt. His story of collapse and changing his life with some intentional decisions was inspiring. It also made me feel good enough to know I could tell my story in *Life Remixed*™.

I was wondering what to do with my life when I discovered my E-Colors. It was yet another light bulb moment, and I used Equilibria's coaching material to get myself up the corporate ladder to a high salary within a few years. All I did was focus on the areas within me that E-Colors identified that needed development. I took the online PDI, which only took 15 minutes, and I was amazed at the results. It was so accurate and showed me that I was a Yellow/Blue, the relating socialiser. My E-Colors showed me that my Green (logical thinking) was my lowest percentage, so I knew what to do. I took lots of exams and achieved qualifications that led to me sitting with directors at some of the UK's largest companies. If you'd like more information on this excellent system, then please head to my HSE Consultancy website: www.hillmontassociates.com/e-colors-pdi and get in touch with me to discuss.

One of the best things I learned about being a really good team player is to allow others to be great at what they do. When I was younger, I thought I had to do everything myself. I still see other people make this common mistake. However, when I realised that I wasn't brilliant at everything, and most importantly, that I didn't have to be, I had the opportunity to step back and allow others to be good at what they do. I also studied and learned that every successful person has a power team around them. Find me a successful person, a multi-millionaire, for instance, and I'll find you the rest of their power team who helped them and supported them through the journey and who also benefited very well themselves.

Remember what I said about doing great things with the money you earn? Well, my larger goal, my purpose (my *why*, if you prefer), is to help people improve their lives in all areas. I will also give to help others get over any crisis or addiction they're facing, or indeed anything that can be detrimental to their lives. I will also create a safe space for homeless people to recover and recreate their lives in a positive way. I was fortunate that when I lost everything materially, my mum was still there with the spare room where I could rebuild my life. From my time volunteering for Crisis at Christmas, I'm well aware that others aren't so lucky, so I would like to and will be able to do more for them. 'Watch this space' on that one.

Bob Proctor has been massive in helping me develop my mind and create an attitude of gratitude for every single thing that has happened in my life. Incurable dis-ease and bankruptcy are two things I wouldn't wish on anyone, and yet they turned out to be hugely influential and positive in changing the direction of my life. Every negative thing that has happened to you will have had a positive effect too. You may have to look a little harder for it. Just know it's there.

I always said to myself that I would meet and show my gratitude to Bob by shaking his hand and thanking him personally for his work. Remember, *thoughts become things*. I held this in my mind, and then I read that because of health reasons, he was no longer coming to Europe to speak at events. So, I thought to myself, right then, I'm going to fly over to the US to meet him, which I duly did. I flew to Phoenix, Arizona, and listened to Bob speak over a three-day weekend seminar, which was both inspirational and a great networking opportunity. I met interesting people that, via the wonders of the internet, I'm still in touch with, and made lots of great connections and gained ideas that came out of that trip. True to my thoughts, visualisation, and decision, I also got to shake Bob's hand and thank him for all that he has put out into the world as he helped me start my recovery.

During this time, I met a wonderful woman called Emma on match. com (online dating can work!). We developed a bond and real appreciation and understanding of each other over time. Please bear in mind that I had done a lot of work on myself to be the man I wanted to be in order to attract Emma. I did much of this personal development well before I met her, and I'll talk more about love and relationships soon. However, as I write this, we've been together for eight years. We got married in 2018, so again I achieved another goal I had set for myself.

When you're in tune with it, the universe aligns. As a birthday present one year, Emma bought me that ticket to see Tony Robbins speak live. We went together for the weekend. Tony spoke for three hours, and it was an excellent experience to hear him, both inspirational and energising. I signed up there and then to attend his Unleash the Power Within (UPW) event in London, again at Excel, which was another amazing experience. At this four-day inspirational long weekend in London, I also walked over two thousand degrees of hot coals to prove to myself, yet again, that by using the power of my mind, anything is possible.

I'd also been thinking about and wanting to write *Life Remixed*™ for many years and never actually managed to find the method or the time. Even though I was earning great money and was grateful for it, the corporate world was sapping all my energy. I was working 60 hours plus a week and was absolutely exhausted. Evenings and weekends were mostly a write-off as I slept through them, and to be honest, to me, this wasn't living. It was a struggle, almost a punishment. Anyone who chooses to work that way for a lifetime has my respect and pity in equal measure!

On the same bill as Tony Robbins that weekend were lots of other speakers. Some of them left me feeling quite cold, and I wasn't sure exactly what they were attempting to achieve (or sell me on). Then this smiling, happy Welsh guy called Kevin Green came out onto the stage and spoke for a couple of hours on property, gold and silver, and other business and wealth-building strategies. I was really fascinated as I had done a couple of property deals previously. However, they hadn't turned the profit I expected in a quick enough time. I wanted to learn more and knew I needed some guidance towards our financial freedom. I also needed to have more time to complete my goal of writing this book, so I listened intently to Kevin, and I understood that this was the guy who had the strategies to give me exactly what I needed: time and money freedom.

Kevin inspired me so much that day at Excel in London that I read his book *The Rich Rules* and signed up for a three-day program he was hosting at a Heathrow hotel shortly after, and there and then, I signed up for a two-year coaching program to be taken through all of his Kevin Green Wealth (KGW) wealth-building strategies.

I'm so grateful to Kevin for what he does. He really is driven by helping people achieve their goals, and he has shared his own personal goal of making one-million millionaires. I absolutely love that. Just imagine all the good that one-million millionaires could do in the world.

We took on our business coach through KGW. He, along with Kevin and the rest of the KGW coaches, helped Emma and me through a challenging period. I was working, admittedly earning a great salary; however, the stress of it was having a huge impact on my energy and my body. As I've told you, my knees had swollen up beyond recognition, and at times the rheumatologist was draining up to a litre of fluid out of each leg and pumping me full of steroids to keep me moving. Once again, I could hardly walk, and I knew by now that the cause was stress and diet. It was another painful time for everyone. Pain can lead to change, and once again, I knew it had to.

Kevin spoke so eloquently from the stage that day about his good health and how living his own life as an entrepreneur had allowed him to stay in great health throughout his life. I really identified with this as I was always an entrepreneur as a DJ and record producer, but now I was working for someone else, unhappy and in a lot of pain. I had always preferred to be my own boss, and here I was struggling with my health again.

I'd always enjoyed being self-employed, so I knew at some point it was time to go back to working for myself, only this time I'd create my success by listening to Bob Proctor, Tony Robbins, and Kevin Green to ensure I would have multiple businesses and streams of income, and also by copying Kevin with his UK property portfolio and wealth strategies. I knew with certainty that this is the way for us to grow and be well equipped and able to cope with any crisis the world would have in store. It turns out I was right.

After a hugely challenging couple of years with my knees, I managed to plan my escape and get out of the full-time corporate job, and I'm glad to say I haven't looked back. So, if your job is costing you too much right now, it's time to make a plan and then take action on it. Your mental and physical health is too high a price to pay simply for a pay packet.

I have found that doing something that makes you happy adds years to your life, but more importantly, it adds life to your years! Have a chat with yourself and answer the questions below. The answers will help show you your future.

- Do you like your job?
- Are you putting up with it because the thought of changing fills you with fear?
- Do you feel stuck or feel that you have no other option?
- Will your outlook change if you look for the positives of this current job?
- Is the pay worth the stress?

After I went through that list, I got my answers. Using Kevin Green's strategies, I knew what to do, and I'm happy to say I've now managed to rebuild my life exactly to my plan, creating multiple businesses and sources of income. I give service and add value to each business in turn throughout the day. This means each business pays me money at different times of the month and year, meaning I can relax. I can do what I like, when I like, with whom I like. I get up when I like, work when I like, holiday when I like, and design and choose my work-life balance daily.

I've been fortunate to meet an excellent success team in Kevin Green's network. Big thanks to the whole KGW team for the love and support.

Due to this wonderful set of choices and people, I've managed to recover once again from an incurable dis-ease and feel so much more at ease again working for myself, this time without the toxins and toxic habits.

Twice now I've recovered, so I can categorically say that the impact of stress and a poor diet can cause an auto-immune condition (AS) to flare up. From my own experience, there is a direct correlation from our mental health to stress on our immune system, and that is the main reason why I have had an incurable auto-immune dis-ease flare up twice. As soon as I improved my diet and, more importantly, became at ease again, the dis-ease went away, twice.

I've made my decision now to stay happy and healthy for the rest of my days and to help others do the same in any way I can.

Nowadays, I enjoy building companies with great people. I always prefer co-operation to competition. I found that the music and DJ world and parts of the corporate world that I was working in could be hugely competitive. People were always undermining each other, and for no good reason that I could see. Perhaps it was people trying to get ahead. You may have some experience of that yourself. When I saw those behaviours, I was always reminded of Napoleon Hill's definition of a genius as someone who can make life pay whatever they desire without hurting others.

I knew those work arenas weren't for me and my body kept giving me stark reminders in my knees. I now have the scars from various operations to remind me of the stress I was under. I work smarter now to ensure I never sink back into that state.

If I can make these changes from the lows I've been in, so can you. Ask yourself, what are you battling with right now? What is causing you the most stress? Can you cope with it? Do you have difficult people in your life? Can you cope with them? Do you reach for comfort food or alcohol when you perceive that someone has made you feel bad? Is sugar or alcohol a problem for you? Do you have a dis-ease in your body? These are important questions that you need to answer for a happy, healthy, and wealthy life.

All of this is really about becoming self-aware, finding your passions and working on them, having multiple sources of income, and having a plan B/C/D/E/F/G and beyond to ensure that you can live your best life, happy, free, and in good health, both mentally and physically.

Do you remember I shared with you the story about the doctor who told me that my symptoms might go away if I left stressful situations? He clearly understood the impact of stress on the body.

I recovered once before, and exactly the same thing happened when I left the corporate world to start working for myself again. So now, as well as being a health and happiness coach, I'm also a business and wealth coach with Kevin Green Wealth (KGW). I coach Kevin's clients towards earning their financial freedom, which gives me great joy. I also share knowledge and inspiration to help them create their business ideas. My life is on purpose right there.

My key advice on money is that you are the master; money is merely the servant for you to achieve your freedom. Take responsibility, add value, give great service, and get in the flow, and you'll always be wealthy wherever you are in the world. If I were you, I'd also book and attend one of Kevin Green's 3-day seminars around the world to see what he has to say about business and wealth. It's thanks to him that I've had the time and the energy to write this book, and I'll be forever grateful to him for that.

. . . . . .

CHAPTER 9 – REMIX OPPORTUNITIES

- Be the best version of yourself.
- Money makes us more of what we already are.
- Money is the servant, and you are the master.
- Money is the tool, and freedom is the goal.
- Give service and add value.
- Provide more service to more people, and your income will improve.
- Create multiple sources of income.
- Create your own economy.
- Read Kevin's book *The Rich Rules*.
- Attend a Kevin Green business and wealth training event.
- Success leaves clues.
- Find someone who is living the way you would like to live and copy them.
- Invest in yourself; it is the ultimate self-love.

With Bob Proctor and Sandy Gallagher in Arizona

Me and my business coach Kevin Green.

For more photos from Chapter 9, go to www.markwilkinsonofficial.com/life-remixed.

CHAPTER 10

FAITH

*A person who doesn't read has no advantage over
a person who can't read.*

– Mark Twain

We become the books we read.

– Matthew Kelly

A LOT OF THE GREAT TEACHERS and authors I've mentioned have similar messages. However, they deliver the messages in their own unique way and in line with their own knowledge and purpose. I have read every one of my recommended books myself and used the information for my own life. Most people would say that 'knowledge is power', but is it really? Let's think about that for a moment as I know some incredibly well-read, knowledgeable people who aren't rich; so is knowledge really power? I also know some people who learned directly from coaches and mentors who understand how to be happy, healthy, and wealthy, and those people are super-rich.

So, the phrase 'knowledge is power' is not completely accurate. The *application* of knowledge is where the power is. From wherever you are right now, you really must apply the knowledge for yourself to see how it works. You have to be responsible for all your results to this date, and only then can you take massive and direct action to be able to get

205

great results. And it's not massive action for a day, or a week, or even a month – this is action for a lifetime. And when you do get on the path of developing yourself, inevitably, your outer world improves and becomes a reflection of your inner happiness and confidence.

You have to have faith in yourself and faith in the unseen to be successful. Remember that believing is seeing. When I had lost everything and had absolutely nothing material to my name, I still had choices. I didn't have any special reason to have faith or to believe that I was going to be able to rebuild my life successfully. At the time, I had given my entire life to music.

What I did get was the understanding that I'd actually been successful many times before in life, and I chose then to cultivate a huge belief and faith in myself that I could do it again, and even better this time. If I took the skills that I used successfully before, added some new skills and kept learning, I could be successful in all areas. I could add value to other people's lives. That was what I needed: faith in myself that I could do it.

I learned that nothing of note has ever happened in a comfort zone. By now, I also knew that I didn't need any toxins in my body to improve my life. Lots of coaches had told me that everything I wanted and desired was already within me, so I decided that now was the time to find that out.

In an earlier chapter, after I shut my book on my favourite beach, Nai Harn, in Phuket, Thailand, I decided to come back to the UK to prove myself. I was inspired and decided to get further educated. So, it's time to tell the full story of my recovery from bankruptcy. I knew I had to have faith in myself and move out of my comfort zones in order to achieve it.

So, I found myself back in London in an exam room at 40 years of age. It was a weird experience going from an international touring nightclub DJ to finding myself sitting in an exam room. How had I ended up here?! I thought I'd left all that behind when I left school. However, as I've discovered since, the more qualified I am and the more responsibility I am willing to take, the more money I receive. So now I'm absolutely committed to being a great student of life. I listen and learn from every wise, intelligent person who is living the way I like to live. I can also learn many things from the people that I don't click with. There is always a lesson and message from every person and in every situation.

Back in the exam room, I managed to pass the NEBOSH HSE (Health, Safety and Environment) course. I sat the exams after only four weeks of studying. Shortly after, whilst waiting for the results, it was New Year's Day 2012, and I was lucky enough to be sitting in the VIP area at Ministry of Sound in London. A big guy came over and introduced himself, saying we had some mutual friends. Unbeknownst to me at the time, he was one of the lead project managers at the 02 Arena in London. After he finished laughing about my potential career change, he suggested I come over and speak with the O2 HSE Manager at that time.

I think it's fascinating to see the connections and the opportunities that open up to you when you make your intentions clear in life. The Universe has a way of supporting you! Within a few short weeks, they had put me in touch with the team who were providing the HSE support for the 2012 London Olympic Park as well as all of the venues being used. Once again, the Universe and the law of attraction took a hand when I went for the interview at Canary Wharf on a Monday. I was asked if I could start the next day, and by Thursday of that week, the boss, a great guy and a former Surrey cricketer who I clicked with immediately, took me out for a drink and a chat about the works coming up.

The following day, I was sitting at my new desk in Canary Wharf, and please bear in mind that I was only a few days into my first ever HSE job. I got a call that a senior manager was coming down from the 18th floor. I was told, 'She needs to have a word with you about a test event at the weekend'. My first thought: *I'm only on the 11th floor. She must be seven floors better than me!*

I quickly found out that the current HSE Manager for the London Olympic stadium was off sick, and they needed me to cover! It turns out that without me, they couldn't run the first Olympic test event.

What could I say? Of course! I quickly remembered *Crocodile Dundee* star Paul Hogan's famous quote: 'Bite off more than you can chew, and then chew as fast as you can!' So I obviously said yes, although inside I was thinking, *What have I done!* I don't think I slept too well that night!

As it turned out, I worked on the stadium for eight months, and it was absolutely fantastic. I left just before the games as I was given the opportunity to move to a full-time role at Heathrow Airport. The commute from Hampton Hill to Stratford was killing me. Two hours each way. I quickly learned that with an 8 to 10 hour day and that commute, I was really exhausted. The job at Heathrow was 30 minutes from my house with a raise, so it was really a no-brainer, plus I'd always loved the airport, and I reasoned that it was pretty much recession-proof (I didn't know about Covid-19 then, of course!). I also knew I had to help my mum as we needed to buy out her long-term partner from the family home.

I was 42, and this was when I really started to come of age. Napoleon Hill's classic *Think and Grow Rich,* where he studied 500 millionaires for 25 years, states that a human being's most important and influential years on this planet are 45–65, so I was just warming up. I could feel the faith I had in myself and the Universe start to filter into my results. No longer was I a DJ chancing my arm, taking a risk in life, living hand to mouth. I had quickly become a respectable, hard-working HSE Manager in events and construction. I remember saying to a good friend, 'I used to go to bed at 6am, now I get up at 6am. My life has turned upside down!' He looked at me and laughed. 'Wilkie, it's turned the right way up, mate.'

The first 18 months at Heathrow was fantastic. Like the Olympics, it is a wonderful place to work. There is a lot of respect for workers, and most things are delivered in an organised and timely fashion. Also, there is maximum respect and service given to the passengers. It was during this time that I met Emma, who has now become my wife.

Much as I enjoyed the interaction with most of the lads every day, I knew I needed to move up the ladder much quicker to recover my finances. I was advised by a very good friend to bypass a lot of politics and to leave Heathrow and come back in a different and hopefully more senior position. I would have to put a lot of faith in myself and the process to achieve this because I had no concept that this strategy would actually work. I believed in the advice and myself enough, though, so I decided to go for it. I spoke to the same team that I worked for at the Olympics, and they told me they had a short-term three-month contract in Saudi Arabia coming up. It was a perfect opportunity to move for a short contract and come back.

On this contract, I achieved a financial goal I had set when I had nothing, to now be earning £400 a day. Bob Proctor had said to set a goal that seems so big that when you achieve it, you'll know it's because of the information I had learned. I was ecstatic as I had proved the power of mind over matter yet again. £0 a day to £400 a day in under three years. Result, right, what's next?

Coming back to the UK, I continued gaining more qualifications and was offered the opportunity to become the HSE Manager for all of the commercial construction areas of Heathrow Airport, a real honour for me at that time. This included retail and property and covered the entire 10-mile radius of the UK's largest airport. As a job goes, it was pretty special, just like the Olympic stadium was. I was still miles outside of my comfort zone, but I mostly enjoyed it. Learning while I was earning great money in a senior position was fine with me.

Another piece of advice I received and acted on is that 'everything you desire in your life is just the other side of your greatest fear'. This one fascinated me as being a DJ, I had travelled the world and played in front of hundreds of thousands of people over a 20-year period. I'd felt that buzz, the heart rate pounding, the excitement of a crowd loving the music all night long. It was the greatest feeling ever!

However, despite that, I knew that my biggest fear was actually public speaking. In fact, it is actually a little bit deeper than that. It's more like a fear of rejection. In the DJ days, if and when I played a record that cleared the dance floor (which did happen occasionally!), it really distressed me. I'd always change the record as quickly as I could to get the crowd back on the floor. I knew I had to overcome this fear of rejection, this need for everyone to like me, to be truly successful.

So, what would you do? I could've joined a public speaking club like Toastmasters (which I later have), but I decided to continue to learn while I earn and take a job where I had to stand up and speak in front of a large number of people giving the HSE Inductions at the airport to up to 60 staff and contractors at a time, on a weekly basis. It was one of the most nerve-wracking things that I had done up to that point. Removing the music and the barrier of a DJ booth, leaving just me and a few slides, was scary! I chose to do it, though, and I was well paid for it, plus I got more confident as the weeks went by. I now regularly speak at conferences and events. Life is always a work in progress, and every single time I deliver something in public from a stage, I congratulate myself for doing a good job and then keep improving.

I kept on believing in myself, studying, and taking more exams. I passed an NVQ5 in HSE and became a Graduate Member of IOSH (Grad IOSH – Institute of Safety and Health). Another pay raise and more responsibility followed. After a busy week working, I would dedicate my Saturdays to studying. It wasn't easy, but I had set a goal and was determined to achieve it.

I saw Kevin Green speak publicly for the first time around this time and realised he was going to be able to show me the strategies to escape the corporate grind I was in. Now don't get me wrong. Heathrow is a wonderful place to work. However, as I've said, with my entrepreneurial spirit, working long hours for someone else for 25 years plus was never going to be high on my list of priorities.

I became a Chartered Member of IOSH (CMIOSH) by taking more exams, and when my time at Heathrow came to an end, I was disappointed but ready for my next opportunity.

Not long after, I was offered a senior position at another company. During the time I was there, I studied and passed an NVQ7 Masters equivalent in Strategic Management and Leadership. I also became a Fellow of the ILM (FInstLM – Institute of Leadership and Management) and have since decided that my next qualification will be a PhD. I am really looking forward to becoming a PhD, as then I'll have completed the journey from DJ to Dr! Achieving all of this has taken a huge amount of faith in myself to succeed. We can all achieve anything we would like when we set our minds to it.

Once I'd heard Kevin Green speak again on his three-day training at Heathrow, I signed up and completed the two-year KGW wealth coaching programme. During this time, Emma and I moved to a lovely house in South West London where we continue to develop businesses and buy property to move towards our passive income goals. Five months after moving in, we got married. All of these are huge leaps of faith but so rewarding, and I'm so happy to be feeling healthy and achieving my purpose, vision, and goals.

Once I made the decision, I was focused enough to be able to put a plan in place to escape the corporate world. I had actually been planning it for 12 months, so when the time was right, I took another leap of faith. However, I was calm about it. When I got home after the last day of my corporate job, Emma had put up a big poster that said, 'Congratulations, you've been talking about doing this for a while, now let's make a success of it.' We had a good laugh about it, and I slept well that night. I felt relieved that the healing and the next chapter of my life could begin.

I've since been dubbed a 'serial entrepreneur' as I now build multiple businesses for income now and for our future. I love them all. They're like my children. I love and nurture and help them grow, adding value and giving service to as many people as possible on the journey.

As I continue to enjoy working for personal and business growth, and due to the wonders of the internet, I now coach people from anywhere in the world. This is complete freedom and a wonderful way to live.

Life Remixed™ is about helping you find your wonderful, happy, healthy way to live using the tools that I'm sharing with you in this book. You can learn more on my website at www.markwilkinsonofficial.com.

One thing that I know for sure is when I was younger, I didn't have much faith in myself or anyone else. I was chaotic, in turmoil, misguided, and I wasn't the best young man I could be. You've read how and why it happened now. That's all the story. I now feel, over the years, I've moved from that inner turmoil to inner peace, and trust me, that is a wonderful journey to be on. I've committed to a better life and made it happen; you can do the same. It hasn't been easy; however, it is some-thing that I've worked on daily, something that I continue to work on, to grow, protect, love, and cultivate. My inner peace would not be worth trading for £10 million, trust me.

I don't blame anyone for how I grew up now. What would be the point? Everyone does the best they can with the information they have at the time. I do understand that fear and anger that I felt ended up leading me into the depths of incurable dis-ease and bankruptcy. The good news is from those moments of deep despair has come the opportunity to see that we can choose our thoughts, feelings, and actions which create our future. It became obvious to me, and I hope to you too, that the best option would be to choose to have absolute faith that life is perfect, and everything works out. Life's lessons happen exactly as they are meant to. Believing in yourself and having faith in yourself is just about the best thing you can ever do.

Faith and fear have a lot in common. They both require you to believe in something that you cannot see, and yet so many human beings choose to live in fear rather than choose to have faith in themselves and the Universe. The human mind cannot have faith and fear on the same subject at the same time. In that case, it really is your decision to choose one or the other. You get to decide right now. Would you prefer to be fearful on any given subject or choose to have faith? Personally, I think you gotta have faith.

. . . . . .

CHAPTER 10 – REMIX OPPORTUNITIES

- Faith and fear both require you to believe in something that you cannot see.
- You can choose to have faith in the unseen right now.
- Start with yourself and have faith in you.
- Get educated.
- Take action.
- Work on your purpose, vision, and goals every day.
- Everything you want is just the other side of your greatest fear.

Public speaking, bringing the joy.

For more photos from Chapter 10, go to www.markwilkinsonofficial.com/life-remixed.

CHAPTER 11

HAPPY

If you want to be happy, be.

– Leo Tolstoy

Folks are usually about as happy as they make their minds up to be.

– Abraham Lincoln

When you complain, you make yourself a victim. Leave the situation, change the situation, or accept the situation. All else is madness.

– Eckhart Tolle

AFTER I HAD CALMED DOWN MY OWN THINKING and had a period of respite and recovery, I started to attract different types of people and situations. I also wanted to meet a calm female partner that I could share my life journey with. The only problem was that I really didn't know where I'd meet someone like that. I'd met all my previous girlfriends in nightclubs over the years and wasn't going there so much anymore. Pubs were also out due to the fact I didn't drink alcohol anymore either. There are only so many times you can smile and watch other people get really drunk and tell you the same story over and over. I only wanted to meet positive, supportive, and uplifting types of women.

A friend recommended that I attend a beginner's philosophy class at the London School of Economic Science in Marylebone. Funnily enough, before he was famous, one of the stars from a Channel 4 dating programme was in the same class, and I ended up DJing at a party for him at the London Hilton Hotel on Park Lane. It was a great evening, as I remember!

By attending that philosophy class, I realised that I had come quite a long way on my self-development journey. The classes were excellent, and the people were open and friendly. I was able to be myself, listen, and also share things I had learned, as well as understand a more philosophical approach from others. One of the things I learned was that happiness is our natural state, and yet we (humanity) seem to work so hard not to have it. Pleasure is what we seek outside of ourselves to try and *make ourselves happy*, but force negates, and the pleasure we feel is usually fleeting. If you want to be happy, 'just be' is a great statement. It's very simple, and yet the world itself and some of the people in it can be challenged by this. We must understand, however, that it is their journey. Sometimes our work colleagues or even our nearest and dearest can seem to want to knock us off course, and that, my friend, is all part of the constant test of life. People can be well-intended and caring and looking out for us, most of the time, though, they'll be talking from their own experiences, which could be negative and aren't actually helping us move forward. Instead of people using terms like 'be careful', 'better safe than sorry', or 'drive safe', if people use more positive words, perhaps it could help us all be more courageous and just go for it without any fear. Richard Branson's parents always told him to go for it, and he's done well! I'll talk more about the tests of life and love in relationships in Chapter 13.

As I wrote previously, my dad had been a very religious man. He attended the Salvation Army in Teddington every Sunday, but his mental health had suffered throughout his life, and he struggled during the time I knew him. I quite naturally connected these two things, thinking that religion had sent my dad a bit off the charts. However, once I started studying more and more, I realised it wasn't religion that had caused my dad's problems. They had stemmed, I believe, from undiagnosed PTSD after WWII.

The more I studied philosophy, the more I realised that philosophy, religion, and science (including quantum physics) are all giving a very similar message. It's just the terminology that is different. That's also true with personal development. Every great teacher, author, or study project may have the same basic ingredients that I'm sharing with you in this book, but it will be delivered in their own unique style. You must choose the teacher or coach you connect with the best and then go for it.

When the penny dropped for me, I realised that each time I read a new book, I was going a bit deeper, then a bit deeper, getting closer each time to my true self, and by doing so, I unearthed basic wisdom and happiness within myself. I realised that they were right. All the answers I had ever been searching for were already within me!

Armed with the knowledge I'm sharing with you, I've now gone out into the world and done my best to help and share positive energy with others. It's my life's mission now. Not everyone has been receptive, especially in the corporate business world as I climbed that ladder. I still believe that there is work to be done so that those who are willing can understand and appreciate personality diversity, their potential, and the laws of the universe.

You may not know much about universal laws. Many people don't. We all know and understand the law of gravity that states if I drop something, then it's going to hit the floor, and of course, it stops us from floating off into space! How much do you know about the others, though?

Here is a list of 12 universal laws with my simple definition of each:

The Law of Universal Oneness – Everything in this universe is connected.

The Law of Attraction – What we believe, we receive, as like attracts like.

The Law of Vibration – Everything vibrates, we live in an ocean of motion, nothing rests; we attract what we vibrate in harmony with.

The Law of Correspondence – Prominent patterns will repeat themselves unless we change them.

The Law of Inspired Action – Take inspired action towards making our thoughts and feelings come true.

The Law of Cause and Effect – Whatever we put out into the world will return to us – referred to as Karma.

The Law of Compensation – You will always be compensated for your efforts and contribution, whatever it is, however much or however little.

The Law of Perpetual Transmutation of Energy – Everything in the universe is constantly changing; change is the only constant.

The Law of Relativity – There really is no 'good' or 'bad', but it is simply our thinking that makes it so.

The Law of Gender – Everything in this universe is composed of complementary male and female energy – referred to as yin and yang.

The Law of Polarity – Everything in the Universe has an opposite.

The Law of Rhythm – Everything has a cycle and a rhythm; when we come to understand that all things can and will change, we can come to a place of peace when they do.

There is a school of thought that says, 'Master the universal laws, and you will master life.' All successful people I've met have tuned into these laws, either consciously or unconsciously. I will leave it to you to investigate these laws further for yourself. Suffice it to say that I believe it's true that once you've mastered these laws, nothing can or will knock you off course. You will enjoy every moment of your existence on this planet, which ultimately must be the goal.

Being completely clean and having given up all toxins, I was able to think clearly and work on total acceptance of myself. It took lots of patience and continual work inside my mind to truly be able to say to myself when looking in a mirror, 'Mark, I love and totally accept you as you are right now.'

Louise Hay says in her amazing book, You Can Heal Your Life, that in her experience of coaching and asking people to do mirror work, how difficult the majority of people find it, and I concur. I found it massively difficult myself, and I've asked many other people on their journey, and they generally avoid the subject and laugh, admitting they've never tried it and probably never will. Then, when they're complaining, this is the moment that I ask them, 'How much do you want to change?'

Standing in front of the mirror and telling yourself that you love every part of yourself is a challenge. Most people won't do it. However, when you can totally accept and love who you are, the rewards are wonderful. Yes, it is a challenge, and yet it is absolutely one of the keys to true happiness. Try it for yourself for as long as it takes. Let me know how you get on. If you find it difficult, I promise it does get easier.

In the main, we are also born out of love, and therefore love is within each and every one of us. So, if you truly want to experience true love, look within yourself, and you'll find every answer you'll ever need. I started with loving and totally accepting myself first. You can do it too, and a quick caveat to that is if you spend a period of introspection and you don't particularly like what you find, then it's totally within your power to change it by changing the way you think.

Start with true love for yourself, and then everything else in your life will begin to move into place. Use the universal laws to learn and grow and be a wonderful member of society. Add value and give service wherever you go, and you will always be wealthy. There is also a school of thought that Jesus and the apostles were actually millionaires, travelling around performing miracles for all they came into contact with. Think on that for a while. Makes sense to me. It's much easier to perform miracles when you're a millionaire.

Also, in line with Buddhism, my belief now is that I'm on the first leg of my eternal journey, and when the time comes, I will die peacefully with a smile on my face. With that in mind, I have no fear of death now and can live a happy, calm life while I'm here. I really don't sweat any of the small stuff anymore, and any problem that I'm faced with now is small stuff.

I just love all the time, accepting everyone and understanding that everyone is doing the best they can with the knowledge they have at this moment. It doesn't mean I'm going to like everything that everyone does and choose to hang out with them. If their thoughts, words, and actions are not in harmony with my own, then we will not be attracted to each other, and we will not want to spend our time with each other anyway. Now that I live this way, life is simple.

Also, any experience that I have now, I can put into this context. Having faced an incurable dis-ease and bankruptcy means that I now totally accept any experience that comes my way. For a start, I know that I have created it, so I always take responsibility for it. I also totally accept the other person who has their own way of living, their own journey, and we may or may not be in harmony with each other. I've tried this out in personal and business relationships as well as with an ex-boss or two in the corporate world, and I have learned now not to have any emotional attachment to anything in life that is unimportant.

With no emotional attachment, I don't have to recover from anything when it ends. I can just accept the experience, learn from it, be grateful for the lesson, and move on to the next stage of my life. This has stood me in good stead and allows me, I believe, to be an excellent coach in all areas of life, helping others achieve, understand, and recover from whatever is happening or has happened to them.

Of course, I am emotionally attached to my loved ones, my wife, and my family, as they are the most important people in my life and fully deserve my love, acceptance, appreciation, and support.

I believe I'm a spirit having a human experience in my body. We are just passing through a short time on this planet, so I enjoy being as effective as I possibly can while I am here. Every night as my head hits the pillow, I simply say to myself, 'I love you all,' and that's aimed to my close family, to all my friends, and also to the whole of humanity. I hope that's not too deep for you. It's the truth for me, and it works.

Trust me, I really have fun with this stuff, and so can you. I live in the moment as much as I can. Of course, we must plan certain things; however, I no longer get lost looking back in anger or forward in fear. I use my time to look around myself with the awareness that I have built.

Life is *incredible* when you decide to make it so. Life is easy when you decide to make it so. Life is happy when you decide to make it so. I wish you nothing but love, of course. Let's keep the happiness going and pay it forward.

. . . . . .

CHAPTER 11 – REMIX OPPORTUNITIES

- Calm down, speed up.
- Know, understand, and put into action the universal laws.
- Love is total acceptance.
- You can heal your life.
- Clear your mind, live in the present, be happy.

Happy.

For more photos from Chapter 11, go to www.markwilkinsonofficial.com/life-remixed.

CHAPTER 12

TESTIFY

If you are not the hero of your own story, then you're missing the whole point of your humanity.

– Steve Maraboli

It is the story that matters, not just the ending.

– Paul Lockhart

Everything you want is just the other side of your greatest fear.

– Bob Proctor

Everything you want is on the other side of those burning hot coals, mate.

– Mat Patey

ONCE YOU'VE STARTED TO MAKE CHANGES, expanded your knowledge, and tried and tested new strategies, you'll find out what works for you. You'll really feel that you need to share what you've learned with as many other people as possible. When I was younger, I found 100 ways to be unsuccessful; as I've grown, I found there are only a few ways to be truly happy and successful, and yet these few ways that I'm sharing with you in this book are not always common knowledge.

I went from resident DJ at Ministry of Sound to a successful international touring DJ, then down to an unemployed and broken person, and then making the decision to start to make my way up all over again. I started again at the bottom in construction when it wasn't a need but a must. This time, I got highly qualified enough to end up as a senior member at the UK's largest airport and a large residential construction company. I made this rebuilding happen through living outside of my comfort zone and overcoming my fears every single day. Admittedly, throughout the journey, I did struggle at times, but I took the lesson each time and will not allow negativity into my life again. I've also overcome my biggest fear of public speaking.

Now it's time for you to find your biggest fear and face it. Everything you would like in your life is just beyond your biggest fear. Can you name it now? What do you think it would be? What's holding you back? Be honest with yourself and write it below. You can spend the next day, week, month, or year facing it and growing through it. First, you just need to know what it is.

My greatest fear is _____

_____

I will overcome this by _____

_____

In *Think and Grow Rich* by Napoleon Hill, he states that there are six basic fears, and most human beings suffer from at least one, or indeed all six at once, at one time or another in their lives.

These six basic fears are:

1. Poverty
2. Criticism
3. Ill Health
4. Loss of Love
5. Old Age
6. Death

In my own experience, my fears can still come up. My fears are 'I am not enough' and 'I won't be loved'. I acknowledge them but don't let them take root. I replace them quickly with positive, loving, and kind messages to myself. 'I am enough' and 'I am love' generally do the trick.

I've also found that fear and excitement are very similar, and it's time to turn your fears into excitement and dance through life with enthusiasm and a smile on your face. Did you know that the word 'enthusiasm' actually comes from two Greek words: *en* meaning 'within' and *theos* meaning 'God'? So, the word *enthusiasm* literally means *God within*. It was used to describe people who possessed god-like abilities or were very strong, God-inspired, and full of wisdom and convictions. Interesting eh!

I know that from time to time throughout my life, I've suffered from each of those six fears from *Think and Grow Rich*. I'm wondering how many of you will hold your hands up and say that you have felt one or all of these? You may even be feeling these fears right now. I'm here to tell you that it is perfectly normal and OK to recognise that these fears can raise themselves in each and every one of us at any time. Facing these fears and replacing them with faith in life is vital.

Andy Duphrane said in *The Shawshank Redemption*, 'Get busy living or get busy dying.' Positive thoughts and actions equal living. Negative thoughts and actions equal dying. You get to choose, so choose life!

A really big moment for me, even as I was suffering the savage knee problems at the time, was when I attended Tony Robbins' Unleash the Power Within (UPW) event in London. My wife isn't a huge fan of going to these kinds of events, but I knew that I had to go to keep learning and keep growing. It was day one at Excel in London, and during the day, to keep the energy fresh, Tony gets everyone to stand up and walk around and hug a new friend (which some people I know wouldn't like). I was fine with it, so I stood up and turned around, and two rows behind me was a guy who was two or three inches taller than me, so we ended up giving each other a big hug. His name is Mat. He's a wonderful guy and has become a great friend, which is why I quote him at the start of this chapter.

I turned up to UPW, walking incredibly slowly with huge, inflamed knees. To be honest, the only real requirement that I put on myself was to get through the day. As I shuffled in, I heard a loud shout of 'WILKIE!'. Incredibly, I turned around to see my friend and celebrity DJ, Brandon Block, who was also there for the weekend. We hung out together for the four days, and we loved and supported each other's journey throughout UPW and still do to this day, which is wonderful in itself.

At the end of day one, I was getting ready to leave and go back to my local hotel, have some dinner, take it easy, and rest my extremely sore legs. However, Mat and his friends Seb and Steve, who had all been to UPW before, said to me that I had to do the firewalk scheduled for the end of day one. I said, 'No way.' I'm only here to hear Tony speak, not to hobble across 2,000 degrees of burning hot coals, thanks very much, chaps!

Then Mat came out with the quote at the start of this chapter: 'Everything you want is on the other side of those burning hot coals, mate.' He totally got me with that one, and I ended up with my shoes and socks off, hobbling through the Excel exhibition centre in London at night, out into the car park with 10,000 other people preparing to walk across six paces of burning hot coals. To say it was an experience would be an understatement, and yet I knew he was right. I knew my recovery and the rest of my healthy life meant that I had to take on this challenge and face those fears.

I put myself 'in state' as Tony had spent the day preparing us to do, and I marched across those burning hot embers, all the while, people were cheering me on. We all celebrated together like crazy once I'd crossed. Some two and a half years later, as I write this, Mat was 100% right. Interestingly Mat, Seb, my wife Emma, and I are now all friends and business partners in a property development company.

It is my journey towards testifying about these amazing things that have happened which keeps me happy. Writing this book is a big step forward. Coaching other people towards their own highest high is also huge for me. Standing up and being counted, not being afraid to show people my emotions, and being able to live my purpose is such a joyful experience.

The way I have overcome my fear of being judged and criticized was difficult at first, but it is now reasonably simple that I'm out the other side of it. Remember: what anyone else thinks of you is none of your business. Just let that sink in again for a moment. In fact, take a few minutes right now to really think about it. How much time do we waste thinking or worrying about what other people think of us? If you're anything like I used to be, the answer will be a lot!

As soon as I heard that it's none of my business what others think, it was like a huge weight was lifted. I can't control it anyway, so why do I care? It was the most freeing piece of information that I had ever heard. Sometimes I wish I'd heard it when I was a lot younger. However, I might not have been listening then. They say when the student is ready, the teacher will come, and that day, I was 100% ready. It's amazing how much more free time I have now to create things – this book, businesses, great relationships, you name it. I'm creating like crazy every minute of the day. The good news is it is within your power too.

My journey towards becoming a really great public speaker is not dissimilar to my journey from being a young DJ to becoming a resident at London's top super club Ministry of Sound. As I was such an avid learner, and before I became a coach, Kevin Green regularly asked me to give testimonials to 500 people for his training courses. I also made sure I always put my knowledge into practice. I've come a long way since the guy who was shaking and nervous, giving health and safety inductions at Heathrow Airport. I think when you understand that life is just a journey and that you could be kind to yourself along the way, encourage yourself, congratulate yourself, and be grateful to yourself (and to everyone else who has helped you along the way), then life can become a true heaven on earth experience.

As you've read, I'm completely comfortable sharing with others about my personal development and business success that I'm now achieving. I want every single one of you to come out of reading this book with a fresh mindset and an opportunity to recreate yourself and then share what has worked for you.

I'm not interested in how old (or young) you are. You can have results or excuses, but not both. It is never too late to make a difference in your life and in other people's lives. Get comfortable being a successful person. Get comfortable helping other people when they need you.

Life Remixed™ is my testimony, and I'm really hoping that it helps you and anyone else you decide to share it with. To learn, grow, and smile more, to enjoy it all – that's the purpose of why we're here.

. . . . . .

CHAPTER 12 – REMIX OPPORTUNITIES

- Identify, face, and overcome the six basic fears.
- What anyone thinks of you is none of your business.
- Stand up and be counted.
- Attend a Life Remixed™ event.
- Attend a Tony Robbins UPW event.
- Attend a Kevin Green KGW event.
- Share your story – testify – you'll help someone else.

I always fancied being a singer.

For more photos from Chapter 12, go to www.markwilkinsonofficial.com/life-remixed.

CHAPTER 13

NOW THAT WE FOUND LOVE

The most loving women are the women who will test you the most

– David Deida

One of the deepest feminine pleasures is when a man stands full, present, and unreactive in the midst of his woman's emotional storms

– David Deida

The hardest question I ever had to answer about love and relationships was 'What is it about me that is attracting all this drama?'

– Mark Wilkinson

I'VE LEFT THIS CHAPTER NEAR THE END of *Life Remixed*™, and yet by rights, it could be right up at the front because, without love, we struggle to live. Love is the foundation of our being. As babies, we would literally die without someone loving us. And as we grow into life, without love and the right relationships, we can find ourselves in both mental and physical pain, which can lead to the degradation of our mind, body, and spirit. When I say relationships, I'm talking about every relationship we have, with ourselves, our families, our partner or spouse, and of course, the people we work with. We often spend more time with them than with our own families!

As a young touring DJ, I simply could not get a relationship with a girlfriend to last for more than two years at the maximum. Every single time I thought I'd met 'the one', within two years, we were apart. I just couldn't fathom it. I was a successful DJ and music man who just couldn't sustain an intimate relationship. I realised I had a certain fear of intimacy myself, which definitely helped accelerate the breakups. Plus, it didn't help that once I'd attracted a beautiful woman, I would often be on the lookout for another one. I suppose I could say I was never satisfied and enjoyed the thrill of the chase. I was continually successful in attracting women because I almost always had a girlfriend around me, and yet, all the dramas and ups and downs were tough to take for all involved. I was addicted to the *ups* of meeting somebody new and that excitement of the new love buzz, and clearly equally addicted to the *downs* of the drama and heartbreak when it didn't work out, some of which ended up being crushing.

I know now that a lesson is repeated until it is learned, and that pain has a message for us. There was a repeating pattern for many years. It was only when I started to learn and become aware of what I was doing that I could change it.

In Chapter 3, I talked about how my DJ partner at the time came out with a great line when I was moaning about love and heartbreak. He said, 'When we're sick, we go to the doctors, and yet when we don't feel good mentally, where do we go?' It was a good point and one I took on board.

I mentioned earlier that I reached out for some therapy and was lucky enough (I thought by chance, but as we now know by the law of attraction) to team up with an excellent therapist who helped me as I peeled away some layers of myself that needed dealing with before I could move forward.

In therapy, we covered all kinds of subjects, including the death of my father when I was 18, my challenging relationship with my mother when I was younger, and the numerous relationship breakdowns, which I had put down to my DJ and travelling lifestyle, rather than any personal issues that I needed to address in myself. But, as I've said before, once the can of personal development is open, you can't put the top back on. So, the journey began with me wanting to rid myself of the pain and to learn to be a better man, to create a loving home life with a wonderful woman who, at that moment, was only in my imagination.

Continuing my search to understand love, I started with Tony Robbins' Get the Edge program on CDs, where Tony delivers two full-on days on relationships. This was amazing and perfect timing for me (of course). I studied hard and listened to it on repeat many times, especially when driving around in my car. I did every exercise on multiple occasions and learned some very important lessons. I will add that this was a rare moment in my love life where I was wilfully single, so I could take the time to understand myself better. I found it easier to work on myself when I didn't have any other distractions.

One of the exercises, in particular, was very effective, and I've used it with many coaching clients who are looking to improve or attract their perfect partner. We can try this together right now, whether you're single or in a relationship. As a single guy, I was tasked with making a list of all the things that I would desire in my perfect partner. Or, if you're in a relationship right now, you can list all the things you would like your partner to be, do, and have right now.

If you're struggling with any of this, you can try it another way. It is well-known that most people know exactly what they don't want in a partner. People have got all the reasons and things they don't like from previous experience, so if need be, you may find it easier to make a list of all the things that you don't like in a partner, all the things that you don't want your partner to be. That may be an easier list for you to make, right? We'll come back to that in a moment. For now, write down ten qualities that you would like your partner to be, do, and have. I'll go first:

1. Loving
2. Kind
3. Generous
4. Attractive
5. Funny
6. Caring

7. Supportive

8. Adventurous

9. Confident

10. Happy

Now you go:

1. _____

2. _____

3. _____

4. _____

5. _____

6. _____

7. _____

8. _____

9. _____

10. _____

Was it easier to be positive?

Or did you need to make a separate list of all the negative things you don't want instead? Either way is fine. If it was easier to go for the negative, then make sure that you list all of those negatives that you definitely *don't want* to see in your partner! Get all those out on paper.

Once you've made that negative list (and this is the fun bit), all you have to do now is write down *the exact opposites of your negatives* to find out the qualities of the person you would like to share your life with. All those positive qualities that you love on your list are now your ten relationship goals.

When I first looked at my positive list of relationship goals, I thought that there was definitely going to be a woman in the UK who would be able to tick all these boxes for me and more, and then the real bomb dropped. Tony stated that to attract that person with all the positive qualities on your list, *you must be, do, and have all of those qualities yourself first* before you can attract those qualities in someone else because, of course, like attracts like!

With all my previous studies, I understood this quickly and also realised that I'd been making a mistake my entire adult life. I realised I shouldn't go looking for love from someone else. First, I had to look deep inside myself to find true love. Once I'd found a real love for myself, only then could I truly love another. When I could totally accept myself, then I could totally accept another. I took some time here and did some deep thinking, some soul searching, and some looking in the mirror.

Please take this as an important lesson. Wherever you are right now in your life, start to work on becoming everything you would like in your ideal partner first. Once you can be everything on your ideal partner list, finding it all within yourself first, then you can find the love you desire with that special someone. Fill yourself up first, and then you can overflow and give to another.

It could be with someone new, or it could be with your current partner. If you are willing to change yourself for the better, you will begin to see changes in your partner too. This was and still is amazingly simple and yet wonderful information to have for your own personal growth. I hope you use this information wisely. Many people go through their whole lives and miss this wonderful opportunity to grow, always looking for someone else to love them, and not understanding that it all starts within themselves.

With all the learning we have been through together so far in *Life Remixed™*, this is one of the most important chapters. Your relationship with yourself and your intimate partner is your foundation, and you cannot attract what you aren't. Now look back at your list and ask yourself, can I be all of those things? Am I willing to work more on myself to attract the wonderful person I deserve to share my life with? As you've got this far, I know the answer is yes, you can do it. You just have to decide to do so. As I've said before, everything starts with your decision.

Once you really get this, you can design your own life and attract your life partner, exactly how you would like them to be. Remember what I've said about love being total acceptance? So many people in our society don't particularly like themselves and go to someone else for validation and love. Or they distract themselves with food, toxins, or the many distractions available to us (as I did for years). However, it's not really possible or fair for you to expect someone else to love you how you want to be loved, certainly not for a whole lifetime. That's completely your job, so decide to do it and make it happen for yourself.

The greatest relationship on every level is between two people who truly love and accept themselves first, then give that love and acceptance to each other from there.

As a calm, confident, loving, and giving single person, you will attract someone who is also giving from their heart. Or if you're in a challenging relationship with the wrong person (for you), it will quickly become clear as they will be taking and not giving back to you in the way that you desire. Once you notice this, you can start to make better decisions from a position of clear awareness and love for yourself. When you love yourself, you won't allow someone to mistreat you in any way. You'll also never be lonely again. You will only nourish yourself with good vibrations, so get used to those good vibrations being in your life!

If you are in a relationship now that needs improving, start by improving yourself. If your partner truly loves you, then they will start to grow with you, and it will turn into a wonderful journey of improvement together.

I mentioned in an earlier chapter that Eckhart Tolle says in *The Power of Now*, 'When one partner becomes enlightened, one of two things will happen. You'll either grow together with interest and love or separate like oil and water.' I've lived through both experiences.

These are positive life lessons and things we can all learn to grow together from a deeper understanding. I went through this whole process of forgiveness, gratitude, and acceptance of myself over a couple of years. I started by looking for the little miracles when I gave total heartfelt gratitude to every person I met throughout my day. I found people responded and smiled back to me more often than not. I found that life became a far more joyous experience. I realised that I could base my comeback from the dis-ease, relationship breakups, and bankruptcy by living this way, using the universal laws from the previous chapter.

My belief is there is good in every one of us and available for every one of us. The majority of the people on this planet are decent, giving, and loving individuals.

As I write today, in 2021, and I am happier, healthier, and wealthier than I have ever been. I'm married and live with a wonderful woman in a wonderful house. We have multiple sources of income and are in a good place, always striving to give more service to more people and driving each other on.

So, I can testify – right here, right now – that everything I have learned, put into practice, and am sharing on these pages really works! Make your decisions wisely and study with and follow the good information and the right instructions from great and successful people. Read or listen to the right books that resonate with you and watch the right uplifting movies. There are loads of them on Netflix, Prime, YouTube, and others. Apply the knowledge you learn for yourself. Study people who are already living how you would like to live. When you do, it will be inevitable that you will develop into someone who attracts all the good things that you currently desire. This will include all the love and great relationships that you desire in your life.

Inevitably, one great teacher always shares information that leads to another, and you'll notice I have credited many people in this book for helping me to learn and grow. After I'd created my perfect partner in my mind, I picked up a recommendation to check out David Deida, who had written the book mentioned earlier called *The Way of the Superior Man*, which has had a profound effect on me. Please do not be put off by the title, as it is not about being superior to anyone else. It is based on the concept that rather than being a mediocre man (as I was while I was growing up), we can become a superior one – an improved version of ourselves, lads!

Ladies, have you met any mediocre men? I'd say probably yes, right? I know, as I used to be one! The book is about being a man who gives his all, who understands the demands of work, women, and sexual desire. He gives his all despite the struggles, tests, trials, and challenges of life. It's an amazing book, and I hope you read it soon after this one. There is a link to it under recommended reading at www.markwilkinsonofficial.com.

We all have masculine and feminine within us. This is obvious as we're made up of 50% of our mothers and 50% of our fathers. Some of us grow up as boys with more masculine traits, and some of us as girls with more feminine traits. However, as well as masculine men and feminine women, there are feminine men and masculine women in the world, and there are more balanced people and couples too. On this journey of self-discovery, it is worth thinking about which traits are stronger within you.

Coming now as I do from a place of love and understanding of the masculine and feminine within us all, I understand that on a basic level, the masculine is always searching for *freedom*, and the feminine is always searching for *fullness*. Thinking about that, all of a sudden, every relationship I'd ever been in began to make sense. I was constantly searching for freedom by DJing, partying, drinking, indulging in my other addictions, travelling the world, and chasing the dream for that hit record and mega success. And all my feminine girlfriends were searching for their fullness by wanting me to be present and loving, living together, and for them to fill the house with pictures of family, flowers, and all those little knickknacks that a masculine person would never think of having around the house.

The best relationships are based on an awareness of this fun game and an appreciation and understanding of each other's requirements – masculine freedom and feminine fullness – and neither partner making a big issue about it, but just loving and understanding each other from a true and present awareness. When articulating this to a few male and female friends and hearing their feedback, I understood and knew that in my next big relationship, I would be able to understand better and handle the challenges ahead.

In my younger mind, I had always assumed that my partner would be the friendliest person towards me all the time. After all, we're on the same team pulling in the same direction and wanting the same things all the time, right? So obviously, we will be 100% supportive of each other all the time, right?

The truth is actually quite different in a relationship of masculine and feminine polarity. We're not friends; we're intimate partners, and there is a big difference. From the masculine point of view, everything in life with the feminine is either a test or a celebration. There is no grey area here – test or celebration, all the time. Really think about that. The more I thought about it, the more I came to realise from my own experiences that, again, this is true. I've even spoken to many of the feminine people I know, and they have confirmed 'the testing' to be true, so it's up to the masculine to grab this information and pass the tests. Step up!

This could be in any relationship in your life. *The feminine in the relationship is always testing the masculine.* I've got news for you: you cannot escape it. Even changing to a new partner will never let you escape it. Although each feminine person has a temperature, hotter or cooler, the masculine must find the best temperature for them, one they can handle. That happens, as I've said, by us being the person we would like to attract first. If you want a calm partner, then you'd better be calm yourself first. The masculine must also work on themselves to be able to find the humour in the testing, then learn the strategies that bring happiness and joy to the relationship.

Here's a summary for masculine people: find a feminine partner whose tests you can pass with humour and love, and you'll find true happiness.

As I said, I've asked many feminine people about all of this. They have almost all agreed that they spend much of their time testing their masculine partner to make sure that they are trustworthy, that they are worthy of their love, that they are loving and present and there for them when they need them. The testing can go on and on for days and sometimes even weeks before there is a celebration. Some masculine people might call the testing 'nagging' and not enjoy it, and here's the thing. If you're being tested and you turn round and react angrily or run away to the pub or lose control of your emotions in some way, then immediately you have failed the test. If you fail the test, there will not be a celebration.

However, if you continually pass the test by being present, smiling, laughing, loving, and meeting the test with humour, continuing to show love. (Don't try and fix the issue, don't try and talk about it or give your solution unless asked for. Just listen and show love.) Then the celebration will follow. The celebration could be a date, a nice evening out or at home, or even (with a bit of luck) intimacy. However, not long after any celebration, the testing will start again. The superior masculine person enjoys these tests, finds the humour in them, and rises to pass them every time.

Let me share a couple of great descriptions of this that I could visualise and therefore really helped me.

The masculine can be like the land: solid, dependable, and always there. You know you can count on them. The feminine is like the weather. Sometimes the sun is shining, and it is the most beautiful place in the world. You feel fantastic and warmed through, and it's beautiful. Other times, it is raining hard with thunder and lightning, and you don't feel as good. But the weather comes and goes in cycles like feminine moods, and it's OK. A strong masculine person learns to smile in the storm as well as enjoy the sunshine.

In another visual description, the masculine can be like the beach, always there and dependable. The feminine is like the sea. Sometimes the tide is in and is lapping all over the beach, which feels great and close and warm. And then other times, the tide goes out so far away, and you're standing there on the beach thinking, please come back, and eventually, the tide does come back, and the beach is still there: strong, dependable, loving, caring.

For a young man continually learning to improve himself, to be more loving, more caring, more present to his feminine partner and to the world, these descriptions are gold. Perhaps they resonate with you. When you have the skills and know-how to break the feminine cycle with love and affection using words of love and encouragement, you will be happy and successful. Being present, passing every test, and enjoying every moment is truly the way to happiness.

I realised that my partner wasn't necessarily going to seem to be my best friend all the time. She would test me to make sure that I was wholly with her and a loving and caring masculine man she could trust. Believe me when I say that as a younger chap, I failed these feminine tests many times.

Another great tip for the masculine is that in order to live your purpose, you must make quality time every day with no distractions, no screens (iPhone, iPad, laptop, TV) and really listen to your feminine partner. Look into their eyes and ask how they're feeling. If you can do that consistently each day, you will then find that you are free to carry on living your mission for the rest of the day without distraction. Your partner will release you to do your work, live your purpose, or enjoy your hobby. Seriously try this together. The feminine will thank you for absolute attention when you're truly present and listening. And you'll both be happier as a result.

Dimple Thakrar, a great relationship coach that I met at Harry Singha's World Class Speakers Academy (also recommended, by the way!), gave some great information on the three needs of the feminine, which are to be *safe*, *seen*, and *heard*. Add that to the three needs of the masculine of *sex*, *praise*, and *respect*, and you have the whole spectrum. These needs have been passed down through the ages. Take care of these three things for each other, and life will be wonderful. And please remember that I am not referring just to women and men here, but to the feminine and masculine, both of which are within us all.

This great understanding has allowed me to become very aware and successful in my marriage. I've been with Emma for eight years now, and we've been married for the last three. In the greater scheme of things, I know it's early days, and yet I know it feels right. I feel good myself and understand our relationship better than I ever have any other before. I was 42 when I met Emma, and I feel hugely grateful that I'd been through so many challenges in my younger life and that I felt the need to reach out and learn why I was so unsuccessful in relationships!

Learning how and why I'd been so unsuccessful led me into learning how to turn it around, and these days I'm the happiest man around. I enjoy all the testing. It's fun, and I always show my love no matter whether it's sunny or cloudy or even raining in our relationship. One of the main reasons for this is that as the masculine partner, I know I'm largely responsible for the state of the relationship. I've found a woman who tests me just the right amount, a woman whose tests I can pass on a daily basis with a smile on my face. It's a relationship where I can be myself and still feel loved and cared for, even smiling my way through the rain.

Early on in our relationship, we also completed the Equilibria Personality Diversity Indicator (PDI) assessment that I mentioned earlier (www.equilibria.com/PDI-home). E-Colors helped us understand each other and our communication styles on a much deeper level. I shared already that I used it in my career change to go from unemployed to communicating with the board of directors. Well, it also worked wonders for Emma and me to understand each other better. Please do the online Equilibria PDI questionnaire yourself and, even better, share the experience with your partner, colleagues, and families. Find out your E-Colors now!

What it showed was that I am predominantly the socialiser (surprise surprise) and top colour Yellow. Emma is predominantly the strategic, logical thinker, with top colour Green. What we found really interesting is that I am all about the 'who' and Emma is all about the 'how'. Where Emma is strong (logical thinking), I am not as strong and vice versa. What a great way to understand each other and work together as a team to have a fully rounded relationship of love and support through the journey.

In relationships, it's important to recognise your masculine gift is purpose, direction, and decision, and always offer your decisions in a loving way. If you're a masculine person, then share those decisions without fear, show your leadership, always listen to your partner, and then offer your own decision. If you're a feminine person, then relax and let your partner share their decisions. Make space for the good you desire. You can both enjoy these feelings and this process. I've seen couples where the feminine partner ends up in their masculine energy and making all the decisions for the couple and family, which eventually the masculine partner can end up resenting. They're doing this because the masculine hasn't stepped up. They don't trust enough to let them do it. Perhaps this resonates with you. Of course, every relationship is different and made of masculine and feminine in both sexes, as I've mentioned.

However, after reading this, I hope you'll research further on relationships. I'm happy to share my success by hosting online and live events around health and happiness, which will include relationships. I'm always here to help, to be your Health and Happiness Coach, taking you to your highest levels of success in both love and relationships. Once your relationship is steady and there are no dramas, the rest of life becomes so much easier to succeed in. Along with your inner self, your intimate relationship is your foundation, so please make sure it's solid. It is much easier to succeed in business when you have strong relationship foundations.

As I've discovered, the remedy for addiction is true connection. As you know, I was addicted to many things as a young man. Most, if not all, were short term pleasures but ended up negative and self-destructive. Since I've kicked alcohol and straightened up my act, I can now connect with people through my own love and acceptance. Through these connections, I am no longer addicted to negativity and self-destruction. What I enjoy nowadays is your success in all areas of your life, and by thinking this way, the law of attraction states that my life must be successful too.

. . . . . .

CHAPTER 13 – REMIX OPPORTUNITIES

- Your intimate relationship is your foundation – choose carefully and wisely.
- A lesson is repeated until it is learned.
- Pain has a message, emotional or physical. Make sure to listen.
- Ask for help and advice when you need it.
- Everything in your relationship is either a test or a celebration.
- The remedy to addiction is connection.

Our wedding day.

For more photos from Chapter 13, go to www.markwilkinsonofficial.com/life-remixed.

CHAPTER 14

CELEBRATION

I believe in miracles, don't you?

– The Jackson Sisters

I'm still standing.

– Elton John

*One of the saddest things in life must be to get to
the end and look back in regret, knowing that you could have
been, done and had so much more.*

– Robin Sharma

Motivation is what gets you started; habit is what keeps you going.

– Jim Rohn

Life begins at the end of your comfort zone.

– Neale Donald Walsch

Success is something you attract by the person you become.

– Jim Rohn

I WAS SO CLOSE TO calling this chapter 'I Believe in Miracles' as I really do now. Here is the evidence:

- I've recovered twice from an incurable dis-ease.
- I've gone from unable to walk to running marathons.
- I've gone from bankrupt to financially free.
- I've finally written this book after ten years of thinking about it.

There are only two ways to live your life: *One is as though nothing is a miracle. The other is as though everything is a miracle.*

All of the above is wonderful evidence (to me) that miracles really do exist. As long as you can learn to create a positive mental attitude and to love and value your own life, then great things happen. They did for me, and they will for you.

Elton John sang, 'I'm still standing, after all this time, feeling like a true survivor, feeling like a little kid.' I feel much the same now!

Despite my parents' challenges and having an addictive personality myself at a young age, then getting into music, sex, and toxic substances, I've still managed to come out the other side and develop into a man that I can, at last, be happy with.

Success in health, wealth, and relationships is vital for anyone to have a happy life. You must have all three, and you can't be truly successful if one is missing. Health is wealth and definitely the number one priority, especially as we get older. The true meaning of wealth is not just about money but includes living with purpose and having a healthy mind, body, and spirit, as well as financial security.

Here is great advice to build your life from the ground up:

1. Keep healthy and stay that way.
2. Love and accept yourself, find another person who loves and accepts themself, and enjoy a wonderful lifetime of giving love to each other in a relationship.
3. Work on adding value and giving service to grow your wealth and financial security.

All too often, though, we don't believe that this life is possible for us. Some of us don't believe that we deserve this success. We struggle through life from drama to drama, blaming everyone else for our issues and problems. It can be difficult to realise that you do actually deserve success, to understand that you are worthy of all the great things in life, and then commit to doing the inner work that navigates you towards success in all of these areas.

Two fantastic pieces of advice that were given to me when I was feeling down on myself and unsuccessful were these:

Stop being so hard on yourself.

Make a list of all your successes from as far back as you can remember.

I've actually made this list and put it on a daily reminder. The list goes back to being four years old. Notice that I put this list in the present tense so I can attract more of the things I desire, and so that the successes continue. Using 'I am' and 'I have' sends a powerful statement as it means you have already achieved your desire. (The last few items on my list are still to be achieved.)

Now every time I fulfil an achievement, I always add a few more to the end of the list to keep striving and to have a few more goals to continue to work for.

Where I am really successful:

Ride a bike – aged 4

Ride a motorbike – aged 16

Passed driving test – aged 17

First job at a bank – aged 17

Learned to DJ – aged 18

Music business/DJ/producer/remixer – aged 18 to 38

Radio presenter – various times throughout my music career

Starting over – aged 39

Running marathons – aged 39

Crisis volunteer – aged 39

Passed the NEBOSH exam – aged 40

Established an HSE career – aged 40 to date; worked at the Olympic Stadium, Heathrow Airport, a large residential construction company, and now my own consultancy Hillmont Associates Ltd

Passed motorbike test – aged 42 (bought a Honda 800cc, then Suzuki 1800cc, then Triumph Rocket 2300cc)

Regular public speaking – aged 43

Passed NVQ5 – aged 43

Purchased a Lexus RX450, first luxury hybrid car – aged 44

Property development and investment – aged 45 to present

Chartered Member of Institute of Safety and Health (CMIOSH) – aged 45

Tony Robbins UPW firewalk – aged 47

Bought a home together with Emma – aged 47

Got married – aged 48

Passed NVQ7 Masters – Strategic Management & Leadership – aged 48

Fellow of the Institute of Leadership & Management (FInstLM) – aged 48

Set up multiple sources of income – aged 48

Recovered good health (again) – aged 49

Kevin Green Wealth (KGW) Business coach – aged 49

Financially free – aged 49

Life Remixed™ book published – aged 50

Future Goals

NVQ8 PhD in Directional Leadership

New Triumph Rocket 3 (2500cc)

Multiple worldwide businesses by helping others achieve their dreams

1,000 worldwide properties

His & hers sports cars

We split our time between London, Spain, Dubai, Thailand, and Miami.

As I write, the last few items on the list are all goals and life's coming attractions, things that we are working towards either achieving, doing, or having. It's always great to have goals, and it's always great to enjoy the journey of working towards them. Then, when the time is right, they will happen. Achieving each one of them feels wonderful as we become better people each time.

I cannot convey the importance of committing to always learning new skills in life enough. Every day is a school day. I've become a sponge for new information. I only really started learning the important things in life when I had my biggest challenges, though.

After 20 years as a DJ, when I was stripped back to the bone, unhappy, and left with poor health and no material goods to show for all my efforts, it was then I had to dig deep and commit to learning these new things. However, now I feel hugely thankful for these experiences as they changed the course of my life. I learned new mindset skills and went through this personal development journey. By doing so, I also became more comfortable with general study and learning, which I'd rejected when I was younger.

Completing my NEBOSH HSE course at around 40 years of age and going on from there to become CMIOSH and then achieve NVQ7 Masters & FInstLM in just a few short years took effort and a lot of additional work in my evenings and weekends, but it was all worth it. The more developed I became and the more qualified I got, the more service I could provide and the more money I received. That cycle goes on and on, and my services are now worth a lot more money to more people. Added to that, I am happy to take more responsibility because I feel growing confidence daily in my own abilities, and I'm also fully qualified to do so. All of this is open to you too.

I realise that not everyone works in this way, and not everyone has to. Some people prefer simple, practical advice and then to go out in the world and make their own way. They don't want or need qualifications to be effective, and to be honest, the only reason I did them was that they seemed to be required in the circles I was moving in at that time. Thankfully, I'm also blessed to have a half-decent academic brain, meaning that I could study and pull myself back up pretty quickly after the dis-ease and bankruptcy.

Once I heard them, I also followed Kevin Green's practical instructions closely, and this meant that I could seriously commit to writing *Life Remixed*™ so I can now share with you everything that is possible when you set your mind to achieve some seriously big goals. We all have the same amount of time on this planet. It's about the energy we bring to our days that counts.

As I've said, the importance of having a really good coach is something that I would highly recommend for you to have in any area of your life that you would like to improve. I studied from afar with Tony Robbins and Bob Proctor. I also did distance learning on academic courses with help from other skilled people around me each time. However, when I first heard Kevin Green speak on stage, I knew this was the guy I wanted to work with directly and move forward with in life by studying his wealth strategies. I knew he had the keys to my freedom to be able to write this book. I can't thank him enough for what he does.

After studying Kevin's strategies, I managed to leave the corporate job that I was in within 15 months of applying what he had taught me. I knew I had to make a break for entrepreneurial freedom for my own mental and physical health. I needed to recover after the stress I had put myself through over a number of years working for other people in order to recover from bankruptcy.

With my previous DJ and entrepreneurial experience, I knew I could now start my own companies and grow in all areas of my life. By having worked as a DJ and record producer, I knew I could be self-sufficient, and most importantly of all, be happy and healthy again, and I'd love the process of who I'd become while achieving it!

Even when I was unhappy at work, I knew it was just a moment in time and that I'd eventually come through it. I also knew that one of my most important strategies is goal setting, so as part of my escape plan, I started by writing down my perfect day. I thought about what it would look like and what it would feel like. I also wrote down my perfect year and my perfect life.

Here's my perfect day:

- Wake up, drink water, and exercise.
- Eat healthily, and only when I'm hungry.
- Live my purpose and passions, give service, add value, and earn money.
- Relax in the evening.
- Have a warm bath and sleep well for 7–8 hours.

Here's my perfect year and life with Emma:

- *January to April*: Manage all our businesses and coaching while enjoying the winter sun in Southeast Asia.
- *May to December*: Live our lives enjoying the weather in London, Spain, Dubai, and Miami, and spending Christmas with our extended family and friends.

In Chapter 8, I mentioned that I found a nutritional coach who ran blood, stool, and food allergy tests. He described the results as 'carnage' because I was so intolerant to almost every type of food. But now, as I write, over 12 months later, and after following his guidance, my body is now stable once again with no signs of ankylosing spondylitis (AS). I know now in my heart I am at ease again, like when I was running the marathons. I am also at ease with the love of a good woman and doing what I love to do every day, in a good financial situation, safe, and secure.

It is not a coincidence that the two most challenging and life-changing health issues have hit me when I have been under the most amount of stress in life. During these times, my body broke down and stopped supporting me. The first time some people could say that my lifestyle played a part, and I can accept that. However, the second time it took me down, I hadn't drunk alcohol for ten years or more, so my body has made me acutely aware of the impact that negative stress has upon me. I'm happy to say I've now become aware enough to listen to my body fully, so I was able to make the changes that were required to recover again.

I wonder, could this be resonating with you? Are you in any pain, mentally or physically? Are you suffering from a dis-ease? If you're really honest with yourself, where could this be coming from? Reach out to me and let me know. Come to one of our events. I know I can help. All pain has a message, and we just have to find out what it is.

Socrates said, 'An unexamined life is not worth living.' As a younger man, in my case, this was very true. If you're facing any life challenges right now, it's time to look deep within yourself to find the solutions. From my own experience, I know you can.

My challenge now is to fully recover the strength in my legs. To that end, I have another coach, my personal trainer at David Lloyd Gym in Hampton. He pushes and guides me towards keeping my body strong for the wonderful life ahead.

Every challenge we face in life is either a crisis or an opportunity. Nowadays, I look for the opportunity in everything. It wasn't always the case, however. It was only the lowest of lows that lead me to change my thinking. My perceptions on health and money were changed when I lost both. I learned not to give up, to keep going, to be persistent. I spoke to myself in a positive way. *Mark, you've succeeded once, so you can do it again. You can do this!*

Failure is simply a part of success, a learning event. It all depends on your outlook and your perspective. I urge you to keep positive no matter what your current experience. Please look for the good in everything. I know it's definitely there. Sometimes you might have to look a bit deeper for it, but I know you'll find it.

In line with your continuous improvement, ask yourself some basic questions every year and set new goals each time. There is a helpful list of questions at the back of *Think and Grow Rich* by Napoleon Hill. One of the suggestions from the 500 millionaires that he studied for over 25 years was to complete an annual review. There are 50 questions at the back of the book for you to answer, and I complete this review for myself every year.

To be successful in relationships, remember to go into it looking to give as much as you can. If you have an open heart, feel confident in yourself, and you're full of love, you'll have already attracted the right type of person who will also be there to give to you. Your relationship will be wonderful. If you're currently single and looking to meet some-one, remember to set the values of the type of person you're looking to meet and to make sure you meet those values yourself. If you don't, work to become the person you'd like to attract.

The next step is to write out your relationship marketing plan. We do have a wonderful tool at our disposal called the internet. Nowadays, you can set out a profile online and populate it with all your likes and dislikes. If you do decide to meet someone in person after you've spoken online, then you already know that they're interested in you, in knowing more about you, because they're on a date specifically to meet you! I met my wife on Match.com. I went on a few unsuccessful dates before I met her, admittedly, but if you persist, like anything in life, online dating can work really well.

The *responsibility is the key to freedom* quote wouldn't have made any sense to me when I was younger. I remember being told at my father's wake, 'You're the man of the house now.' I was an 18-year-old with a fledgling addiction problem. I wasn't ready to hear that – far from it. I was hurting. However, I've now come to understand that quote, and I realise that the moment you accept total responsibility for everything is the moment you claim the power to change anything in your life. That is when you have complete freedom to choose. That in itself is the golden ticket, worth more than all the material things I have accumulated in the last ten years.

I will always study myself as an individual as I know I can keep improving. I am fascinated by all of humanity, plus learning more about business and wealth gives me focus for the rest of my life. I love all people, and I'm fascinated by why we do the things we do.

My business and money studies include credit rating management, business development, investments, and how to manage and improve all aspects of a wealthy life. Something that always interests me is that most multimillionaires went bankrupt in their thirties. I suppose going through that event removes the fear of money, plus it allows the experience to be in our memories, so everything we do ensures that it won't happen again. It certainly feels that way for me.

You can remix your life too. You just have to decide to do it. Make the decision to become the person you would like to be, the person you've always wanted to be, the person you know you can be. All these achievements are within you right now. Align your thoughts, feelings, and actions to develop the attitude and great habits as part of the person you're working to be. I've shared the strategies to get you there in these pages.

I hope you're enjoying the journey of your life right now, and I suggest that you go back through the book and do all of the recommended exercises over and over again. Remember, repetition is mastery. To decide and commit is the only way to be, do, and have anything of note in this life.

If you've enjoyed reading *Life Remixed*™ and learning the strategies on how to remix your life and you'd like to continue on your journey with us, please sign up on my website to receive all our latest information and news. I'm across all social media channels and would love to connect with you there too.

Go to www.markwilkinsonofficial.com to get in touch with me and the team.

Our social media channels are:

- Facebook: www.facebook.com/markwilkinsonliferemixed
- Twitter: www.twitter.com/djmarkwilkinson
- LinkedIn: www.linkedin.com/in/markwilkinson14
- YouTube: www.youtube.com/c/MarkWilkinsonOfficial

Tell us what you would like, and we'll show you how to get it.

Now let's celebrate!

. . . . . .

CHAPTER 14 – REMIX OPPORTUNITIES

- Believe in miracles.
- Happiness starts within you.
- Be happy first, then attract other happy people.
- You are successful every day that you can be here to give.
- Remix your life to exactly how you would like it to be.
- Believe in yourself.
- You've got this.
- Big love.

Fifty!

For more photos from Chapter 14, go to www.markwilkinsonofficial.com/life-remixed.

END NOTES

i   https://theboot.com/addictions-com-drugs-in-music-study/#:~:-text=A%20new%20study%20claims%20that,the%20recreational%20use%20of%20drugs.

ii   https://theboombox.com/which-music-genre-mentions-drugs-the-most-its-not-hip-hop/#:~:text=According%20to%20Addiction.com%2C%20%22,in%20one%20way%20or%20another.&text=Jay%20Z%20has%20made%20238,in%20second%20with%20305%20references.

iii   https://maps.org/research/mdma

RECOMMENDED READING AND STUDY LIST

These people and books helped me recover my health, wealth, and happiness. I am forever grateful to each and every one of them for their work. Immerse yourself.

The Secret – Rhonda Byrne (Book/Movie Netflix) – What you think about is what you bring about.

You Can Heal Your Life – Louise Hay (Book/Audio) – Discusses potential emotional reasons behind dis-ease.

Think and Grow Rich – Napoleon Hill (Book/Audio) – Hill studied 500 millionaires for 25 years.

The Way of the Superior Man – David Deida (Book) – I followed his book to succeed in my relationships.

The Rich Rules – Kevin Green (Book) – I follow Kevin's rules for business and investing.

At the End of The Day – Lewis & Laura Senior (Book) – Inspired by Lewis' own collapse, this is an empowering story.

As A Man Thinketh – James Allen (Book) – Especially read the Serenity chapter.

It's Not About the Money – Bob Proctor (Book) – It really isn't.

You Were Born Rich – Bob Proctor (Book) – You really were.

The Science of Getting Rich – Bob Proctor (DVD) – There is a science to it.

The Happiness Gap – Will Foster (Book) – Use gratitude, acceptance, and living in the present.

You2 (You squared) (Book) – Price Pritchett – Provides a high-velocity formula for multiplying your personal effectiveness in quantum leaps.

The Richest Man in Babylon (Book) – George S Clayson – This classic is an important book on money.

The Science of Getting Rich – Wallace Wattles (Book) – The movie *The Secret* was inspired by this book.

Get the Edge – Anthony Robbins (Audio) – This is an inspiring 7-day audio program.

Unleash the Power Within (UPW) – Anthony Robbins – This 4-day seminar is a great entry to committing to your development.

The Miracle Morning – Hal Elrod (Book) – Transform your life before 8am.

The Power – Rhonda Byrne (Book) – This is the follow-up book to *The Secret.*

Heal (on Netflix) – This is an excellent health documentary.

Feel the Fear and Do It Anyway – Susan Jeffers (Book) – Face your fears.

Rich Dad, Poor Dad – Robert Kiyosaki – (Book) – Kevin Green worked with Robert Kiyosaki.

Peaceful Warrior – Dan Millman (Book/Movie) – A part-fictional, part-autobiographical book based upon the early life of the author.

Doctor, Your Medicine Is Killing Me – Pete Coussa – (Book) – Presents the dangers of over-medicating.

Body for Life – Bill Phillips (Book/Audio) – Provides some good workout tips.

An Open Heart – Dalai Lama (Book) – Contains wonderful advice for living.

Conversations with God – Neale Donald Walsch (Books/Movie) – Written when Walsch was homeless; this is a wonderful recovery and redemption story.

The Monk Who Sold His Ferrari – Robin Sharma (Book) – A lawyer is forced to confront the spiritual crisis of his out-of-balance life.

How to Win Friends and Influence People – Dale Carnegie (Book) – This is a classic how-to book.

How to Develop Self-Confidence & Influence People by Public Speaking – Dale Carnegie (Book) – This book does exactly what it says on the cover.

Skinny Bastard/Skinny Bitch (Diet Books) – These books contain life-changing diet information.

The Power of Now – Eckhart Tolle (Book) – Don't read this book first; build up to it!

Sugar Blues – William Duffy – (Book) – This is a classic dietary book.

Super Juice Me – Jason Vale – (YouTube documentary/Books/App/Programs) – Jason's energy is great.

Fat, Sick & Nearly Dead – Joe Cross – This is a Netflix documentary with juice recipes. A great life turnaround story.

COACHES AND INSPIRATIONS

Tony Robbins – Personal development

Bob Proctor – Mind

Kevin Green – Wealth and business

Lewis Senior, Equilibria – Understanding people and realising potential

Harry Singha – Public speaking

Dimple Thakrar – Relationships

Dave Hompes – Nutrition

Joe Moriarty (David Lloyd) – Personal training

ARE YOU LOOKING FOR A COACH TO SUPPORT YOUR LIFE REMIX?

Mark Wilkinson has been extremely successful at remixing his own life to where it is now with multiple businesses, wealth, marriage, harmony and focus. Whatever part of your life you're looking to remix, Mark can coach you through the journey to help you identify and create the life you want!

Reflecting on the lessons from his own life, he now shares his knowledge and techniques to help others, with a natural ability to connect with people of all ages.

If you're contemplating reaching out to a life coach or just need someone to speak to to help you remix a particular part of life that you would like to change, Mark offers friendly, straight talking, positive support.

You deserve health, wealth and happiness, It is achievable and Mark can show you how!

12 MONTHS TO REMIX YOUR LIFE

Pay Per Session / Pay As You Go	12 Months To Remix Your Life	Life Remixed Mastermind Club
Share what you'd like to achieve and Mark will show you how to get there.	Maximise your Life Remixed coaching with 2 sessions a month and free access to the Life Remixed Mastermind Club.	VIP Member Only Access Monthly Mastermind Zoom Call Private WhatsApp Group Private Facebook Group Accountability Buddy

For more information about Mark Wilkinson
and the 12 Months to Remix Your Life programs, visit
https://markwilkinsonofficial.com/coach

ABOUT THE AUTHOR

MARK WILKINSON is a multiple business owner, coach, speaker, and published author. Originally, music was Mark's life as an international house music DJ and record producer. He was resident DJ at the famed Ministry of Sound in London, played music in 65 different countries, and achieved a UK Top 10 hit!

At 33 years of age, Mark collapsed with an incurable disease. It was the start of a hellish experience as his body froze up over the next 18 months resulting in him being unable to walk. He was in constant agony and lived on painkillers. His loss of health and financial setbacks eventually led to bankruptcy, depression, loneliness, and suicidal thoughts.

On a detox in Scotland, Mark was given a DVD of *The Secret*. In it, he learned from Bob Proctor that disease is two words: dis-ease. This brand-new information completely opened Mark's mind to new ways of thinking, feeling, and being. He began to study philosophy and personal development to detoxify and cure his body, eventually completing four marathons.

After hitting rock bottom, Mark took positive action, overcame his health issues, and re-educated himself in a new career in construction Health and Safety. He worked at the London Olympic Stadium for the 2012 Games and then at London Heathrow Airport as HSE Manager overseeing their entire commercial construction portfolio. He next became Head of HSE at a division of a residential home developer having overall HSE responsibility on a 90-acre, £1 billion project.

During this time, Mark Wilkinson was introduced to the UK's largest landlord and self-made millionaire, Kevin Green, and completed his Kevin Green Wealth (KGW) property wealth coaching programme. As a result, Mark was asked to join the KGW coaching team to share his knowledge of business, property investing, and wealth management.

In 2018, Mark set up his own Health and Safety consultancy, which meant he could also focus on his various property businesses and develop as a coach and speaker.

Mark Wilkinson's debut book *Life Remixed*™ launched in February 2021. The book tells the story of his roller coaster life as a DJ, how he lost everything, and how he remixed his life.

Mark is now a Fellow of the Institute of Leadership & Management (FInstLM) and a Chartered Member of the Institute of Safety and Health (CMIOSH). He holds an NVQ7 Master's in Strategic Management and Leadership (MPhil) and plans to study next for a PhD in Directional Leadership. He is also an E-Colors practitioner and coach.

For more information about Mark, please visit:

www.markwilkinsonofficial.com

www.liferemixed.co.uk

CHARITIES SUPPORTED BY MARK WILKINSON

Here are the charities supported by Mark and *Life Remixed*™ (in alphabetical order).

Crisis

www.crisis.org.uk

While volunteering for Crisis on a number of occasions, I was able to see how my life could have turned out if my mum was not there to help me when I lost everything. Crisis provides vital help so people can rebuild their lives and are supported out of homelessness for good.

JENGA

www.jengauganda.org

My friend Robby Keane set up this charity a number of years ago. JENGA Community Development Outreach is a non-profit charity that provides the basic essentials of life to the most vulnerable and needy people of Mbale, Uganda, East Africa.

Last Night A DJ Saved My Life

www.lastnightadjsavedmylife.org

A charity started by Jonny Lee in Ibiza. As a DJ, I help and support many fundraising events and initiatives to support children in crisis around the world.

MACS

www.macs.org.uk

I was so honoured to be sponsored by and raise money for my first marathon by MACS (Microphthalmia, Anophthalmia and Coloboma Support), the UK's national charity for children born without eyes or with underdeveloped eyes.

National Axial Spondyloarthritis Society

https://nass.co.uk/

National Axial Spondyloarthritis Society (NASS) is the only charity in the UK that is dedicated to supporting people affected by axial SpA. If you think you have axial SpA (AS) or are affected by the disease you can contact NASS on 020 8741 1515 or visit the charity's website, www.nass.co.uk

Giving a Voice to Creativity!

With every donation, a voice will be given to
the creativity that lies within the hearts of
our children living with diverse challenges.

By making this difference, children that may
not have been given the opportunity to have their
Heart Heard will have the freedom to create
beautiful works of art and musical creations.

Donate by visiting
HeartstobeHeard.com

We thank you.

Printed in Great Britain
by Amazon